OUR CAMPAIGNS;

OR, THE

MARCHES, BIVOUACS, BATTLES, INCIDENTS OF CAMP LIFE AND HISTORY OF OUR REGIMENT DURING ITS THREE YEARS TERM OF SERVICE.

TOGETHER WITH

A SKETCH OF THE ARMY OF THE POTOMAC, UNDER GENERALS McCLELLAN, BURNSIDE, HOOKER, MEADE AND GRANT.

By E. M. WOODWARD,
Adjutant, Second Pa. Reserves.

PHILADELPHIA:
JOHN E. POTTER AND COMPANY,
617 SANSOM STREET.

TO

The Officers and Men of the Second Reserve,

AND

TO THE MEMORY OF THEIR DEAD,

This Volume

IS RESPECTFULLY DEDICATED,

BY

THEIR COMRADE,

THE AUTHOR.

INTRODUCTORY.

THE object in writing this volume, is to give in a clear and lucid manner the history of THE SECOND REGIMENT PENNSYLVANIA RESERVE VOLUNTEER CORPS, and an insight into the life of a soldier. To connect it properly with the movements of the army, it is deemed necessary briefly to sketch the campaigns of the "ARMY OF THE POTOMAC," under Generals MCCLELLAN, BURNSIDE, HOOKER, MEADE and GRANT, from its formation until June, 1864, when the regiment's term of three years expired and it was mustered out. The short, arduous and decisive campaign of "The Army of Virginia" under General POPE, is also sketched."

The Author's journal, kept on the field, and his "Picket" letters in the *Sunday Transcript*, written on the spot with the official reports of Commanders, furnish the material. If the recital of the incidents of the camps, the marches, the bivouacs, the battles and the joys, the sorrows, the pleasures, the sufferings, the glories and the defeats, will revive in the memory of the participants, the scenes gone by, or interest the reader, it will be the highest source of gratification to the author.

E. M. W.

CONTENTS.

CHAPTER I.

CHAPTER II.

CHAPTER III.

CHAPTER IV.

CHAPTER V.

CHAPTER VI.

CHAPTER VII.

CHAPTER VIII.

CHAPTER IX.

CHAPTER X.

CHAPTER XI.

CHAPTER XII.

CHAPTER XIII.

CHAPTER XIV.

CHAPTER XV.

CHAPTER XVI.

CHAPTER XVII.

CHAPTER XVIII.

CHAPTER XIX.

CHAPTER XX.

CHAPTER XXI.

CHAPTER XXII.

CHAPTER XXIII.

CHAPTER XXIV.

CHAPTER XXV.

CHAPTER XXVI.

CHAPTER XXVII.

APPENDIX A.

APPENDIX B.

APPENDIX C.

Our Campaigns.

CHAPTER I.

THE GREAT REBELLION.

MANY men of discernment, who had watched the politics of the country for years past, and the gradual but steady moulding of public opinion in the North and South, had long foreseen the approaching storm, that was to test the great question of the stability of the Government and institutions established by our fathers, and many pure patriots of both sections, guided by the light of history in their judgments, foreseeing the fearful consequences that would inevitably follow, sought to avoid or at least postpone the calamity by concessions and compromises, while others, equally patriotic and sincere, deemed it best to bear the bosom to the storm and suffer the consequences at once, rather than by delay, permit the nation to be bound hand and foot to the car of Southern institutions.

Under the Government of the United States, which Alexander H. Stephens, the Vice-President of the "Southern Confederacy," in November, 1860, pronounced "the most beneficent Government of which history gives us any account," and which Jefferson Davis, the President in the session of 1860–61 said was, "the best Government ever instituted by man, unexceptionably administered, and under which the people have been prosperous beyond comparison with any other people whose career has been recorded in history," the citizens of all sections of the country and of every class felt only its power and influence to protect and prosper. Possessing a continent under one Government and one flag, free from the evils of standing armies and expensive fleets, free from imposts and export duties among themselves, free from export duties to foreign countries and internal revenue taxes, being one people in fact with a substantial community of origin, language, belief and law, (the great ties that hold society together,) having struggled, suffered and triumphed together, with their glories and defeats in common, with a Constitution springing from the free consent of all with ample provisions for its peaceful alteration or modification, with one section a commercial and manufacturing, another grain and stock growing, and a third whose great staple was cotton and tobacco, they of all people on God's earth should have lived in peace and contentment. But the South saw that in wealth and prosperity the North was far outstripping her, and alas, instead of seeking for the cause and trying to remedy the fault, they affected to despise the superior industry and energy of the North, preferring a system of labor that gave wealth and luxuriant ease to the few, at the expense of the prosperity and elevation of the masses, and the degradation of labor.

Fearing that slavery would become isolated they sought to maintain the balance of power in the Senate by the extension of slave territory, and the creation of slave States which their population and resources did not warrant. Nor did they confine themselves to the territorial limits of the United States. Already had the Government purchased for them the territories now forming the slave States of Louisiana, Arkansas, Missouri and Florida, and already had it engaged in a war with a sister Republic to annex and open to them the vast State of Texas. And more than this, the Government underhandedly favored the fillibustering expeditions of the marauders, Lopez and Walker, for the conquest of Cuba, Lower California and Central America, that they might be annexed to the Union and opened to slavery. With these, Mexico, and the Southern States, the Southern dream of a mighty empire, enabled to secure the good offices and favors of mercenary and monarchical Europe, and to bid defiance to Republican America, arose in golden visions before their eyes, and ambitious men were willing to destroy the Government and constitution of their country, and wade through seas of blood to power and position. Yet they were anxious to remain in the Union and enjoy all the advantages of it, as long as they could continue to control its councils, which they had done from the foundation of the Government.

As early as 1820, the Missouri Compromise was passed, which was the first and most respected of all. In admitting Missouri as a slave State, it stipulated that slavery should not be introduced north of the line of thirty-six, thirty degrees of latitude, its southern boundary, but that limit so long accepted, the South complained of, and Mr. Douglas introduced a bill annulling the same, and substituting "squatter sovereignty," which drew from Congress the right to interfere in the question of slavery in the territories. The South soon discovered that the superior population and resources of the North enabled them to settle the territories of Kansas and Nebraska with their hardy workmen, who decreed liberty to the land. This unexpected turn of events, which should have been foreseen, caused them to change their theory, and they invoked the power of Congress to interfere in the slave question in the territories against "squatter sovereignty," and demanded that its decision should be trampled under foot. The miserable and imbecile conduct of Presidents Pierce and Buchanan in permitting a civil war to exist in Kansas for so long a period without making any effort to stay it, is alas too well known to need comment.

It is only necessary to say that the Southerners defeated in their trials of popular vote, force of arms and congressional legislation, although assisted by a powerful and obedient Administration, turned their attention in a new direction and obtained a decision from the Supreme Court of the United States—the Dred Scott decree. In the preamble of this celebrated decision of the highest judicial power of the Government, there is proclaimed two principles: first, that there is no difference between a slave and any other kind of property; secondly, that all American citizens may settle every where with their property. With the right of property understood in this wise no State had the power either to abolish slavery, or to forbid the introduction of slaves, and, therefore, there was no legal power to prevent a Southerner from settling in a free State with all his slaves. But this is not all that was demanded. The subservient Administration was given up to the will of the Southerners and the mails ceased to carry letters, journals and books, which excited their suspicion.

In 1832, under the leadership of John C. Calhoun, the long dreamed of vision of empire that had haunted the brain of their ambitious and reckless politicians, first made its appearance in the nullification act of the legislature of South Carolina, but that stern old patriot Andrew Jackson, who declared that "The Union must and shall be preserved," met it with firm resolution, and his demand for the immediate disbanding of the State troops nipped it in the bud. From that time, however, the spirit of disunion had been assiduously disseminated in the South, and every issue that had arisen between the two sections, had been met by them with the threat of secession. The Hall of the august Senate had witnessed the drawing of firearms, and its sanctity had been violated by brutal assaults upon its members, and threats were freely made by the "fire-eaters" to break up the sessions of Congress in blood. Yet the North submitted to these degradations for the sake of peace, and bowed the head to the demands of the South for the sake of the Union.

At last, in 1860, the two great political parties met to make their nominations for President and establish their platforms. The disunionists first showed their treason by betraying their party and breaking up its convention, because the true democrats would not bow their heads to their will. The seceders then called a convention and nominated John C. Breckenridge, who is now a leader in this infamous rebellion, and declared that the election of Mr. Lincoln, their opponent, would be followed by the dissolution of the Union. The North heard the threat; if they had submissively yielded to it once more, all dignity, self-respect and mental liberty would have been lost. They knew the consequence; secession was rebellion, rebellion was a commercial crisis, was the political weakening of the country, and the unsettling of many fortunes. It was the loss of all Southern trade, the loss of all capital invested in the South, the loss of all debts owed by the South. But the great spirit of the North that had bowed so often to the dictates of a Southern minority for the sake of the Union and peace, arose in its majestic dignity and proclaimed that the will of the majority should be expressed regardless of threats and consequences.

Prior to the election for President, the Governor of South Carolina had recommended both Houses of the Legislature to take measures in advance for the secession of the State in case Mr. Lincoln should be elected; and a special commission was nominated, and held permanent session. In Texas, Senator Wigfall, in speaking of Mr. Breckenridge, did not hesitate to say, "If any other candidate is elected, look for stormy weather. There may be a confederation, indeed, but it will not number more than thirty-three States." Senators Jefferson Davis of Mississippi, and Judah P. Benjamin of Louisiana, (Secretary of War of the Confederate States,) held no less explicit language, announcing that at the first elec-

2

toral defeat of the South, it would set about forming a separate confederation, long since demanded by its true interests. It was even freely proclaimed through their papers, "that Mr. Lincoln should not be inaugurated if elected."

The Presidential election took place on the 6th of November, 1860, and resulted in the choice of Abraham Lincoln; Messrs. Bell and Douglas, who were equally exceptionable to the secessionists, receiving a joint vote in almost all the Southern States, larger than that cast for Mr. Breckenridge, who was the embodiment of the secession principles. Yet in the face of this direct refusal of the majority of the southerners to endorse Mr. Breckinridge ,and the principles he represented, the unprincipled and ambitious leaders set diligently to work to accomplish their long cherished and diabolical design of destroying the Government of their fathers, that they might rise to power and position. By resolutions of their Legislatures, and unauthorized conventions, studious misrepresentations of their press, and inflammatory appeals to the masses they at last succeeded in "firing the Southern heart," and preparing it for the awful crime of fratricide.

On the 20th of December, a few days after the result of the election was known, the Legislature of South Carolina, a State with a white population of two hundred and seventy-six thousand, or about half that of the city of Philadelphia, passed an ordinance of secession, and declared herself a free and sovereign State. She did in fact the same thing in 1832, but the firm and resolute Andrew Jackson, with a stroke of the pen awed into submission and silence all. Would to God for one month's rule of the old patriot and hero in 1860. This action of South Carolina produced a deep sensation throughout all sections of the country, and the people of the North could not realize the earnestness of the atrocious deed.

But in rapid succession followed other acts, that too

plainly showed that madness had usurped the throne of reason, and that "those whom the Gods wish to destroy they first make mad."

On the 3d of January, 1861, Forts Pulaski and Jackson, in the harbor of Savannah, were taken possession of by State troops, by order of the Governor of Georgia, under the pretext of preventing them from falling into the hands of mobs!

On the 9th, the State Convention of Mississippi passed an ordinance of secession by a vote of eighty-four to fifteen.

On the 11th, the State Convention of Alabama passed an ordinance of secession by a vote of sixty-one to thirty-nine, and invited the other slaveholding States to send delegates to a Convention to be held on the 4th day of February, in Montgomery, Alabama.

Soon after all the United States forts and arsenals along the Atlantic and Gulf coast and on the Mississippi river, with the mints, custom-houses and other Federal buildings in the South were seized. Batteries were erected on the Mississippi river, and its navigation obstructed. Beside the above States, Florida, Georgia, Louisiana and Texas seceded.

On the 4th, a Convention of the seceded States convened at Montgomery, Alabama, and elected Howell Cobb, the late Secretary of the Treasury, President.

On the 9th, the Southern Congress, at Montgomery, Alabama, elected Jefferson Davis of Mississippi, President, and Alexander H. Stephens of Georgia, Vice-President of the Southern Confederacy for one year. The Constitution of the United States, with amendments, was adopted.

On the 16th, Mr. Davis, at Montgomery, declared in a speech, that the South will hold her own, and force all who oppose them, "to smell Southern powder and feel Southern steel."

During this time, a little over two months only, the most bitter feeling of hatred and animosity was engendered against Northerners residing in the South, and school teachers and mistresses were shipped north, whipped, tarred and feathered, or hung, according to the whims or passions of the mobs. Merchants were robbed, honest men, who had resided among them for years, were notified to leave without time to collect their debts or dispose of their property. Traders on the Mississippi were driven from their barges by lawless mobs, their goods plundered and their lives jeopardized. Yet, while the military force of the United States could be used to drive squatters from their cabins on the Government lands in Kansas in the middle of winter, the right of the Government to use it to protect its own property, sustain the supremacy of its laws, and suppress insurrection, was denied. Such is the deplorable course secession had run during the last days of Mr. Buchanan's Administration, and so far from raising his voice or hand to save our beloved Union from destruction, he encouraged them in their treason by his imbecility and silent acquisition, until at last, in a message to Congress, he actually denied the power of the Government under the Constitution to coerce the seceding States—*i. e.*, to maintain the supremacy of its own laws.

And what was his Cabinet? The hot-bed of treason and secession! On the 8th of January, Jacob Thompson of Misssissippi, resigned his position as Secretary of the Interior, because aid was granted to Major Anderson, at Fort Sumter. The next day the *Constitution*, the Government organ at Washington, attacked Secretary Holt, for sending aid to Major Anderson, and defended Mr. Thompson for resigning, and the United States subtreasurer refused to pay the salaries to Major Anderson and his command. Howell Cobb, the Secretary of the Treasury resigned, and was chosen President of the Convention of the seceding States, convened at Montgomery, Alabama. John B. Floyd of Virginia, Secretary of War, after stripping the arsenals of the Northern States of their arms, ordnance, and ammunition, colleagued with

Russell, Bailey, and others in stealing over $6,000,000 worth of trust bonds, resigned, and on the 29th of February, the Grand Jury of the District of Columbia presented charges against him for mal-administration in office, and conspiring against the Government. And even Isaac Toucey of Connecticut, Secretary of the Navy, had ordered to foreign stations all the available vessels of the navy, leaving at home only the ships in ordinary.

Can any one suppose that these chosen counsellors of the President, who daily debated at the meetings of the Cabinet the great questions that had agitated the country for so long a time, had succeeded in deluding Mr. Buchanan in regard to their real views and intentions? Can any one suppose that the leading statesmen of the South who always had free access to the White House, and were welcomed to the hospitalities of the President, could so utterly deceive him in regard to their designs? Could it be possible that a man of the ability of Mr. Buchanan, with his familiarity with the politics of the country, and long intercourse with the leading men of the nation, could have been blinded as to the intentions of the arch-traitors and "fire-eaters" of the South? No! It requires too much credulity and charity to answer in the negative. But let us put the most charitable construction on his actions that we can, and what shall we say of them? That the poor old dotard was in the traces and could not kick out; that he was bound hand and foot and had not the strength to release himself, and that he quietly acquiesced in their treasonable designs, hoping that the Government would be reconstructed upon a firmer basis by those who had treason in their hearts. The great principle of popular suffrage was to be violated, the broad arena stretching to the Pacific, and far to the south was to be given up to human bondage. The African slave trade, with all its loathsome horrors, was to be re-opened, and for what? To preserve a dishonorable peace, that soon would be broken.

But, thank God, the Administration of Mr. Buchanan

was coming to a close, and through the dark clouds that empaled the Nation, a bright ray of hope shone upon the horizon as Abraham Lincoln appeared upon the ship of state and seized the helm.

The nation breathed freer, and patriots felt our Government was a reality, and not a rope of sand.

CHAPTER II.

SUMTER AND THE FLAG FIRED ON—THE AIM AND DESIGN OF THE LEADERS OF THE REBELLION—JUSTIFICATION OF THE COURSE OF PRESIDENT LINCOLN.

No President ever assumed the cares of State under more inauspicious circumstances than Mr. Lincoln did. Seven States had already seceded from the Union and were marshalling their armies to maintain their independence at the point of the bayonet, and the arch-traitors were using all their insidious wiles to seduce the remaining slave States from their allegiance to the Federal Government. From the Forum, Pulpit and Press was proclaimed the foulest treason, and the boast made that the "Stars and Bars" would soon float in triumph over the National Capitol. A large portion of the army had been surrendered by General Twiggs, in Texas, the remainder of it was on the Pacific coast, or scattered through the Territories of Utah and New Mexico, or stationed on our distant frontiers, while six hundred men were the entire available force which the Government was able to concentrate at Washington to secure the peaceful inauguration of the President. All the available vessels of the navy were stationed in distant seas. Many of the purest patriots despaired of the Republic, foreign nations proclaimed its doom was sealed, and "hope for a season bade the world farewell," while the hallowed light of Liberty paled before the gathering storm. But the steadfast chief heeded not the storm that swept across the land, but serene, firm and immovable, held aloft the lamp of hope, while he gathered the scattered strength of the Nation and matured his plans for its preservation.

On the 11th of April, Leroy P. Walker, rebel Secretary of War, demanded the surrender of Fort Sumter, to which Major Anderson replied, that his sense of honor and his obligations to the Government prevented a compliance. The next morning at two o'clock the rebel General Beauregard sent word to Major Anderson that if he would evacuate, he would not be fired upon, to which the Major replied, that, if not otherwise ordered or provisioned, he would be forced to evacuate by noon of the 15th inst. But the peaceful possession of the fort was not what the traitors desired; they wanted blood "to fire the Southern heart."

In two hours afterwards, the batteries and fortifications in Charleston harbor, seventeen in number, opened fire upon the fort, which was returned by Major Anderson, and kept up on both sides all day without harm on either side, excepting the dismounting of two of Anderson's guns. A slow fire was kept up all night, and resumed with great vigor early the next morning. At eight A. M., the officers' quarters took fire from a shell. Soon after a number of hand grenades and shells caught fire and exploded within the fort. At twelve o'clock, the whole roof of the barracks were in flames, and the magazine being in great danger, ninety barrels of gunpowder were taken out and thrown into the sea. The heat, smoke, and galling fire gradually exhausted the garrison, and nearly suffocated them. At one P. M., after sustaining an attack of thirty-three hours, the fort was surrendered, the garrison being permitted to carry away the flag and all company arms and private property. A salute of fifty guns was fired, and the glorious old flag was hauled down, and the emblem of liberty and hope of the down-trodden and oppressed of the world gave place to the flag of treason.

The greatest crime that was ever committed against liberty and mankind was now consummated. Heaven itself revolted at the act, and sent the hissing missiles of death harmlessly on their course. The North was stupefied, and stood aghast at the enormity of the crime, being unable to realize that the flag of such glorious memories should have been fired upon by those whom they looked upon as brothers, and whom they supposed would have given the best blood of their hearts to save from dishonor.

But let us consider for one moment what was the aim and design of the rebel leaders. Already a confederate flag of fifteen stars, one star for each slave State, inclusive of Delaware and Maryland, had been flung to the breeze, and it was solemnly proclaimed that the Confederacy would never yield any portion of the territory claimed. This virtually, and in fact, included Washington. On the fatal 12th of April, 1861, while the tidings of the assault on Sumter were travelling over the wires, the Rebel Secretary of War, in the presence of Jefferson Davis and his colleagues, and of five thousand hearers, declared that before the end of May "the flag which now flaunted the breeze would float over the dome of the Capitol at Washington."

In pursuance of this original plan of the leaders of the rebellion, the capture of Washington has been continually had in view, not merely for the sake of its public buildings, as the capital of the Confederacy, but as the necessary preliminary to the absorption of the Border States, and for the moral effect in the eyes of Europe of possessing the metropolis of the Union. In speaking of this matter, the Hon. Edward Everett, in his address at the consecration of the National Cemetery, at Gettysburg, says: "the occupation of the National Capital, with the seizure of the public archives and of the treaties with foreign powers was an essential feature. This was in substance, within my personal knowledge, admitted, in the winter of 1860–61, by one of the most influential leaders of the rebellion, and it was fondly thought that this object could be effected by a bold and sudden movement on the 4th of March, 1861. There is abundant proof also, that a darker project was contemplated, if not by the responsible chiefs of the rebellion, yet by nameless ruffians, willing to play a subsidiary and murderous part in the treasonable drama. It was accordingly maintained by the rebel emissaries abroad, in the circles to which they found access, that the new American minister ought not, when he arrived, to be received as the envoy of the United States, inasmuch as before that time Washington would be captured, and the Capital of the Nation, and the archives and muniments of the Government would be in the possession of the Confederates."

And what is secession but rebellion? Rebellion, like any other revolutionary act, may be morally justified by the extremity of oppression. In monarchical governments revolution is frequently justifiable, as the cartridge-box is the only means by which the popular opinion can be expressed. But in our country the solution of all our political differences was wisely left to the decision of the ballot-box, which had heretofore served us upon every occasion, and had ever been respected.

Andrew Jackson, in his Proclamation against the Nullification Act, in December, 1832, says: "And then add, if you can, without horror and remorse, this happy Union we will dissolve; this picture of peace and prosperity we will deface; this free intercourse we will interrupt; these fertile fields we will deluge with blood; the protection of that glorious flag we renounce; the very name of Americans we discard. And for what, mistaken men, for what do you throw away these inestimable blessings? For what would you exchange your share in the advantages and honor of the Union? In the dream of separate independence—a dream interrupted by bloody conflicts with your neighbors, and a vile dependency on a foreign power." * * * "Its destroyers you cannot be. You may disturb its peace—you may interrupt the course of its prosperity—you may cloud its reputation for stability, but its tranquillity will be restored, its prosperity will return, and the stain upon its national character will be transferred and remain an eternal blot on the memory of those who caused the disorder."

"Having the fullest confidence in the justness of the legal and constitutional opinions of my duties, which has been expressed, I rely, with equal confidence, on your undivided support in my determination to execute the laws, to preserve the Union by all constitutional means, to arrest, if possible, by moderate but firm measures, the necessity of a recourse to force; and, if it be the will of Heaven, that the recurrence of its primeval curse on man for the shedding of a brother's blood should fall upon our land, that it be not called down by any offensive act on the part of the United States."

Such was the language of that sterling patriot when treason first raised its head in South Carolina.

Was Mr. Lincoln justified in his determination to maintain the Union at all hazards, or should he have submitted peaceably to its dissolution? A peaceable dissolution was impossible, except by the surrender of the National Capital and the border States of Delaware, Maryland, Kentucky, Tennessee, and Missouri, all of which at the late election had gone against the South by casting their electoral votes for Mr. Bell, excepting Missouri, which went for Mr. Douglas. And more than this, all of them had sent delegates to meet those from the Northern States in a peace conference, and showed unmistakably their attachment to the Union. Delaware and Maryland refused to secede, Virginia elected Union delegates to the State Convention and refused to adopt the rebel constitution. Kentucky subsequently elected nine Union members of Congress and one secession, Tennessee had elected a majority of Union delegates to a State convention and refused to hold a convention, and Missouri subsequently elected Union delegates to its State convention. Could the Government withdraw its protection and support from the union-loving people of those States and surrender its Capital to traitors who would soon become a foreign and hostile nation? Could the Government voluntarily surrender the navigation of the Mississippi river, the great outlet of the Western States to the Gulf of Mexico? Could a great Nation submit to its political death and destruction without an effort for self-preservation? No, God forbid it, yet Americans have argued these questions in the affirmative, but only those who were deceived themselves, or were trying to deceive others. But Mr. Lincoln, the chosen of the people, the instrument of God, was inspired with the knowledge that he held not only the destiny of the country, but of liberty throughout the world in his hand, and rose equal to the emergency.

Throughout his inaugural address, he is firm, without being provoking. The limits of concession are clearly marked out, and a conciliatory spirit is maintained. The President, while manifesting the most pacific disposition, distinctly declares he will abandon none of the rights of the Government, but will leave to others the odium of aggression. He declares secession is unconstitutional, and nothing can induce him to consent to the destruction of the Union. That he will endeavor to shun a war, that he will not be the aggressor, but that he will fulfill the duty of preserving federal property and collect federal taxes in the South. "In your hands," says Mr. Lincoln, "my dissatisfied fellow-citizens, in yours and not mine, is found the terrible question of civil war. The Government will not attack you; you will have no conflict, if you are not the aggressors. You have not, on your part, an oath registered in heaven to destroy the Government, whilst I, on my side, am about to take the most solemn oath to maintain, to protect and defend it."

If Mr. Lincoln had acted otherwise than he did, he would have been derelict in his duty to his God, his country and mankind, and when the intelligence of the assault upon Fort Sumter was received, the issuing of his proclamation calling for seventy-five thousand volunteers to maintain the laws of the United States over the seceding States, and admonishing the rebels to lay down their arms and quietly submit to the laws within twenty days, was but the response of the great American heart. And America's reply to the proclamation was such an uprising of free men as the world never witnessed before. Where ever it was received, it produced the wildest excitement and enthusiasm, the booming gun, the pealing bell, and rattling drum, announced it throughout the land, until from the broad Atlantic it rolled across the plains and echoed over the snow-clad peaks to the Pacific.

CHAPTER III.

WAR FOR THE UNION—PENNSYLVANIA'S RESPONSE—ORGANIZATION OF THE RESERVES—COLONELS MANN'S, MARSH'S, AND DE KORPONAY'S REGIMENTS—CAMP WASHINGTON—QUAINT NAMES—WHISKEY IN A MUSKET BARREL—GETTING THE COUNTERSIGN.

IN Philadelphia business was suspended, flags were thrown to the breeze in every street, rendezvous were opened in every section, and placards calling for volunteers, covered the walls of every corner. Recruiting parties traversed the city in every direction, followed by crowds of men eager to enroll their names, the armories of the volunteer companies were crowded to overflowing with men drilling night and day, the public parks of the city were given up for the same purpose, and the quietude of the Sabbath was forgotten amidst the preparation for war. The citizens furnished armories free of rent, and such of the volunteers as could not support themselves without work were fed on the bountiful supply of the neighborhood. The lady congregations of the different churches set themselves diligently to work supplying the volunteers with shirts, drawers, socks and other clothing and contributions of all sorts were freely given. The generous impulses of the heart of a nation never flowed freer. The soldiers rode free on the cars, and went free to all places of amusement. The only trouble the men had was to find companies that were sure of acceptance, and some who had good reputations numbered two hundred and fifty and three hundred men, while all were rapidly filling up. In fact twenty thousand men could have been raised in the city in one week.

The quota assigned to Pennsylvania was fourteen regiments, and in four days after the call six hundred men—the first to arrive for its defence—were placed in the National Capitol, and ten days later twenty-five regiments were organized and put in the field, eleven more being furnished by the State than called for. In fact, such was the patriotic ardor of the people, that the Adjutant-General of the State, in his Annual Report for 1861, states, that the services of about thirty additional regiments had to be refused, making in all more than two-thirds of the requisition of the President. Eight of these regiments were from Philadelphia, but there were scores of full companies that were not accepted. The second call for volunteers was made upon the State in May. The allotted share to Pennsylvania was ten regiments; but the General Government would not allow these to be raised, but simply credited the State with them, as she had already furnished more than her two quotas.

The extra session of the Legislature of Pennsylvania convened on the 30th day of April, in pursuance of the proclamation of the Governor, fully appreciating the gigantic task the North had before them, wisely and patriotically resolved, in accordance with Governor Curtin's recommendation, to organize, arm, equip and discipline a division to be called the "Reserve Volunteer Corps of the Commonwealth," and to be composed of thirteen regiments of infantry, one regiment of cavalry, and one regiment of light artillery, to be held in readiness to obey any requisition the President might make on the State for troops. In organizing this division, the conception of which originated with the Governor, the greatest difficulty he experienced was, not in finding officers and men to fill it, but to select between the numerous applicants who beset him night and day, not only in the executive chamber and public streets of the Capital, but even in his bed room. His Excellency having resolved that the division should be a true type of Pennsylvanians, proportioned it among the different counties, so that every township should be represented in it.

Among the regiments organized in Philadelphia, at that time, were those known as Mann's, March's, and De Korponay's, from the first of which eight companies were accepted, from the second seven, and from the third five. All these were mustered into the State service about the latter part of May, by Captain Henry J. Biddle, Assistant Adjutant-General of the Division, at the Girard House, where the men went through the most severe medical examination by the surgeons, who required every man to strip, and rejected all who had the least blemish or defect. "Never," said Dr. Henry H. Smith, the Surgeon-General of the State, "were a finer formed or more hardy body of men collected together in one division."

Gabriel De Korponay commenced the organization of his regiment about the middle of April, and among the captains who joined with him were George A. Woodward, "Pennsylvania Rifles;" J. Orr Finnie, "Scotch Rifles;" E. M. Woodward, "Taggart Guards;" P. I. Smith, "Consolidation Guards;" and I. W. Kimble, "Hatborough Guards." These captains were selected by the Governor from DeKorponay's regiment.

Wm. B. Mann commenced the organization of his regiment about the same time, and the companies chosen by the Governor were Captains P. McDonough, "Governor's Rangers;" James N. Byrne, "Hibernia Target Company;" R. Ellis, "Governor's Rangers;" T. Bringhurst, "Governor's Guards;" T. Mealey, "Independent Rangers;" William Knox, "Constitutional Rangers;" Robert McClure, "Quaker City Guards;" and Wm. S. Thompson, "Montgomery Guards," (of Bristol, Pa.) All these companies were soon filled up to the maximum number, but the men were in such a feverish state of excitement for fear they would not be mustered in, that difficulty was experienced in inducing them to stay long with any company that appeared to hang fire. Thus, after a few days recruiting, most of them had the necessary number of men, but after they had drilled awhile, they left to join other companies that they supposed were more likely to be accepted. But their places were readily filled by others who came from other companies under the same impression. Almost all the soldiers were supplied with flannel shirts and other articles of clothing by the congregations of the different churches; most prominent among which in their liberality was patriotic Old Christ Church, which distributed no less than four thousand five hundred and seventy-two articles of clothing, most of which were made by the ladies of the church.

On the 29th of May, the seven Philadelphia companies of Colonel Mann's regiment left the city for Camp Washington, Easton, Pa., where they arrived during the afternoon. Prior to their departure they marched to the residence of the colonel at the corner of Fifth and Green streets, where they were presented with a magnificent and richly trimmed silk flag by a number of ladies, the presentation being made by Daniel Dougherty, Esq.

On the morning of the 30th, the four Philadelphia companies of Colonel De Korponay's regiment, with the "Ontario Guards," Captain Horatio G. Sickel, formed on Broad street near Green, and under the command of Captain Sickel, marched to Master and America streets, where they took a special train on the North Pennsylvania Railroad, for Easton, at which place they arrived during the afternoon, aud marched out to camp; quarters were assigned them to the right of Colonel Mann's regiment.

The camp was on the Fair Grounds of the Farmers' and Mechanics' Institute, which covered about thirty-five acres, situated on a level elevation about one and a-half miles west of Easton, and three-quarters of a mile north of the Lehigh river, in Northampton county. On the east and north sides of the enclosure were long rows of bunk rooms, three of which were assigned to each company. In front of each company's quarters were situated the kitchens, facing inward, and in their rear were the officers' quarters facing outwards. To the west, occupying about two-thirds of the enclosure, was the race course, and in the centre was situated the large and capacious Fair buildings of imposing appearance and equal to any of its kind in the State. From its roof rose a large and stately dome, from the balcony of which was presented a magnificent view of the surrounding country. To the north, far in the distance, lie the Kittatinny or Blue Ridge mountains, pierced on the right by the Delaware Water Gap, in the centre by the Wind Gap, and on the left by the Lehigh Water Gap. The intervening country is interspersed with rolling hills and gentle valleys, farm houses, and villages with their tapering spires, the most prominent of which are the Moravian towns of Bethlehem and Nazareth. On the south, from the Lehigh, the country gradually rises for the distance of two miles, where it is shut in by the lesser spurs of the Blue Ridge. On the east rolls the broad Delaware, and beyond it stretches in the distance the rolling country of New Jersey.

The men immediately upon their arrival were furnished with tincups, plates, spoons, knives and forks, a day's rations, and plenty of straw to sleep upon. The next day was spent in getting things in order, and by the following morning they were settled down and ready to commence the routine of camp. Colonel Mann, commanding the camp, issued the following "calls" to be sounded: Reveille, 4 A. M.; Drill, 4½; Recall, 6, Breakfast, 7; Guard Mounting, 7½; Fatigue, 7¾; Sick Call, 8; Drill, 9; Recall, 10; Orderlies' Call, 12 M.; Dinner, 12½ P. M.; Drill, 6; Recall, 7; Supper, 7½; Tattoo, 9; Taps, 9½. Four roll calls were had each day, and in a little while every thing worked with the regularity of machinery. During the intervals between drills, the men amused themselves in various ways, mostly in one-half sleeping, while the other half deviled them. Quoits, foot-ball, boxing and sparring, singing and playing, and all sorts of pranks were continually going on, and altogether they appeared the happiest and merriest set of men in the world.

One of the most interesting scenes was the policing the camp. The guard of the previous day had liberty from 10 A. M., until 4 P. M., and the next day were required to perform the police duty of the camp. Armed with rakes and hickory brooms, they gathered the straw, rubbish and old bones into heaps, to be removed in wagons. This duty is always disliked by soldiers, as in fact all work is, but as they marched out, with their implements at a "shoulder," it was with the mock ceremony of troops leaving for "the sacred soil of Virginia," and many "a good-by" and "God bless you" was heard, as their puckered lips whistled out "The girl I left behind me."

A few days after our arrival, Colonel March's seven companies came into camp, and others soon after followed, and by the 12th of June, there were twenty-five companies, numbering one thousand nine hundred and fifty-six officers and men present. As no clothing or blankets were as yet furnished by Government, and as the men had brought nothing with them except what they stood in, they soon presented a rather ragged appearance, which, however, did not in the least affect their buoyant spirits. The citizens of the borough of Easton, however, with a noble generosity took the matter in hand, and determined to do all in their power to render the soldiers comfortable. A Ladies' Aid Society was formed, which furnished every necessary supply of clothing, blankets, comfortables, flannels, jellies, etc., for the hospital, and a large number of quilts, pantaloons, shirts, towels, etc., for the camp.

The soldiers will always remember with gratitude, the kindness of the citizens of Easton, which was bestowed upon them without ostentation. The food furnished was abundant, and of the best quality, consisting of fresh beef, wheat bread, potatoes, rice, beans, bacon, coffee, sugar and small stores, but considerable sickness prevailed among the men, arising from the free use of limestone water, to which they were unaccustomed, but there was no serious illness. In the place of a well, the supply came from a large cistern, in which was caught the rain water from the roof of the Fair building, and that hauled from the borough of Easton in casks. As a sanitary precaution the whole camp was vaccinated, and to promote the general health, the men were taken to the Lehigh three times a week, where they enjoyed the luxury of bathing. Upon such occasions there would sometimes be a thousand men in the water at once, and they hugely enjoyed the sport of diving, splashing and paddling around in general. The great feat among the expert swimmers, was to cross and recross the river without resting.

Among the first things that agitated the brains of the men, was to devise quaint names and mottoes to place over the doors of their quarters, and although they were not purely classical, some of them were typical of those who adopted them.

Commencing on the extreme south of the eastern side, was Captain McDonough's company, with "Fourth Ward, City of Philadelphia;" "Fort McCandless, Sergeant Dillon commanding;" "Fort Mann, Lieutenant John J. Gill commanding;" "Fort ———, Lieutenant J. D. Schock commanding." On the right of this was "The Quaker City Head Quarters;" "Camp McClure;" "Fort Wm F.

Blundin;" "Quaker Bridal Chamber;" "Calahan Hall;" "Live and let live." Next, "Fort James N. Byrnes;" "Screws;" "Hibernia Fire Engine Company;" "Bird in Hand;" "Finney House." Next, "Continental Hotel," "The Rose Cottage;" "Dart's Head Quarters:" "Hard Corner Sharps;" "The Old House at Home;" "Independent Rangers;" "Nailer's Head Quarters;" "Gay Rooster;" "Diamond Hall;" "Don't Tread on me;" "Minerva Hall;" "Git up and Git;" "Old Lebanon Garden, Captain Mealey."

Next, "Happy Home of the Constitutional Rangers, Captain William Knox;" "Punch Bowl Hotel;" "Black Horse Hotel;" "Astor House;" "Ellsworth Hotel;" "The Government keeps us, and we will keep the Government;" "Cohocksink Hotel;" "District Attorney's Office;" *Notice,* "Upon any liquors being brought in, the moral character of applicants to practice at the Bar, must be strictly inquired into." Next, "Bristol Boys, Captain Wm. S. Thompson;" "Bower of Love;" "Happy Crew;" "The Old School House;" "The Old Spring House;" "Hole in the Wall;" "Montgomery Guards;" Next, "Einwechter's Head Quarters;" "Tenth and Eleventh Street Depot, Exchange Tickets, Seven cents;" "The Serious Family;" "Out for a Day's shooting."

Next, "Ontario House, Captain Horatio G. Sickel;" "Donaghy's Inn;" "Bill Pool Club;" "We Respect all, and Fear none;" "Never Sink;" "Live Oak;" "Kensington Boys;" "Hike out and Simmer down." Next, "Balmoral Castle;" "Scotch Rifles, Captain J. Orr Finnie;" "Wallace's Cave, Lieutenant J. B. Fletcher;" "De Korponay;" "Struther's Retreat;" "Poney Hall." Next, "Penn Rifles, Captain George A. Woodward;" "De Korponay;" "The Flag Wyoming." Next, "Taggart Guards;" "De Korponay Bricks;" "Sunday Mercury, Captain E. M. Woodward;" "Spicket's Head Quarters;" "Railroad House;" "The abode of Virtue." Next, "Consolidation Guards, Captain P. I. Smith;" "De Korponay Pidgeon Box;" "Gay and Happy;" "Fort Defiance." Next, "Hatborough Guards, Captain I. W. Kimble;" "Free and Easy;" "Happy Family."

Next, "Wide Awake Hall, Captain Wm. D. Curtis;" "Long Island, of Reading;" "Keystone Hook and Ladder Company;" "Elephant Guards." Next, "The Star of North Birdsboro', Captain Jacob Lenhart;" "Fort Sumter;" "Japanese Hotel;" "Arctic Circle;" "Death to Traitors;" "Jeff Davis at the Sheriff's Ball;" "The Blue Eyed Stranger;" "Moonlight Assassinators;" "Mount Vernon;" "Washington and Lincoln;" "Victory or Death;" "White Hall, Newtown, Captain David V. Feaster;" "Traitor Hunters;" "Love and Glory;" "Game Chickens;" "Ellsworth Avengers;" "Rebel Killers;" "Hard Scrabble Rangers;" "Chester County Volunteers;" "Never Surrender;" "The Wheat Field;" "The Red Curtin;" "Susquehanna Tigers;" "Gloria Dei;" "Ellsworth's Heart," etc.

Guard mounting in the morning was an interesting ceremony, the guard numbering one hundred and two men, which, with the band, made a fine display. Of course, it could not be supposed with so many young men in camp, many of whom were for the first time free from the restraints of home, they would all conduct themselves with the strictest decorum. In fact there were many of them who looked upon the arrangement as a grand pic-nic or excursion, and were bound to enjoy themselves as much as possible, and took particular delight in dodging the guard. But four men from each company, inclusive of the old guard, were permitted to be absent from camp at a time, but quite a number more managed to get out without authority. Almost every bunk had its "rat hole" dug under the back partition, through which the boys made their exit despite the guard. Some of these gentlemen upon their return would be caught, and put in the guard house, but it being soon discovered that it afforded a most easy means of egress, Colonel Mann determined to build one of logs inside of the enclosure with only a small aperture for ingress and egress. This was pronounced by the men to be a real "Black house of refuge," and served most admirably the purpose intended, but really it was quite amusing to see the artful dodges resorted to by some of the inmates to overcome the difficulties.

An "officer of the day," on one occasion, upon visiting the guard house, found the guard and one of the prisoners in a violent altercation, the guard with his musket between the logs trying to bayonet the prisoner. Complimenting the guard upon the zeal displayed, he was privately cautioned not to wound any of the prisoners, and advised to take no notice of the naughty names they called him. The officer afterwards was highly edified to learn that the guard having his musket barrel filled with whiskey, was engaged in treating the prisoner when surprised by him.

With the countersign an officer or private could enter the camp at any time of night, but it was seldom given to the men, yet some of them were cute enough to get it, when wanted. The most successful one in this arrangement was an eccentric genius in Company A, who managed to get in and out almost every night. His *modus operandi* was taking a musket and crawling up to one of the guards and telling him he was on the next post and had forgotten the countersign. Some times he would take half a company out with him, when they would go to town and have a grand time dancing. The men upon such occasions seldom went to excess or troubled the citizens, but were inordinately fond of singing patriotic songs at unseasonable hours of the night, which disturbed the quietude of the town, but the borough watchmen never interfered with them. Colonel Mann, however, was not unmindful of his duty to the citizens, and sent out nightly patrols to pick up the boys who should be in bed, and they seldom had any trouble in persuading their comrades to return with them.

In fair weather the camp presented an animated appearance, it being the fashionable resort of the neighboring farmers and the citizens of Easton, particularly on Sundays, when in addition to the evening "dress parade," the troops, headed by their band, passed in review before Colonel Mann, and marched around the race course. The female visitors to the camp were not always of the most refined and unexceptionble class, and although they possessed much patriotism and love for the soldiers, it occasionally was found necessary to drum them out, and although it produced much merriment to the spectators, it was rather distasteful to the individuals themselves.

While laying at Camp Washington, the remains of John Lerch, of Captain Dachrodt's company, First Regiment Pennsylvania Volunteers (three months men) were sent to Easton for interment. The funeral obsequies was performed by the Taggart Guards, Lieutenant J. K. Brown, and the Constitutional Rangers, Captain Thomas Bringhurst, the battalion being under the command of Captain Woodward. The ceremony was very imposing, Pomp's Cornet Band, with muffled drums, playing the "Dead March in Saul."

The funeral of young Moyer of the same regiment, also took place; the escort consisting of the "Williamsburg Legion," Captain F. Burger; the "Quaker City Guards," Captain R. M. McClure; the "Harmer Guards," Captain Thomas F. B. Tapper; the "Hatborough Rifles, Captain I. W. Kimble; the "Governor's Rangers," Lieutenant George Young; the "Dickson Guards," Lieutenant J. B. Baker; the "Reed Guards," Lieutenant P. M. Davis; the "Able Guards," Lieutenant Thomas G. O'Hara; the "Governor's Guards," J. D. Edwards, the "Governor's Rangers," Lieutenant John D. Schock; the battalion being under the command of Captain Ellis. It was many years since Easton had witnessed such funeral ceremonies.

CHAPTER IV.

ORGANIZATION OF THE SECOND, THIRD AND FOURTH RESERVES. DISSATISFACTION THEREWITH. ELECTION OF FIELD OFFICERS. WATCHED AND FANNED ALL NIGHT. DEPARTURE OF THE FOURTH AND THIRD REGIMENTS.

ON the 14th of June, General McCall visited the camp to organize the regiments, supposing the independent companies had formed voluntary associations with one or the other of the three colonels who had parts of their regiments quartered there. Not finding such to be the case, however, after a consultation with Colonel Mann, the general issued an order for the organization of the camp, which order, after stating that "the best interests of the service demanded that the companies brought together at this camp shall be organized at the earliest day, practicable," went on to say, "it would be desirable that the proposed organization should be arranged by the voluntary association of companies." He concluded by ordering that if such voluntary association could not be effected by the 19th inst., inclusive, the "organization would be conducted in the following manner: The ten companies which first arrived in camp and in the order they are now quartered, will constitute a regiment, to be known as the Second regiment; the next ten will form the Third regiment, and the last ten will form the Fourth regiment of the Pennsylvania Reserve Volunteer Corps. Each regiment so formed, will proceed without delay to elect their field officers." The companies, as quartered, were: First, eight of Colonel Mann's and two independent; next, five of Colonel De Korponay's; next, five independent; next and last, seven of Colonel Marsh's and three independent.

On the 20th, General McCall again visited the camp, and in the evening convened the captains at the commissary's building, and proceeded to organize the regiments.

As no voluntary associations had been effected, the order was read, when Lieutenant H. Clay Beatty arose and stated that as Captain Thompson's company did not arrive until several days after De Korponay's had, he should not be thrown into the first division. Against this the De Korponay companies earnestly protested, maintaining that as they were the companies assigned to the colonel by the Governor, they could not be taken from him, and as Captain Thompson's company had been accepted by the Governor as one of Colonel Mann's, he rightfully belonged to him, and that the mere fact of the delay of a few days in his arrival in camp, where quarters had been assigned, and kept for him, did not alter the case. After considerable argument, the General announced that the names of Captains Thompson and Sickel and four of De Korponay's captains be placed in a hat, and the question of which two companies should go to Colonel Mann, be decided by lot.

This gave two chances to one against Colonel De Korponay. Lieutenant Henry A. Scheetz, aid-de-camp to General McCall, drew the slips, and the first two names drawn were Captains G. A. Woodward and E. M. Woodward. This destroyed all hope of the De Korponay regiment. It cannot be denied, the officers and men were deeply attached to De Korponay, and the effect of this blow upon them was severely felt. A captain of one of the companies detached, threw himself upon his hands and wept like a child, and his company broke out in open mutiny, and attempted to seize a number of muskets in a neighboring officer's quarters. It was with the utmost difficulty the other De Korponay's companies could be kept quiet, and in fact it was deemed necessary to order out the whole camp for the purpose. Though defeated, the De Korponay companies desired to remain together, for which purpose, Captains Smith and Finnie of the Third regiment exchanged with Captains Thompson and McClure of the Second regiment.

The three regiments having now been formed, elections were held in them the next day for Field Officers, which resulted as follows:

Second Regiment.—Colonel, Wm. B. Mann. Lieutenant-Colonel, Albert L. Magilton. Major, Wm. McCandless.

Third Regiment.—Horatio G. Sickel. Lieutenant-Colonel, Wm. S. Thompson. Major, Richard H. Woolworth.

Fourth Regiment.—Colonel, Robert G. March. Lieutenant-Colonel, John F. Gaul. Major, Robert M. McClure.

The four De Korponay companies of the Second Regiment, cast a unanimous vote for Colonel De Korponay and Lieutenant-Colonel A. L. Snowden.

Soon after, the men commenced receiving clothing from the State, the first instalment, consisting of twenty blankets and forty pair of shoes for each company, and some time after their complete outfit and arms came.

The Fourth of July in due course of time rolled round, and was duly celebrated with the usual festivities appropriate for the occasion. Of course the liberty of the camp was much enlarged, and the number of passes to town largely increased, while a still larger proportion of "absent without leave," managed to get out. Although many of the patriots' brains became in a highly inflammatory state, every thing passed off in good humor, and taking all things into consideration, they had a very happy and jovial time. As a precautionary measure, heavy details were sent from camp to patrol the town and collect the disabled, who were conveyed to camp and carefully stowed away in their bunks, until they became refreshed with sleep.

For the better accommodation of the sick, a large hospital was erected near the centre of the race course, in a wooded grove, to which was attached a laboratory, kitchen, washing and dining rooms. This building was appropriated to the Second Regiment, the hospitals of the Third and Fourth Regiments being located at the Head-quarters of their respective colonels.

One day upon the arrival of the Philadelphia train at South Easton, a young soldier who was "slightly inebriated," fell through the trestle work upon a coal pile below, a distance of twenty feet, and his Captain and one of the Surgeon's being there, immediately went to his assistance, but before their arrival he had got up and started for camp. Fearing he was internally hurt, they started in pursuit, and soon overtaking him, detained him until an ambulance could be sent for. Night came, but no ambulance, so he was put in a carriage, conveyed to camp, stripped, examined and lapped up in warm blankets and put to bed in his bunk. In the meantime the ambulance came down the street in search of the wounded soldier, and finding a "green shirter," stretched upon a cellar door, he was carefully picked up and conveyed with brotherly care to the Camp Hospital, where two of his comrades were detailed to watch over and fan him through the night.

Through the long and weary hours, faithfully did they perform their charge, with a love and watchfulness known only among comrades. The morning came, but the soldier still slept, until at last the Surgeon approaching him, gently woke him up. "Andy, my boy, how do you feel?" "Feel," replied the bewildered boy, as he gazed upon the strange scene around him, "feel, why where am I? what has happened to me?" "Ah, Andy," replied the Surgeon in a kind and gentle voice, as he stripped off the bed clothing to examine him, "I fear you are seriously hurt; you fell through the tressel work at South Easton, and the only wonder is, it did not kill you instantly. Draw your leg up and stretch it out." Andy with some misgivings, slowly obeyed. "Draw up the other one—now stretch out your arms." "Does that hurt you," said the Surgeon as he pressed his ribs and breast. "No, sir," replied Andy.

"See here, young man," said the Surgeon, beginning to smell a rat, "I guess you were drunk last night, get up out of that bed and travel." "Well," replied Andy as the truth flashed upon him, and a comical expression came over his face, "I think you guess right, but Doctor, hadn't you better set those broken bones of mine first?" As Andy passed down the ward, a tittering was heard among the patients, and some unable to repress their smiles, covered their heads with their blankets, and gave vent to hearty laughter. A quiet old gentleman who witnessed the scene, called Andy to one side as he passed through the laboratory, and gave him a drink of brandy, remarking, that "that would set his bones all right." Andy enjoyed the arrangement wonderfully, and was always afterwards on the best terms with the Surgeon. The young man who fell through the tressel work, was on drill the next morning as sound as ever.

On the 14th, His Excellency, Andrew G. Curtin, Governor of the State arrived, and a review of the troops was ordered. The men were dressed in their light blue pants, neat dark blue blouses, and fatigue caps, with their muskets and brasses as bright as new dollars. Being thrown into column of companies, they passed in review before His Excellency, who was surrounded by his staff. The affair was very creditable for newly organized troops, and the Governor expressed himself much pleased.

The next day, Major H. D. Maxwell, the Paymaster-General of the State of Pennsylvania, arrived in camp and commenced paying off the Second Regiment, but when he got through with two companies, orders were received for the Fourth to prepare to march, so the payment of the Second was suspended, and that of the Fourth commenced and got through within a short time.

On the 16th, the Fourth, Colonel March, left the camp and proceeded by rail to Harrisburg. The payment of the Second and Third Regiments was resumed and soon completed, and on the 22d, the Third, Colonel Sickel, was ordered to Harrisburg.

CHAPTER V.

DEPARTURE OF THE SECOND. ITS ROSTER. CAMP CURTIN. LEAVE THE STATE WITHOUT BEING MUSTERED INTO THE UNITED STATES SERVICE. MARCHING WITHOUT ORDERS. BALTIMORE. SANDY HOOK. DISCONTENT AMONG THE MEN. REFUSAL TO TAKE THE OATH. SENT HOME IN DISGRACE. STRANGE MISMANAGEMENT. MARCH TO BERLIN.

THE news of the disastrous battle of Bull Run being received, orders were issued for the Second Regiment to prepare to move on the morning of the 24th of July, and accordingly about nine o'clock, they bid farewell to the camp, and marched through Easton across the Lehigh to the depot. Pomp's Cornet Band escorted them, the bells were rung, the citizens cheered, and the ladies waved their handkerchiefs. The organization of the Regiment was as follows:

Colonel, Wm. B. Mann. Lieutenant-Colonel, A. L. Magilton. Major, Wm. McCandless. Adjutant, ———. Quartermaster, Charles F. Hoyt. Surgeon, Thomas B. Reed. Assistant Surgeon, J. W. Lodge. Sergeant Major, Augustus T. Cross. Quartermaster Sergeant, Wesley S. Mann.

Company A.—Captain, G. A. Woodward. First Lieutenant, R. H. Loudon. Second Lieutenant, Horace Neide.

Company B.—Captain, P. McDonough. First Lieutenant, John D. Schock. Second Lieutenant, John J. Gill.

Company C.—Captain, James N. Byrnes. First Lieutenant, John B. Robinson. Second Lieutenant, Frank Fox.

Company D.—Captain, R. Ellis. First Lieutenant, John Curley. Second Lieutenant, George Young.

Company E.—Captain, J. Orr Finnie. First Lieutenant, J. Baxter Fletcher. Second Lieutenant, Alexander Black.

Company F.—Captain, Thomas Bringhurst. First Lieutenant, George W. Kite. Second Lieutenant, William J. D. Edwards,

Company G.—Captain, E. M. Woodward. First Lieutenant, Henry A. Scheetz. Second Lieutenant, John K. Brown.

Company H.—Captain, Timothy Mealey. First Lieutenant, Peter Summers. Second Lieutenant, — ——.

Company I.—Captain, William Knox. First Lieutenant, Thomas Weir. Second Lieutenant, John H. Jack.

Company K.—Captain, P. I. Smith. First Lieutenant, Isaac J. Harvey. Second Lieutenant, James C. Justus.

Amidst the cheers of the crowd the cars moved off, and the day being excessively warm, the boys soon proceeded to produce ventilation by knocking the sides out of the freight cars, with the butts of their muskets. Although the tops of the cars were crowded, and the bridges on the road were very low, but one man was hurt during the passage, he receiving a severe contusion on the back of the head, that set him so wild, that it required several men to hold him down to prevent his jumping off. Along the route flags were displayed from the houses, and at the villages the populace turned out *en masse* to welcome our passage. About four o'clock in the afternoon we arrived at Harrisburg, and marched out to Camp Curtin, where we enjoyed the novelty and romance of sleeping upon the soft green grass, with nothing but the vault of heaven above us, from which descended a copious shower of rain during the night.

All the regiments of the Reserve, we believe, with but one exception, were mustered into the United States service before leaving the State, and it was Colonel Mann's desire we should also be, but as it would cause a delay of some days, the Colonel was induced by Lieutenant-colonel Magilton, and with the consent of the Governor, to proceed to Baltimore without its being done. Accordingly, at two o'clock the next afternoon we marched to the railroad, and at dark took the cars and proceeded on our way several miles, where we laid on a sideling until near daybreak the next morning, when moving on, we arrived at Baltimore early in the afternoon, and slept that night upon a common opposite the depot.

Upon the regiment being reported to General Dix, who commanded the Department, and he ascertaining we came there without any orders, he declined having any thing to do with us, until he telegraphed to Simon Cameron, the Secretary of War, upon the subject. Mr. Cameron, probably vexed at such unauthorized proceedings, and being on bad terms with Colonel Mann, on account of his defeat in the gubernatorial convention, replied in a very unsatisfactory manner, when it was determined to move the regiment to Sandy Hook, which point was then reported to be threatened by the rebels under General Jackson.

Early on Sunday morning, July 28th, our regiment marched through the city to the depot of the Baltimore and Ohio Railroad, where we took cars for Sandy Hook. It numbered one thousand and one, officers and men, and were as fine a body of soldiers as ever passed through the city. Their neat new uniform, their steady tramp and well-dressed lines, with their martial bearing, attracted the attention of all, and many were the inquiries as to what regiment it was. At the depot they were met by the Union Relief Committee, who supplied them with an abundance of ice-water. On the route to Sandy Hook many American flags were displayed, and at Ellicott's Mills unmistakable signs of loyalty were shown by the waving of handkerchiefs and the cheers of the people. We arrived at the "Point of Rocks," about four P. M., where we found two companies of Vermont three months volunteers, guarding that point. The bridge at this place was burnt by the rebels on the 8th of June, and a huge rock, many tons in weight, tumbled upon the track. The rebels may have been picketing on the opposite bank of the Potomac, but whether they were or not, the boys had the satisfaction of imagining they saw them. After an hour's delay, we started on, finding the road picketed for twelve miles up, the distance to Sandy Hook, where we arrived after dark, and found many of the three months men on their way home, their time having expired, and all the army having that day crossed to the Maryland shore of the Potomac, except a few left to occupy Harper's Ferry, about two miles above. It had been raining hard through the afternoon, the night was exceedingly dark and unpleasant, and after remaining a long while awaiting orders, the men laid down along the road and went to sleep.

The next morning was oppressively hot, and after making coffee, we formed and marched to Pleasant valley, a table-land plateau, about a mile back from, and some four hundred feet above, the Potomac. This valley lays between the mountains known as Maryland Heights, abutting opposite Harper's Ferry, and a spur of the Blue Ridge, terminating on the Potomac, at the village of Knoxville, on the Baltimore and Ohio Railroad, overlooking Harper's Ferry, Sandy Hook, and Knoxville, and commanding the country roads running from the former place towards Hagerstown and Frederick. The location was unassailable, except from the opposite Virginia or Loudon Heights, which would really command the position, but for the existence of obstacles almost insuperable to the placing of any battery there. Here we encamped in a wheat stubble-field, and received our camp equipage and tents.

The night of our arrival, the regiment was reported to General Banks, commanding the Department of the Shenandoah, whose first inquiry was by whose authority we came there, and upon his ascertaining we had come upon our "own hook," he declined to have any thing to do with us, until he communicated with the War Department. The general, however, assigned us camping grounds, and the next day before night, the colonel succeeded in obtaining for the men a part of a ration, by indemnifying the commissary of subsistence from any loss.

Discontent among the men soon commenced showing itself, and was increased from the fact of our being encamped next to the Twenty-eighth Pennsylvania Volunteers, of which De Korponay was Lieutenant-Colonel, and who received their full ration, and of a much better quality than our own. A rumor, that obtained much credence among the men, was put afloat, to the effect, that they being out of the State of Pennsylvania, and not mustered into the United States service, there was no power to hold them. It soon after coming to the knowledge of General Banks that an officer of another regiment was tampering with the men, and had offered to enlist them in his regiment if they would not be mustered in, an order was issued by him prohibiting the enlistment of any of the men, under penalty of cashiering the officer who did so, and directing the drumming out of camp of any of them found enlisted. This discontent, there is not the slightest doubt, was countenanced and encouraged by a field officer of our own regiment, whose object was to bring Colonel Mann into bad repute, and wear the eagles upon his own shoulders. Secret meetings were held by the men, and the ringleaders were led to suppose that if the regiment was broken up, they would be sent to Philadelphia, and that the would-be-colonel would obtain permission to reorganize them, and they would be made officers.

This discontent continued until the 1st of August, when it reached its climax. That afternoon Lieutenant-colonel Fitz John Porter, U. S. A., "the extreme West Pointer," was sent by General Banks to muster the regiment in. Commencing on the right, he discovered mutinous intentions among a portion of the men, which extended to every company in the regiment. This was increased by his very injudicious remarks, he apparently caring very little whether the men were mustered in or not. When they were ordered to hold up their right hand and take the oath of allegiance to their Government, about one-fourth refused to do so. The reasons assigned by them was, that they were armed with smooth-bored muskets, (the only ones the Government at that time could give them,) their crowded tents, (five in each,) bad rations, (better than some of them got at home,) not having overcoats, (in the middle of Summer,) their unwillingness to serve under Colonel Mann, (their own choice,) they, in fact, like all other men who were doing wrong, using every subterfuge to justify their conduct. They were marched to their quarters, and the names of all who had taken the oath, forwarded to headquarters.

The next morning the regiment was again called out to have the oath administered, and to the surprise of all, those who had taken the oath the day before, were required to take it again, they being informed that those who refused would be sent home in disgrace. The consequence of such injudicious proceedings was what might have been expected, and instead of one-fourth, nearly one-third, or three hundred and twenty refused. They were then marched to General Thomas' headquarters, ordered to stack arms, divest themselves of their accoutrements, and strip off their blouses and blue pants, retaining only their linen pants and shirts. An order was then issued detailing eleven officers, leaving five companies without any officers, to conduct them to Philadelphia, it stating, "this order is peremptory, and must not be disobeyed." Late that afternoon they left Sandy Hook in a special train, the men giving Lieutenant-colonel Magilton three cheers at their departure. They conducted themselves very orderly, and at Broad and Prime streets were dismissed to their homes, but how they were received we know not.

The officers having learned Governor Curtin was in the city, proceeded to the Continental Hotel to call upon him, but he at first declined having an interview with them. Having granted one, however, what was their surprise and indignation at being shown a telegram he had just received from General Banks' Assistant Adjutant-general, stating that they, and over three hundred of the men, having refused to take the oath of allegiance, had been sent home in disgrace. A few moments' conversation, however, satisfied His Excellency that a gross and dishonorable deception had been practiced by some officer of the regiment upon General Banks, and he expressed his willingness to issue an order to have the officers mustered in immediately, and furnish them with transportation back to their regiment. But as the officers had been mustered in, the order was unnecessary.

Upon their arrival back at Sandy Hook, they were met with another unaccountable surprise, in finding that the men whom they had left in camp, and who had been sworn into the service twice before, had been called upon that day to take the oath for the third time. "It is necessary," said the men, "for a good soldier to carry a Bible with him to be sworn in on, or he will find himself discharged before he knows anything about it." In fact, many of the men, finding it easier to get out of the service than to stay in it, concluded to go home and enter some other regiment, and out of one thousand and one men who marched through Baltimore two weeks before, but a little over four hundred remained. The men whose officers had been sent home with the deserters, being told they would not return, and that they would be transferred to other companies, left almost in a body.

Who was responsible for such unaccountable and criminally mismanaged proceedings, the reader must judge for himself. It is just to those men to state, though they deserted the flag when almost within sight of the enemy, that, with few exceptions, they entered the service again, and their blood has been poured out upon almost every battle-field of the Army of the Potomac.

On Sunday morning the 11th, the Independent Rangers, of Philadelphia, Captain Wm. McMullin, who were encamped near by, started home, being escorted to the cars by Company D. The next morning, The First City Troop of Philadelphia Light Cavalry, Captain James, broke camp and marched homeward, *via* Hagerstown and Baltimore, being escorted a distance on their way by the Twenty-Eighth Regiment Pennsylvania Volunteers, Colonel Geary. These two companies at the request of the general, had consented to remain some time after their term of service expired, for which they received his thanks.

On the 13th, Colonel Geary received orders to march to the Point of Rocks, twelve miles down the Potomac, and after dark they got into motion, a guide being employed to pilot them by a back road, to prevent the movement being discovered by the enemy. The night was exceedingly dark, and the pilot having intentionally or unintentionally lost the way, and not having any desire to become a stockholder in the colonel's lead mine, thought it prudent to decamp; so the colonel, after hunting around for him for some time, with pistol in hand, turned into a narrow road which proved to be a private lane. As the baggage wagons were passing through the barn yard one of them upset, which was followed by considerable noise, occasioned by the braying of mules, and the shouting and cursing of the teamsters. The colonel went to the house to procure a lantern, but all his pounding, shouting and throwing stones at the windows, produced no effect. At last he heard meek, tremulous voices issuing from the cellar, and discovered the old folks and children in their night clothes, down there praying for deliverance from the battle they supposed was raging around their house.

On the 14th, orders were received to reduce our baggage as much as possible, and to pack up and send to Harrisburg the extra articles left by the deserters. About one A. M., while in the midst of the work, the drums beat the "long roll," and the men dropping every thing, were soon in line with their muskets and cartridge boxes. When Dr. Reed went to the Hospital to get his instruments, he found his patients hurrying on their clothes, against which he remonstrated without avail, and before he could get a guard to enforce his orders, the sick were in the ranks and could not be got out. Leaving the camp "topsy turvy," in charge of the cooks and teamsters, we started off, and hurrying across the canal at Knoxville, proceeded down the towpath to Berlin, about four miles below, where a party of rebs had been firing upon the pickets of the Nineteenth New York, but with no other effect than the knocking over of some camp kettles and the scattering of their contents. Here we stacked arms and stretched ourselves upon the grass watching an old rascal on horseback waving a white flag, and who doubtlessly was calculating our strength.

On the 8th of June, the rebels burnt the long and substantial bridge that spanned the river at this point, and the only wagon communication between the two shores, are the fords above and below the piers. About two weeks back, the rebels brought an old iron twelve-pounder cannon that had its muzzle knocked off, and was fastened with chains to the front wheels of an old wagon, which they posted on the opposite hills to command the village. They thought it prudent to withdraw the same night, and hiding their cannon, they left, intending to return the next night and get it. The Berlinites, however, found it out, and slipping over brought it away, and at night it was stationed on the pier of the bridge, behind a bulwark of hay bales. Being minus of grape shot, they cut the iron braces of the bridge into slugs, which were about as good as anything else to fire out of it. After remaining here until it was ascertained that the rebels had decamped, we about face, and retraced our steps to camp, but all the spirit of the boys was gone, and our march was a quiet one. We arrived about dark, and had a late, but welcome supper.

At this time the Army of the Shenandoah picketed the Potomac for the distance of fifty miles, from Williamsport about twenty miles above the Ferry, until the line joined that of the Army of the Potomac, some thirty miles below. The enemy picketed on the south bank for an equal distance, we having abandoned Virginia, except in the immediate neighborhood of Harper's Ferry.

The greater portion of the rebel army under General Johnson, having joined Beauregard at Manassas, and left the valley of the Shenandoah and the upper Potomac comparatively bare of troops, which relieved all anxiety for the safety of Maryland and Pennsylvania, it was determined to make a corresponding movement of our forces towards Washington, which was not yet considered safe. Therefore, orders were issued on the night of the 16th, to be prepared to march early the next morning with three days cooked rations in haversacks. Fortunately the paymaster, Major Maxwell, arrived that day and paid the regiment off for the twenty-one days owed by the State of Pennsylvania, we having been transferred to the United States service on the 21st of July. This money was very acceptable to the empty pockets of the men, and was duly appreciated by the citizens of Maryland on our march through their State.

CHAPTER VI.

MARCH THROUGH MARYLAND. MUTINY IN THE NINETEENTH NEW YORK MILITIA. GUARDS AFTER WHISKY. DISBANDING OF COMPANIES.

ONE of the most exciting scenes in a soldier's life is the breaking up of camp when they have been lying inactive for some time, and particularly so when it is for the first time in active field service. Although the order to move was not issued until 10 o'clock at night, and rain was falling at the time, the camp fires were soon brightly burning and the men busily engaged in preparing their rations for the march. Early the next morning, before "reveille," the men were all up and stirring, and soon cooked their breakfasts and had everything ready to move. And what a scene of animation it was! The striking of tents, the packing of baggage, the loading of wagons, the falling in of the men, their cheers and songs, intermingled with the strains of martial music, the shouts and curses of the drivers, the braying of mules, the galloping to and fro of orderlies and aids, the rattling drums and hoarse commands—oh, how animated and exciting. "Frank, help me on with my knapsack," "Ben, fix my cartridge box," "Charley, hold my musket while I go for water," "Take my canteen along," shouts a dozen voices, "Who'se got a piece of string," "Give me a cork for my canteen," "Who wants a good blouse," and a thousand other similar expressions are heard through the camps. "Fall in, fall in," is heard, and the noise ceases as the men take their places.

A cold drizzly rain was falling, as the wagons moved from the encampment, and stretched in a long line in a neighboring field, followed by the regiment, clad in heavy blue overcoats. Colonel Thomas, with his staff and the Second U. S. Cavalry dashed past, followed by a battery of the Fourth U. S. Artillery, and one of the Ninth New York. The Twenty-ninth Penna. Vols., Colonel Murphy, passed next, then came the Second Reserve, Colonel Mann, followed by the First Reserve Rifles—the "Bucktails," Colonel Biddle. Next came the Fifth Connecticut, Colonel Ferry, and the Nineteenth New York Volunteers, and a long line of other troops, but the smoke from the burning rubbish of the camp hung heavily upon the earth, partially obscuring the masses of men, presenting a scene at once grand and interesting. "Forward," passed down the line, and to the soul-stirring music of our bands, we took up our march, striking the banks of the Potomac, which we followed for a short distance, when turning to the left, in a northeasterly direction, we halted at intervals to rest the men and let the wagons come up. We passed through Petersville, a small village where a secession flag had lately been flying; but the old flag of our hearts now floated in its stead. In the afternoon we passed through Jefferson, as pretty a village as Maryland can boast of. Our bands struck up lively marches, and smiling faces from Union hearts, and waving handkerchiefs greeted us, as we passed along. We turned to the right toward the Point of Rocks, then to the left towards Frederick, moving over a narrow road through the woods, to the left of which was presented a magnificent scene of rolling hills and wooded valleys, broken in the far distance by the lofty peaks of the Blue Ridge. At dusk we halted to select a bivouacking ground, and then moving off entered a thick woods, where our blazing camp fires were soon surrounded by the wearied soldiers. The flakes rose high in the air; the flames casting their lurid light through the arching branches of the majestic trees; and wrapped in our blankets, with our feet to the fire, we slept peacefully until "reveille." Our march that day was fifteen miles.

The next day we started early, it being cloudy, drizzly and oppressively close, and by noon crossed a branch of the Monocacy, and encamped on its banks in a wheat stubble, having made but six miles. Here we were met by Dr. Hoyt, our quartermaster, who had gone ahead to procure provisions and wood for us.

The next morning, the 19th, we moved at eight o'clock, through a drizzling rain and deep mud, passing through Buckeystown whose inhabitants are of strong secession proclivity. Not a flag was seen or a handkerchief waved to welcome us. The darkies and children were highly delighted with the music and novel sight, the men stayed in the houses and peeped through cracks, but the women's curiosity overcoming them, stood at the doors and windows looking pictures of woful sorrow. About a mile from here we crossed the Monocacy and encamped on its banks, having marched eight miles. Here we found concentrated a large number of other troops. As we did not move the next day, the men had a good time bathing, several thousands of them enjoying it at once, resembling as they sat on the innumerable rocks in the river, flocks of penguins. That night we sent off all our sick to the general hospital at Frederick.

The next morning we struck tents and got into motion early, passing through Urbana, and encamping about noon near Hyattstown, we having marched six miles. There the next day, August 22d, a mutiny broke out in the Nineteenth New York State Militia. This regiment had been sworn into the State service for two years, and transferred to the United States under the President's second call. The term of three months having expired, the men claimed that they were released from further service, and that the Government had no right to continue them in the service for the balance of the two years. In fact, they tried the same game on, that had been so successfully played by the mutineers of our regiment, but they had the wrong man to deal with. The regiment was formed, the wings doubled up, faced inwards and arms stacked. The wings were then marched to the rear, leaving about sixty paces between them, a portion of the articles of war and the governor's orders read to them, and those who were willing to obey, ordered to step to the front. But one hundred and eighty did so. These were placed on guard over the rest, and the "Bucktails" sent for. In the mean time a battery of artillery was unlimbered and placed in position about three hundred yards from them and soon after the "Bucktails" came down on double quick and were formed into two lines. The mutineers remained silent, quietly watching the proceedings, when Colonel Biddle rode up, and giving the necessary orders marched them into the space between his lines, and escorted them to an open field, where they enjoyed the luxury of a broiling sun for the remainder of the day, and a drenching rain all night, which cooled them off and refreshed them wonderfully. The next morning the patriots were so transmogrified, that all but a few returned to duty, and the balance were shipped to the Tortugas. This regiment afterwards proved itself one of the bravest and most gallant in the service, and this little freak of theirs proves that upon such occasions it only requires firmness and judgment to keep men in the right path and prevent them from disgracing themselves.

We remained in camp until noon of that day, when we marched to the southward about one mile, and encamped on the skirt of a fine piece of wood, where the ground was high and dry. Here considerable labor was spent in fixing up our camp, digging sinks and cutting a broad path through the wood for the camp guard to move on. In obedience to orders the baggage was very much reduced, officers being limited to eighty pounds, and the men to what they could carry on their backs. Two axes, one hatchet, five mess-pans, two camp kettles, were allowed to twenty men, and one tent to six. This, at that time was exceedingly limited, but we afterwards learned to look upon it as sufficient for a whole company. On the 24th, Company E, Captain J. Orr Finnie, was ordered to escort a train of one hundred wagons to Washington, which they did successfully, and rejoined us on the march back.

Considerable liquor having been introduced into camp, Colonel Mann ordered Captain ——— with his company and part of K, to seize and destroy all he could find in the neighborhood. Sixteen barrels belonging to a storekeeper at Charlesburg were destroyed, for which the Government paid. But the hardest job was to find the liquor belonging to a man who had followed the regiment from Easton, Pennsylvania. He generally kept his liquor a mile or two off, and went to the huts and farm houses near the camp, and represented himself as a sutler waiting for his team. By the time he sold out his jug of whiskey, the guards would discover his whereabouts, and when they arrived he was gone to refill, and the next day would commence operations at some other cabin. At the railroad station near Buckeystown he played an exceedingly sharp trick on all concerned. A tavern keeper there was doing a lively business at five cents per glass. ——— had but one keg, and wanted to make the most out of it possible, so he got some of the men drunk and succeeded in raising a fight, when he immediately reported it to one of the colonels, who shut the tavern up. Then ——— opened his keg in a bye-place, and sold out at ten cents per glass. But his time soon after came, they caught him, destroyed his liquor, and he was banished from our regiment forever afterwards. He was a fair sample of camp followers.

On the 27th, the First Brigade, Colonel George H. Thomas, consisting of the Second United States Cavalry, one battery Fourth United States Artillery, one battery Ninth New York, the First Rifles, P. R. V. C., "Bucktails," Colonel Biddle; the Second Infantry, P. R. V. C., Colonel Mann; the Twenty-ninth Pennsylvania Volunteers, Colonel Murphy; the Nineteenth New York State Militia, Colonel ———, and the Fifth Connecticut, Colonel Ferry, were reviewed by Major-General Nathaniel P. Banks. The day unfortunately was drizzling, which in a measure spoiled the effect. However, as the cavalry, artillery and infantry wheeled into column, and passed in review, they presented a fine appearance. The bands of each regiment wheeled to the left out of the column in front of the general, and continued playing until the regiment passed, when it followed in the rear. The colonels took their position by the side of the general until their command passed, the officers and colors saluting, and the men coming to a carry. The next afternoon, the Second Brigade was reviewed by the general, but it rained then also.

While lying here, an order was issued by General Banks, disbanding Companies B, F, G and I, on the ground of being "below the legal standard of acceptance," the men being transferred to the other companies of the regiment, and the officers honorably discharged. There were some points in this order worthy of observation. The companies could not be "accepted," although they had been regularly mustered into the United States service nearly a month before, and the officers had been in the exercise and discharge of their duties during that time, and were recognized as such. they subsequently drawing their pay. Again, the officers were "honorably discharged" from the United States service, which the order stated they could not be "accepted" into. But the most important point in regard to the order is, that it was illegal, there being no authority to discharge an officer from the army, except by order of the President of the United States. This is distinctly stated in the Army Regulations of 1861, and was subsequently ad mitted to the author, by the Honorable Simon Cameron, Secretary of War. General Banks, however, had but lately entered upon his military life, and doubtless was ignorant of the laws upon the subject, or else it is hardly to be supposed he would have assumed a power not vested in him, and that too, when he had received orders to send all the Pennsylvania Reserves to General McCall. General McCall entertained the same opinion of the illegality of the order, and protested against it, but Fitz John Porter was indirectly connected with the arrangement, and he, with General Banks, were favorites of Mr. Cameron, and their friends were pushing them for positions, so the Secretary would not revoke an order he acknowledged to be illegal.

This was a gross act of injustice, as the officers were no more responsible for the loss of the men, than if they had been killed in battle, but the colonel finding his ranks greatly reduced, was unwilling to await the slow process of recruiting, and supposing the governor would immediately order four full companies to fill up the regiment, he sanctioned the act. But His Excellency could not be induced to assign companies in their place, and so far from acknowledging the legality of the act, he soon after issued commissions to the officers. The officers discharged were Captains P. McDonough, T. Bringhurst, E. M. Woodward and William Knox. First Lieutenants John D. Schock, George W. Kite, John K. Brown and Thomas Weir. Second Lieutenants John Gill, William Edwards and John H. Jack. One lieutenant of the companies was not discharged, another discharged who had resigned a month before, and had not been mustered into the United States service, and another transferred to a company in which there was no vacancy. Captain McDonough raised another company, joined the regiment at Camp Pierpont, and was subsequently promoted lieutenant-colonel. Captain Woodward entered the ranks along with his men who remained true, was appointed sergeant-major of the regiment and at the battle of Antietam, promoted adjutant. Captain Knox was appointed sutler, and continued with the regiment until May, 1862. Of the lieutenants, John H. Jack returned with Captain McDonough, was wounded at the battle of Bull Run, and promoted captain for gallant conduct. John K. Brown for a year was connected with the brigade commissary. Wm. Edwards entered the Curtin Light Guard as orderly sergeant, and George W. Kite the Ninety-first Regiment Pennsylvania Volunteers. About this time First Lieutenant Isaac J. Harvey, Company K, was detailed to the Signal Corps.

On the 28th, orders were received to draw provisions and prepare to march, and during the evening there was a busy time cooking and packing up. At three o'clock the next morning the reveille sounded, and soon the camp was all astir, and at seven we took up our line of march, the rain descending in torrents, drenching us to the skin. But onward the men pressed through the mud, and about four o'clock in the afternoon, after a tiresome march of only eight miles, went into camp about two miles from Darnestown. The next day Colonel Thomas was detached from the command of our brigade, which devolved upon Colonel Charles J. Biddle, of the "Bucktails." The regiment remained here until the 19th of September, when at eleven o'clock at night the "long roll" awakened the sleepers. Getting under arms and into line, we moved off in a southeasterly direction, and after a march of eight miles arrived at Muddy Branch, a tributary of the Potomac, where we were sent to guard a supply train. Here we remained until the 25th, when we again moved, marching fifteen miles, to Tenallytown, where we joined the Division of Pennsylvania Reserves, under Brigadier-General George A. McCall.

CHAPTER VII.

TENALLYTOWN. VISIT FROM THE PRESIDENT AND GENERAL McCLELLAN. PRESENTATION OF FLAGS. A HAIL-STORM. THE REGIMENTS BRIGADED.

TENALLYTOWN is situated at the junction of the Rockville and Poolesville roads with the Georgetown road, three miles from the latter town, and one mile and a half from the Chain Bridge. Here was erected Fort Pennsylvania, a most important and formidable earthwork, with a broad and deep ditch, heavy abatis, and guns mounted barbette. It was built by the Reserves, details being made from all the regiments for that purpose.

Prior to our arrival several interesting ceremonies took place, among which was a grand review of the Division by His Excellency Mr. Lincoln, attended by his Cabinet, and Major-General George B. McClellan, commanding the Army of the Potomac. The next day the following order was issued and read at the head of the regiments of the Reserves on dress-parade :

HEADQUARTERS PENNSYLVANIA RESERVE VOLUNTEER CORPS,
Camp Tenally, *August* 21*st*, 1861.

Soldiers of the Pennsylvania Reserve! This day must be recognized as a propitious inauguration of your future military history. You have this day passed under the scrutinizing inspection of the Commanding General of the Army of the Potomac, in whose ability to successfully prosecute this war, the confidence of the country is reposed. You have passed in review before the President of the United States and his Cabinet; and both the General and the President have expressed to me their unqualified approval of your soldierlike appearance on review, and of the discipline thus manifestly shown to exist in the corps.

It now rests with you, officers of the Pennsylvania Reserve, to carry out to perfection the work so well begun. Upon you devolves the care of your men; let that be unremitting; let every attention to their wants temper the rigid discipline necessary to the formation of the soldier, and with one heart we will uphold the flag of our State, and place her name among the foremost in the cause of our common country.

GEO. A. McCALL,
Brigadier-General Commanding.

On the 10th of September, the presentation of the flags, the gift of the Society of the Cincinnati, of Pennsylvania, to the Reserves took place. But nine regiments were present, which were drawn up in a large field adjoining the River Road. The color companies of each regiment were marched to the front with their colonel on their right. Soon the swelling notes of a fine band were heard far away in the distance, and as the music approached the guns of Fort Pennsylania and Campbell's batteries of the First Reserve Artillery thundered forth their salutes, which echoed from hill to hill, and reverberated through the valleys until it seemed like the roar of battle. Ere the sound had died away, the First Reserve, Colonel Simmons, and a procession of carriages appeared in view, containing His Excellency the President of the United States, accompanied by his Cabinet, Governor Curtin and General McClellan, with a host of government and Pennsylvania officials, reporters, &c. The flags were produced, and Governor Curtin commenced the presentation, and as each colonel received his regimental flag, he briefly returned thanks for the gift. The presentation being over, the Governor addressed the troops. When he told them that they were his fellow-citizens and Pennsylvanians, and that the honor and faith of Pennsylvania, to the last drop of her blood, and the last dollar of her resources, were pledged to the support of the Government, and the maintenance of our beloved institutions, he mounted the back seat of the carriage, and declaring that he was in full view of thousands of her citizens assembled to carry that determination into effect, the enthusiasm was unbounded, and cheer after cheer went up from thousands of manly throats.

General McCall briefly replied to the Governor, thanking him for the gifts, and giving the assurance that the colors would never be dishonored.

The presentation over, the regiments wheeled into columns of companies and passed in review before the Governor. After this the company attending the President and Governor partook of a collation, in pic-nic style, in the grove fronting General McCall's headquarters. There were several ladies in the party—Mrs. Governor Curtin, Mrs. General Maxwell, and others, whose presence added greatly to the pleasure of the occasion. The greatest sociability prevailed, and all present enjoyed themselves. President Lincoln was in his happiest mood, and was the life of the company. Wit and sentiment ruled the hour, without stiff formality. Through with the repast, they stepped into their carriages, and passing over the Chain Bridge into Virginia, returned to Washington, *via* the Long Bridge.

While we laid here heavy details were made daily

for picket, cattle-guard, or working parties on the fort, besides which Colonel Mann was indefatigable in his efforts to discipline the regiment by constant battalion and company drills. Several demonstrations of the enemy's pickets created alarms in camp, and caused us to get under arms, all of which were pleasant little excitements for the men. On the 7th of October, we were visited by a violent hail-storm accompanied with a high wind. Some of the stones were of the size of bullets, cutting through the tents, and almost driving the horses wild. The storm lasted about a half hour, leaving the atmosphere quite cool. The next day the fall election taking place in our State, the Reserves exercised their right of casting their vote, each company voting at its captain's quarters. About this time Lieutenant-Colonel Magilton resigned.

While we laid here the organization of the regiments into brigades took place.

The First Brigade, Brigadier-General John F. Reynolds, was comprised of the First Rifles, "Bucktails,' Colonel Charles J. Biddle; the First Infantry, Colonel R. Biddle Roberts; the Second Infantry, Colonel William B. Mann; the Fifth Infantry, Colonel Seneca G. Simmons; and the Eighth Infantry, Colonel Geor Hays.

The Second Brigade, Brigadier-General George Gordon Meade, was composed of the Third Infantry, Colonel Horatio G. Sickel; the Fourth Infantry, Colonel A. L. Magilton; the Eleventh Infantry, Colonel T. F. Gallagher; and the Seventh Infantry, Colonel E. B. Harvey.

The Third Brigade, Colonel J. S. McCalmont, was composed of the Sixth Infantry, Colonel W. W. Ricketts; the Ninth Infantry, Colonel Conrad F. Jackson; the Tenth Infantry, Colonel J. S. McCalmont; and the Twelfth Infantry, Colonel John H. Taggart.

The First Reserve Cavalry, Colonel George D. Bayard, and the First Reserve Artillery, Colonel Charles F. Campbell, although attached to the division were not brigaded.

CHAPTER VIII.

CROSSING THE CHAIN BRIDGE. CAMP PIERPONT. THE "LONG ROLL." BEAUREGARD RECONNOITRING. MARCH TO DRAINESVILLE. AN INDISCREET HEN. RETURN TO PIERPONT. BALL'S BLUFF. REVIEW. RESIGNATION OF COLONEL MANN. GRAND REVIEW.

EARLY on the morning of the 9th, General Smith advanced his division from the neighborhood of the Chain Bridge to Langley, where deploying his skirmishers, he pushed forward a brigade on the Drainesville pike, and took possession of Prospect Hill. With his main body, he diverged from the pike at Langley to the left, advancing towards Lewinsville, which village he entered and occupied without opposition, leaving the main portion of his troops at Smoot's Hill, and pushing on a detachment to occupy Miner's Hill.

To occupy this extension of the lines, the same day orders were issued to the Pennsylvania Reserves to march, and in a short time their tents were struck, wagons loaded and men in line. At seven o'clock in the evening our regiment took up its line of march, passing eastward through Tenallytown, and turning to the right, wound down a long, narrow, rough road to the Potomac, along which it moved to the Chain Bridge, and set foot for the first time upon the "sacred soil of Virginia." As the regiments crossed, their bands struck up "Dixie's Land," and their vociferous cheers burst forth, echoing from shore to shore of the rock-bound river. Moving on past Fort Marcy they bivouacked for the night about half a mile beyond Langley, Fairfax county.

The next afternoon the wagons arrived, the tents were pitched, and Camp Pierpont established, named in honor of Frank H. Pierpont, the loyal Governor of Western Virginia. The position assigned to the Reserves was the extreme right of the Army of the Potomac, their picket line extending from the river past Prospect Hill over towards Lewinsville. The camp of the Second was to the right of the Chain Bridge and Drainesville pike, on a low and badly drained piece of ground, at the base of a wooded hill, near the Langley School-House, which was occupied as the head-quarters of the First Brigade.

During the first ten days, the "long roll" was beaten, and the men got under arms five times. On the night of the 11th, the pickets in the neighborhood of Lewinsville were driven in, and the next day the enemy consisting of at least three regiments of infantry, some cavalry and a battery of six guns, were discovered near Miner's Hill, concealed in the woods, which led to the supposition that an attack was meditated the next morning. At noon the drums beat, and the men got into fighting order. General McClellan and staff, including the Comte de Paris and the Duc de Chartres, rode over and remainded during the night at Smoot's house, and at midnight the drums again beat and every preparation was made for an attack.

It was a clear and beautiful night, the moon shone forth in its mild beauty; the stars twinkled with resplendent glory, and not a cloud glided through the sky. The drums beat "the long roll," the trumpets of the cavalry and artillery sounded their shrill blasts, and the bands of the infantry pealed forth their most soul-inspiring strains. The camp-fires burned brightly, the glittering bayonets and sabres flashed in the light, and every heart beat high with hope. At two A. M., various columns of troops, on the Maryland side of the Potomac, were put in motion, and moved across the river to a position from which they could be easily thrown to any point of the line the emergency might require. Among them were some four thousand cavalry and fifty pieces of artillery. But alas, after remaining in position until daylight, chilled with the falling dews, the boys were doomed to disappointment. Beauregard had only been on a reconnoisance in force, to ascertain our position since the recent extension of our front.

About this time Orderly Sergeant Richard Clendining, Company H, was elected Second Lieutenant, vice Robert H. Porter, resigned, July 21st. Also, Sergeant James R. Nightingale, Company C, Second Lieutenant, vice Frank Fox, resigned.

About eleven o'clock on the night of the 18th, orders were issued for the Reserves to prepare to move early the next morning, with three days cooked rations in haversacks, and accordingly there was a busy time that night around the camp-fires. Early in the morning, the regiments were in line, and at seven o'clock they moved off up the pike towards Drainesville. The First Brigade, General Reynolds took the lead with a squadron of the Reserve cavalry, Colonel Bayard in the van, followed by two batteries of the Reserve artillery, Colonel Campbell, the "Bucktails" and infantry with the ambulances, or "avalanches," as the boys called them, bringing up the rear. Crossing Difficult creek, we continued on through Drainesville, and halted to bivouac three miles beyond. Soon after General McClellan rode up and ordered us to fall back about four miles to Thornton's house, at the forks of the Chain Bridge and Leesburg and Alexandria pikes. The artillery was posted to sweep the roads, pickets thrown out, and the men put in a heavy woods, where they slept peacefully.

When we first commenced our retrograde movement many surmises that soon assumed the shape of rumors were set afloat, and as we at that time were incapable of judging of military movements, they received much credence. An orderly came dashing down the road in search of General Reynolds and almost breathlessly informed him, there were "forty thousand rebels coming down upon us." "Forty thousand old fools," replied the General, "go back to where you came from."

The Second Brigade lay that night about three miles in our rear, and the Third about three miles in their rear at Difficult creek, to preserve our communication and prevent our rear being turned, General Smith's division was also moved out the Alexandria and Leesburg turnpike, to cover that road and those leading from Centreville to Drainesville.

The next morning by daylight the boys were up and hard at work cutting down the chestnut trees in the woods to get the nuts, and the squealing of pigs was heard in various directions. An old hen that had been roosting on a tree commenced cackling, which attracted the attention of a soldier who was passing by. "Madam," said the boy, "you had better have kept your mouth shut," as he knocked her off with a stone. These proceedings were however put a stop to, and the boys restricted to the limits of the camp.

On our march up we found a number of houses abandoned by their occupants, who had fled on our approach under the impression we were Mamelukes and Bedouins coming to murder and destroy all we found. At some places we found the furniture carried out on the lawn ready for moving. We also found houses that had been abandoned for some time, their inhabitants having been driven away by their neighbors on account of their Union sentiments.

During the day detachments were sent out to reconnoitre the neighboring roads and country and make a plane-table survey of a great portion of it, and along the Loudon and Hampshire railroad in several places they encountered the enemy's scouts, killing two and wounding four of them. The next morning, the 21st, General McCall having accomplished the object of his advance, in obedience to orders received that morning from General McClellan, returned to camp.

Much comment was made at the time through the public press in regard to this movement, as the battle of "Ball's Bluff" took place upon the day of our return, and we were in a position to have been pushed forward in the enemy's rear, and probably reversed the fortune of the day.

In the official report of General McClellan, he states that General Banks sent a despatch to him on the 20th, that the signal station at Sugar Loaf telegraphed that the enemy had moved away from Leesburg, upon which he telegraphed to General Stone that McCall occupied Drainesville, and desired him to keep a good look-out upon Leesburg, and to make a slight demonstration, to see if the movement had the effect of driving them away. This despatch was received by General Stone at eleven o'clock A. M., and he immediately despatched Captain Philbrick, Fifteenth Massachusetts Volunteers with twenty men on a reconnoissance towards Leesburg, who returned that night and reported having advanced within a mile of the town without finding any enemy. He had then accomplished all that had been expected of him. It is probable that that night he conceived the idea of capturing the town by a brilliant *coup*, and the next day commenced the crossing of infantry, horses and artillery over the broad and rapid river in three scows. The disastrous results of this rash undertaking are well known. General Stone acknowledged before the "Committee on the conduct of the war," that the movement on the 21st originated with himself, and was not ordered by General McClellan.

Upon the return of the Reserves to camp, General McCall was ordered to rest his men, and to hold them in readiness to return to Drainesville at a moment's notice.

The camp of our regiment was moved about a half mile to the north-east, on a fine high and sloping piece of ground, terminating abruptly towards the pike in a steep hill. At the base of this were the quartermaster's and sutler's tents and the guard house. On the crest was located the field and staff, and on the slope the company tents, with a fine parade ground beyond.

About this time First Lieutenant R. H. Loudon, Company A, resigned, and Second Lieutenant Horace Neide was elected to fill the vacancy. Orderly Sergeant John J. Ross was chosen second lieutenant of the same company, and Mr. Neide was appointed adjutant of the regiment. Quartermaster-sergeant Wesley S. Mann having some time before been honorably discharged the service, John L. Benzon was appointed in his place, and William A. Hoyt made commissary-sergeant.

On the 22d, an election was held for lieutenant colonel, which resulted in the unanimous choice of Major William McCandless.

On the 28th, General McCall reviewed the Reserve, consisting of the thirteen regiments of General Reynolds and Meade, and Colonel McCalmont's brigades, the First Reserve Cavalry, Colonel George D. Bayard, and the First Reserve Artillery, Colonel Charles F. Campbell, in front of Johnson's Hill. The field contained but about forty acres, the regiments were formed in divisions closed in mass, which wheeled into column in mass, and moved forward to where General McCall and staff were stationed but before reaching him, the divisions broke into companies at wheeling distance, and passed in review. When the line began thus to uncoil itself, it reached a great distance, and presented a splendid spectacle.

When Colonel Mann raised the regiment, his intention was to remain in the service until Washington was safe, and on the first of November, feeling the object for which he came out was accomplished, he resigned and returned to his profession. While in command of the regiment, he was assiduous in his attention to the welfare of the men, frequently examining their rations, visiting their quarters and the hospital, and tempering the rigid discipline necessary to the formation of a soldier with a fatherly care. With his ability, if he had remained in the service, and had not had his "light put out," the eagles upon his shoulders would have undoubtedly soared until they reached the stars.

While at Tennallytown, the men were kept half of the time in digging earthworks and building forts, and but little time was left to devote to battalion drill. But here it was different, besides the difficulty of getting to Washington was so great, that few cared about taking the trouble to procure a pass. The result was, that a great portion of the time was spent in drilling, and the regiments being all encamped within sight of each other, quite a rivalry sprang up between them, as to which would become the most perfect. The effect was a marked improvement in the discipline of the men.

On the 7th the regiment was paid off by Major Smith. About the same time we exchanged the smooth-bore for the Harper's Ferry rifled muskets.

On the 20th, a grand review of a portion of the Army of the Potomac, took place near Munson's Hill, in a valley, or rather plain, two miles long by one broad, stretching to the east towards Bailey's Cross Roads. The troops, numbering seventy-five thousand, rank and file, were drawn up in a line, forming three sides of a square. Upon the right were cavalry and artillery, and on the left was the Pennsylvania Reserves. Around this immense plain, thousands of people and vehicles were gathered. Munson's Hill was black with them, and the trees and houses were covered with men and boys. Considerable time was occupied in getting the troops into their proper positions, and the centre of the field presented an animated scene, hundreds of aids and orderlies galloping in all directions, carrying orders for the different divisions and brigades.

At twelve o'clock, noon, a cortege consisting of President Lincoln and lady, in an open barouche, followed by Secretaries Seward and Cameron, a host of distinguished civilians and Foreign Ministers arrived, and took post near the flag-staff, in the centre and front of the square. Soon after General McClellan arrived, escorted by the Second and Fifth United States Cavalry, and his Body Guard, and took post to the left of the President, surrounded by his Generals and Staff. A salvo of artillery announced his arrival. The President and Secretaries mounted horses and rode over to the General, and they started on the review. Commencing on the left, they passed down by the Reserves, and as the party, consisting of some three hundred officers, generals and their staffs, rode up, the troops commenced cheering and the bands playing. As they galloped down the line at the rate of fifteen miles an hour, the terrific roar was kept up the whole way through, making the scene intensely thrilling. After passing around, a position was taken, and orders given for the column to pass in review. First came the Reserves, General McCall, which after passing, filed to the right and marched at once to their camp, some ten miles off. Then followed General Heintzleman's Division, which passed to the left, and marched some fifteen miles to their post. The divisions of Generals Smith, Franklin, Blenker, Porter and McDowell, brought up the rear, and each was dismissed and marched directly to its camp. There were seventy regiments of infantry, seventeen batteries, and seven regiments of cavalry, and the time occupied in passing was three hours. They marched in column of division, and if they had been in the usual order, it would have taken twice as long. It was by far the finest review ever witnessed on this continent.

About this time the men commenced preparing winter quarters. These consisted of walls of from four to six logs high, with wedge tents placed over them. Floors of boards or logs were put down, shelves put up, and small sheet-iron stoves put in. From four to six generally bunked together, according to their liking.

CHAPTER IX.

SKIRMISH NEAR DRAINESVILLE. FORAGING EXPEDITION. BATTLE OF DRAINESVILLE VISIT OF GOVERNOR CURTIN. THE BOYS IN WINTER. CAMP LIFE. FIRING FOR MEDALS. PICKETING. "OLD UNCLE BEN." "TAKING FRENCH." NAUGHTY "SELL."

EARLY in the evening of the 26th, Colonel Bayard with five hundred and fifty men of the Reserve Cavalry, started on a scout up the pike. They halted at Difficult Creek, and before daylight, proceeded to Drainesville, and captured four pickets, Charles Coleman, Philip Carper, Dr. Day and son, and three other citizens. On the return a short distance from Drainesville, a volley was fired from the woods, mortally wounding Assistant-surgeon Alexander, and slightly two men. Colonel Bayard and Surgeon Stanton had their horses killed under them.

A portion of the cavalry were immediately dismounted, and entering the woods, killed three and captured six, including Captain Farley, of General Bonham's staff, and Lieutenant Carderees, of South Carolina. Thomas, the brother of Charles Coleman, was shot in the eye and breast, and died a few days afterwards. On the return home of the expedition, they were met by Generals McCall and Reynolds, with the First Brigade of the Reserves, and three batteries of artillery coming to their aid. These Colemans were accused of shooting wounded soldiers, and of cutting the head off of one who escaped from the first Bull Run, which they set upon a pole in front of their tavern, and threw his body to the hogs. Of these accusations there can be little doubt, as much pains were taken to inquire into them, and it was found, that while several of their neighbors acknowledged the fact, others said they had heard of them, and none gave a direct denial. Thomas, however, we presume, is now meditating upon his deeds, surrounded by an infinite host of congenial spirits, whose happiness and comfort is receiving the attention of their beloved master who prompted them to their acts. Captain Farley and Lieutenant Carderees were on a courting expedition to the Misses ———, who lived in the neighborhood, and got themselves into trouble by neglecting their lady loves to go bushwhacking.

On the 29th, Captain McDonough, whose company had been disbanded by General Banks, at Hyattstown, Md., arrived with a new company and was assigned his old letter, B. The lieutenants were John H. Jack and James C. Manton, the former being one of the officers whose company was also disbanded at the same time. This gave us seven companies.

On the 3d of December, the brigade started on a foraging expedition, and proceeded about nine miles up the pike to Mr. Thomas' House, where they captured a large number of wagon loads of corn, etc., that had just been collected by the enemy. Mr. Thomas was an agent for the Confederate Government, and was in the habit of scouring the country and collecting from the inhabitants, much against their will, bedding, blankets, clothing, etc., for the use of the army. The boys returned in the afternoon highly delighted with their expedition.

While the roads were good, General McCall sent his expeditions a considerable distance from camp, reserving the forage near by for winter, but this prudential foresight availed him little, for one day General Smith, whose division laid on our left, sent out an extraordinary strong expedition and swept the whole country in our front, actually gathering within sight of our pickets. This was not considered exactly the fair thing, but further than a good-natured reproof no notice was taken of it.

On the 12th, there was a review of the Reserves. On the 19th we practiced with blank cartridges, and in the evening received orders to be prepared to move at three o'clock the next morning.

THE BATTLE OF DRAINESVILLE.—Early on the morning of December 20, 1861, Brigadier-General Ord, with the "Bucktails," Lieutenant-Colonel Kane, Easton's battery of four guns, and his own brigade, the Third, consisting of the Sixth, Captain W. G. Ent; the Ninth, Colonel C. F. Jackson; the Tenth, Colonel J. S. McCalmont, and the Twelfth, Colonel John H. Taggart, marched through Drainesville and some distance beyond on a foraging expedition, and on their return about two and a half o'clock, they discovered the enemy who were also on a foraging expedition, approaching from the direction of Centreville, on the Alexandria and Leesburg pike, in their rear. This pike joins the Chain Bridge and Leesburg pike a short distance east of Drainesville, near Thornton's house, where there is a heavy woods and high ground. To gain this position was the aim of both parties, and General Ord, by double quicking his command succeeded. The battle soon opened and lasted for one hour and a half with great fury, when General Ord observing the enemy to waver ordered a charge, when they broke and fled, leaving their killed and wounded and two caissons on the field, and were followed by our victorious troops for over a mile. The enemy's force consisted of First Kentucky Rifles, the First and Eleventh Kentucky Infantry, the Tenth Alabama and the Sixth South Carolina volunteers, a regiment of cavalry and a battery of six guns, commanded by Acting Brigadier-general John H. Forney. Their loss in killed and wounded was one hundred and sixty-five men, they acknowledging that of one hundred and fifty. Among their killed was Colonel Tom Taylor, First Kentucky Rifles. Our loss was but seven killed and forty-one wounded, including four officers, among whom was Lieutenant-colonel Kane, slightly. We brought all our killed and wounded, many of the enemy's wounded, eight prisoners, and fifty-eight wagon loads of forage to camp. General McCall arrived upon the field during the action and took command.

General Reynolds, who had been moved with his brigade to Difficult creek, immediately upon hearing the sound of battle put his column in motion, striking across the country to the left for the purpose of intercepting the enemy in their retreat on the Alexandria and Leesburg pike, but his movement was countermanded by General McCall, whose positive instructions were not to bring on a general engagement. The Second Brigade, General Meade, was also put in motion, and General Hancock's division was ordered to our support. General McClellan proceeded as far as Miner's Hill, where, finding the battle was over, he returned.

This battle was the first victory gained by the Army of the Potomac, and after the disastrous defeats of "Bull Run" and "Ball's Bluff," was hailed with joy by the people of the North.

A few days after the battle, His Excellency, Governor Curtin, visited the Reserves to congratulate them and care for the wounded, and he caused the flags of the regiments that participated in the battle to be sent to Washington, where "Drainesville, December 20, 1861," was inscribed on each of them, after which they were returned to them in the presence of the whole division and an assemblage of distinguished officials and civilians.

On the 14th of January, Lieutenants John B. Robinson and J. Baxter Fletcher, Sergeants Joseph Benison, David H. Pidgeon and Isaac C. Sharp, were detailed to proceed to Philadelphia, on recruiting service.

On the 20th, the regiment was paid off by Major Smith.

Winter now set in, in earnest, and the "sacred soil of Virginia" began to assume very much the appearance of a vast mud-puddle. Almost every day it drizzled, rained and snowed alternately; the sun not blessing us with its genial rays, or Jack Frost coming to our relief to extricate us from the mud. Shoe and clothes brushes were at a discount. Nice young men who formerly prided themselves on their kid gloves and patent leather boots, began to realize the stern necessities of the case, and officers, sergeants, corporals and privates wandered about in a promiscuous mass, floundering and splashing in the mire as happy as young ducks in a mud-puddle. Nature happily has formed man to be contented with circumstances, and what seems the height of misery to the imagination, in reality loses much of its unpleasantness. The boys ate their rations, thought of their sweethearts, slept warmly in their bunks, stood in the mud on guard and shivered on picket, making the best of their situation, occasionally wishing the war was over, and having slight hopes of furloughs in the future.

The reveillé rattles and up springs the soldiers. "Fall in, Company A!" rings down the street; and with variations in the last letter, is repeated over the camp. Out tumble the sleepy boys and range themselves in line in front of their tents. Roll call is soon over and down they run to the neighboring brook where their toilet is performed. Back to their tents and tumbling in they soon have a glowing fire burning, Then comes "peas on trencher," as breakfast is called—for what reason I know not, considering the unvarying bill of fare. But the fascinating summons is always obeyed, and with tin plates and cups, to the music of the "tin plate march," they proceed to the cook's quarters of their own company. The milkless coffee is dipped from a huge kettle, and the salt junk from a pile and with a few wafers of hard tack, the patriots march back to their bunks and enjoy a hearty meal. At eight comes guard mounting—quite an imposing ceremony in clear weather. Then the boys cut their wood and fill their canteens, clean their muskets, sew on buttons, write home, read, cut wooden chains and bone rings, play cards, smoke and talk over old times, and brag about their sweethearts. At noon 'roast beef," is sounded and out turns the redoubtable tin plate band who waddle through the mud to the kitchen, where it is only by their redoubled energies with the more uproarious rattling of merry voices, that the words of discontent and grumbling are drowned. The "roast beef" generally turns out to be an article known to the soldiers as "salt horse," which sometimes gives way to its fresh kindred, or bean soup, but is usually only varied with salt pork. The afternoon glides away like the morning, and then comes the unchangeable "hard tack and coffee." At nine, tattoo beats, and the regimental bands commencing on the right of each brigade begin playing and by the time they have ceased the half hour has expired for taps to sound, when all lights are extinguished and sounds cease. This is the routine of camp in bad weather, but when the ground will permit, drilling and bayonet exercise take place in the morning and afternoon, besides the "dress parade" of the evening.

About this time target practice became quite popular and the crack of muskets was heard daily in the rear of the camp. Company C, Captain Byrnes, was presented with four handsome silver medals by the members of Hibernia Engine Company of Philadelphia, which were fired for on the banks of the Potomac. The target was well riddled, and the prizes won by Corporal Thomas Wood, William Miller, Edward Concannon and William Derr. About the same time Company H fired for three magnificent silver medals, and the prizes were won by Captain Mealey, Corporal Edward Dubois and Samuel Hershaw. A leather medal, richly decorated with pegs was presented to Andy ———, he making the worst shot. In the regular army they have company and regimental prizes which are fired for yearly, and army prizes that become the private property of the winner.

Although our regiment numbered but seven companies we were required to furnish the guard and picket details of a full regiment, which, though it came rather hard, was cheerfully submitted to. The two companies detailed for picket were up bright and early, and with a day's cooked rations, marched up the pike above the general's quarters, where they were inspected by one of his aids, who verified the detail. They then proceeded to Prospect Hill, where they were divided into three reliefs, and relieved the old picket. Shelters of boughs were here built for the Reserve to lie in, and a considerable portion of the day was spent in cutting wood for the night. Our regiment generally picketed from the pike to the Potomac, but when it laid to the left of the road they made the Ball House their headquarters. Mr. Ball was a violent secessionist, and like most of his clan had abandoned his home and with his family gone south upon the approach of our army. The consequence was, everything soon went to ruin. The trees were cut down, fences turned up, and one board after another disappeared from the house, until the chimney alone marked where it once stood. This was the case all the way down to the Chain Bridge and to Alexandria, the only exceptions being of those who had sense enough to remain at home, and those who had returned from the exile into which they had been driven by their secession neighbours. When the rebellion first broke out, the secessionists, although in the minority, with the aid of Confederate troops drove the Union citizens from their houses, impressing the young men, and plundering and robbing the old and helpless.

An old slave and his wife were all that remained on the farm, and their cabin and little garden were undisturbed. They obtained their daily food from the haversacks of the soldiers, for which, they appeared grateful. They had great faith in the efficacy of prayer, and when "old Uncle Ben" discoursed upon the war, he was wont to observe, "Massa Linkum has a power of men, and them am mighty fond of chickens. I spects Massa Government must be powerfully rich to own all dem wagons and horses." Uncle Ben truly loved the aforesaid gentleman, and frequently inquired if they "had eber experienced religion."

Picketing in pleasant weather was much preferable to

the camp, but on the bleak hills of the Potomac, during the bitter cold nights, the wind came rushing down the valley, penetrating to the very bones. Sometimes the weather was so intensely cold, that the men were relieved every hour. Then it was their pace was quickened on the beat, and in their frail shelters they huddled up together to get warm, the motto being, "united we sleep, divided we freeze."

Some of the men, with bad memories, had considerable trouble in remembering the countersign. One night, when Pat D—— was posted, the corporal gave him the word "Malta." "Now remember, Pat, by thinking of malt from which liquor is made, you can remember it." "Yes, sir," replied Pat. Sometime afterwards, when an officer visited the posts, he interrogated Pat. Pat looked confused for a few moments when his face brightened up as he replied, "and is it rye, sir?" At another time when the word was "Brandywine," one of the men replied, "wine and whiskey," and at another time the word "Toledo" was tortured into "toad eater."

Beyond the picket line was the cavalry patrol, who moved to and fro on the pike, as far as Difficult creek. Sometimes on cold nights the patrols would induce some one of the infantry who was off duty to ride a round for him, while he warmed himself. This, however, he had better not have been caught at.

Of course, the men wished to visit their homes during the winter, and as furloughs could not be granted to all, many were doomed to disappointment. Considerable numbers, however, took a run home for a week or ten days without any authority, which was called "taking French." To accomplish this, they concealed themselves in the army wagons and were smuggled across the Chain Bridge to Washington, where they procured citizens clothes and went north. Many of them, however, were detected by the depot guard in spite of their disguise, for soldiers have a peculiar look and style about them that is easily detected by a practiced eye. And woe unto them that were caught, for the guard-house was their certain resting place until they were sent to their regiments under arrest. None of the Second boys, however, were put to this indignity, but whether it was on account of their virtue or excessive cuteness, the reader must judge for himself. When the Potomac froze over this evil became prevalent in spite of the sure punishment that awaited their return to camp, for the men were willing to stand it for the pleasures of home. However, there is a mode to remedy all evils, so pickets were stationed on the river with orders to shoot down any one who attempted to cross. But home, no matter how humble is the palace of the heart, and some of the boys took the risk and got safely over, and surely it was right to deal leniently with them when they returned.

A short distance beyond Difficult creek was the residence of Mrs. Jackson, the mother of Jim Jackson who killed the lamented Ellsworth. As it was ascertained that her house was a general rendezvous for scouts and spies, whom she harbored and concealed, a squad of cavalry visited it early one morning with an ambulance and escorted her to General McCall's headquarters. Quite a number of concealed weapons and some important sketches of our picket line, that had been corrected to correspond with the changes lately made in it, were captured, so the old lady was sent to Washington.

On the 14th of February, First-Lieutenant Peter Summers, Company H, resigned, and Orderly Sergeant Hugh P. Kennedy was elected to fill the vacancy. About the same time Assistant-surgeon J. W. Lodge resigned, and Doctor John Malone was appointed by Governor Curtin his successor.

Five volunteers from each regiment of the Reserve were called for about this time for the Western flotilla, and the seventy-five men thus obtained from the division formed the crew of the celebrated gunboat Carondolet that ran such a glorious career on the Mississippi.

A very amusing sell was started about this time by

some wags, who circulated in all the regiments, at the same time, a rumor to the effect that any volunteer who would enter the regular army would receive one hundred dollars in cash, and sixty days furlough by applying at headquarters the next morning at ten o'clock. The consequence was that headquarters was literally besieged by the gulled ones, and those who came out of curiosity. The General, observing the crowd, sent one of his staff, "Old Snapping-Turtle," out to inquire the cause of it, who stormed like an old war-horse at the men for being such fools.

On the 3d of March the Reserves were ordered out with "kits complete," and marched to the Chain Bridge and back, a distance of eight miles. On the 5th this was repeated, the object being to prepare the men for the fatigues of the campaign.

CHAPTER X.

OPENING OF THE CAMPAIGN OF 1862. FAREWELL TO PIERPONT. THE MARCH. HAWKHURST'S MILLS. ARMY CORPS. WET AND NOISY NIGHT. "HOLLO BARNEY." ALEXANDRIA. EMBARKATION FOR THE PENINSULA. BY RAILROAD. A NIGHT IN REBEL CABINS. RUINS OF MANASSAS. BULL RUN FIELD. SELLING CIDER. MARCH TO THE RAPPAHANNOCK. CAVALRY SKIRMISH. WASHINTON *vs.* DAVID OF OLD.

FOR the proper elucidation of the subject it will be necessary here to refer to the planning of the campaign that was about opening. Two bases of operations for the Army of the Potomac presented themselves; one submitted by the President, January 31st, from Washington, involving an attack upon Centreville and Manassas direct, or the turning of one or both flanks of those positions, or a combination of those plans. An attack on the left flank involved too long a line of wagon communication, and on the right flank by way of Occoquan if successful by a decisive battle, could not have been followed up with commensurate results. Should the condition of the enemy's troops permit, he could fall back upon other positions, and fight us again and again, or if he was not in a condition to give battle outside of the intrenchments at Richmond, it would have proved difficult and hazardous to have followed him there either by way of Fredericksburg or Gordonsville, as he would have destroyed the railroad bridges and otherwise impeded our progress. Besides a line of communication from Washington to Richmond, through an enemy's country, was impracticable. A direct attack upon Centreville would have been productive of no other results, and a combined attack upon that point and the right flank was impracticable on account of the distance and obstacles intervening between the columns.

The plan submitted by General McClellan, February 3d, was to operate from the lower Chesapeake, making Urbana, on the lower Rappahannock, the point of landing, which is distant from West Point one march, and from Richmond but two. This would have necessitated the abandonment of Manassas, Centreville and the Upper Potomac by the enemy, and if followed with celerity of movements the probable cutting off of Magruder in the Peninsula, and the occupation of Richmond before the enemy's forces could have been concentrated for its defence. The latter proposition was adopted, and as early as February 14th the collection of vessels for the transportation of the army to the lower Potomac was commenced.

On the 9th of March information was received that the enemy having discovered the intended movement, was evacuating Centreville and Manassas, as well as his positions on the upper and lower Potomac. Upon his retiring, he having destroyed all the railroad bridges in his rear, and the roads being almost impassable, it was impossible to inflict the usual damage generally afforded by the withdrawal of a large army in the face of a powerful foe. But as considerable time must elapse before transportation could be collected to convey the army to the lower Potomac, an opportunity was offered to experience the troops on the march and bivouac previous to the campaign, and to get rid of the superfluous baggage which had accumulated in the camp during our long period of inactivity.

Accordingly on the night of the 9th, orders were issued for a general movement of the army the next morning, our regiment being ordered to have four days' cooked rations in haversacks, sixty rounds of cartridges, and kit complete.

At eleven o'clock on the 10th of March, 1862, we got into line, and bidding farewell to our happy home at Pierpont, crossed over the fields to the pike, and took up our line of march. A heavy rain had fallen through the night and during the morning, rendering the roads very muddy, and our backs being green, the knapsacks bore heavily upon us. But all were in excellent spirits, believing we would soon meet the foe, and sooner than fall out to rest, the men threw away their extra clothing, strewing the road along the march with coats, blouses, blankets, etc. We continued up the pike across Difficult Creek to Spring Vale, within three miles of Drainesville, when turning to the left and following a bridle path through the woods and over the hills, we reached about dark the neighborhood of Hunter's Mills, near which, on the Loudon and Hampshire railroad we bivouacked, the night being cold and rainy. Here we remained until the next afternoon, when we marched about two miles to a high elevation near the ruins of Hawkhurst's Mills, where we encamped.

Our encampment was about seventeen miles from Pierpont, two from Fairfax Court House, and eight from the Bull Run battle-field. The scene here was magnificent, particularly at night, when the valleys and hills beneath us for miles around, were lit up with thousands of camp-fires. Here we received our "shelter tents," which experience taught us were the best in use for an army in the field. But at first they were very unpopular, the men calling them "dog houses," and for amusement creeping into them on their hands and knees, and barking out of the ends at each other.

It should have been stated, that on the 8th of March, the President directed the Army of the Potomac to be divided into four corps, in compliance with which, there was assigned to General Irwin McDowell the first, consisting of the divisions of Franklin, McCall and King. To General E. V. Sumner the second, consisting of Richardson, Blenker and Sedgwick. To General S. P. Heintzleman the third, consisting of F. J. Porter, Hooker and Hamilton; and to General E. D. Keyes the fourth, consisting of Couch, Smith and Casey. On the 11th, an order from the President announced, that as General McClellan had personally taken the field, he was relieved from the command of the other military departments, and would retain command of the Department of the Potomac.

It being ascertained that the enemy were in no force north of Warrenton Junction, on the evening of the 14th, during a light fall of rain, we took up our march through the woods, passing on every side bivouacks, and burning bough huts and arbors, the glare from which lighted us upon our road for miles. Reaching the Alexandria and Leesburg Pike, we turned to the right, and passing along it for two miles, about eleven o'clock filed into a dense open woods, where, in spite of the falling rain, our fires soon burnt brightly, and we slept soundly. The next morning early, during a heavy rain, we took up our march, moving across the country to the Drainesville Pike, and turning down it crossed Difficult Creek, passing within four miles of our old home at Pierpont, and entering a woods, moved back again towards the Alexandria and Leesburg Pike by a private road. The rain by this time was falling in torrents, flooding the swampy ground, making the marching most tiresome and fatiguing. Soon the ranks were broken, the men scattering, plunging through the mud, and toiling under their knapsacks, made doubly heavy by their blankets and overcoats becoming saturated with water. Soon they commenced dropping out, and laid scattered through the woods for miles. Upon striking the turnpike again, a long halt was called for the stragglers to catch up, and then moving on, we soon filed into a wood and stacked arms. This was about three o'clock, and although we had marched fifteen miles, we were but three miles from the starting point in the morning, the detour to the left being made on account of the enemy having burned the bridge on the pike over Difficult Creek some months previous.

After much patient labor, we succeeded in getting our fires started, and towards night hot coffee was served out, but such was the violence of the storm, that it was impossible to put up our tents, the most of the men spending the night in cutting wood and standing around the fires. At one time the heavens appeared to out do themselves, opening their flood-gates and pouring down a torrent of water, stifling the wind and flooding all below. The fires were almost instantly extinguished, and then the patriots were aroused to a full appreciation of their position. Not to be thus conquered and subdued by the raging elements, they set up their wild shouts and huzzahs, making the woods and hills for miles around echo with their noise, until by indomitable perseverance, they actually got themselves into a good humor. All that was wanted after they got fully started to complete their happiness, was a fiddle and a "straight four," and then they would have made a full night of it. But morning came, and with it a bright warm sun, Nature appearing to have exhausted herself in the mad rage of the night.

At ten o'clock the next morning, we moved down the pike, passing Falls Church, Munson's Hill, and a long line of fortifications erected at different times by the Union and Confederate troops, and arriving within a mile of Alexandria, moved over the fields to the left, and encamped near the Cemetery and the Fairfax Seminary. On account of the roads, and the sleepless night, the march was rather an inanimate one, but little spirit of joviality being displayed until we met a supply train moving in an opposite direction among whose drivers was a red panted Zouave, the first we had seen. One of the boys found out his name, and as he passed cried out "hallo Barney"—Barney turned round to see who his friend was, when the whole regiment saluted him. At first he was disposed to take it ill-naturedly, and gave full vent to violent gesticulations and oaths, but finding he was "in for it," he jumped upon the seat of the wagon, and commenced dancing and waving his hat. As he passed by our regiment, the next took it up, and for a long way we could hear the shouts of "Barney," and see his red pants dangling in the air. Thus a happy point taken will enliven for a time a whole army.

The war metamorphosed Alexandria from a quiet Old Virginia town into a bustling business place. Almost every house was turned into a store, restaurant or boarding house, all of which did a thriving business from the continual influx of officers, soldiers, government attachés and innumerable teamsters and workmen. Though the sale of liquor was prohibited under severe penalty, and the provost guard continually visited places suspected of the illicit traffic, yet large quantities of it were daily sold. One individual had a barrel up his chimney, another one upon the top of his house, from which he drew it out of a gas jet in a back room, and a third drew it from a private house next door by means of his hydrant. The city possessed not a single attraction for a private residence. As the whole army was now concentrated in the neighborhood, the streets were crowded with soldiers, many of whom went to excesses, though not annoying the citizens or particularly harming themselves, but as the Reserves had not been paid off for some time, and were out of money, they won golden opinions for their good conduct.

The enemy's retreat from Manassas to Gordonsville somewhat modified the plans of the campaign, and at a council of corps commanders held at Fairfax Court House on the 13th, the Peninsula campaign was decided upon, provided the enemy's steamer Merrimac could be neutralized, the army be immediately transported to the Lower Potomac, the navy co-operate in silencing the batteries on the York river, and Washington be made safe. If not, to Richmond via Manassas and the Rappahannock. The embarkation of the army was immediately commenced at Alexandria, Washington and Perryville, and in thirty-seven days after the order was received by the Hon. John Tucker, Assistant-secretary of War, one hundred and twenty-one thousand, five hundred men, fourteen thousand five hundred and ninety-two animals, one thousand one hundred and fifty wagons, forty-four batteries, seventy-four ambulances, besides pontoon bridges, telegraph materials, and the enormous quantity of equipage, etc., required for an army of such magnitude, were transferred to Fortress Monroe with the loss of but eight mules and nine barges, an operation of such magnitude as was without a parallel in this country.

The weather during our encampment here was cold, rainy and unpleasant, rendering the ground mostly unfit for drilling, but every favorable opportunity was taken advantage of for that purpose. We received our full ration and a ration of whisky was served out every rainy night. As the troops who had laid here all winter had cut down and used the wood in the neighborhood, it was scarce, and the boys hearing some regiments of New York troops had embarked for the Peninsula, went over and rummaged their encampments, and procured a rich supply of boards, etc. Some commissary stores were left behind under guard, to which they proceeded to help themselves, under the patriotic impression that as they belonged to Uncle Sam, it was their duty to improve his property by keeping themselves in good fighting order.

On the 2d of April, Captain George A. Woodward was elected Major, First Lieutenant Horace Neide, Captain, and Orderly Sergeant Daniel H. Connors, First Lieutenant. After the election the Major regaled the men on ale, and his opponent on whisky, which made what is termed a "stone wall," some portion of which toppled over during the night.

About this time a company of Pennsylvanians, under the command of Lieutenant John M. Clark, who had been attached to the First District of Columbia Volunteers, were nominally transferred to our regiment, taking letter F, but were assigned by General McCall to take charge of the extra line of caissons for the artillery battalion of the Reserves.

Our Corps de Armee, being detached from the Army of the Potomac, constituted an independent command—the Department of the Rappahannock—under General McDowell, designed to cover Washington. We prepared to move south, first having the cartridges increased to one hundred per man.

Early on the morning of the 9th, we struck tents, and strapping them on our knapsacks, with three days' cooked rations in haversacks, moved off. A severe storm of alternate rain, hail and snow, which had been falling for several days, was prevailing, rendering the roads and fields we passed over in many places knee-deep in mud. Passing down between Forts Ellsworth and Lyons, we marched about three miles to the Orange and Alexandria railroad where we halted to await transportation. Here we stood six hours shivering in the mud, with our heavy knapsacks upon our backs, but about three o'clock the cars arrived and our brigade embarked and we got under way. Our journey was without any incident of interest, and at nine o'clock in the evening the train halted about two miles beyond Bull Run creek, in front of a large deserted encampment of huts, that had been built and occupied by the enemy during the winter. We had anticipated a hard night of it, in the open fields without fires, so these proved a perfect god-send to us, as the snow was deep and the storm was raging with fury, and many of the men had been exposed through the day on platform cars, so closely huddled together that they could hardly move. We were in the cabins but a few moments before bright crackling fires were burning in the ample chimney-places and we were partaking of a bountiful supper of hot coffee, crackers and junk. As we sat around the cheerful fires enjoying our pipes, we soon forgot the exposure of the day and the storm that was raging without, and then stretching ourselves upon the clay floor we enjoyed a good night's sleep.

The next morning at eight o'clock we formed and marched up the railroad about three miles, the surrounding country presenting a scene of desolation, being stripped of fences and wood. On either side were deserted huts, camps, broken wagons, caissons, barrels and boxes.

At Manassas Junction were the vast ruins of the depot and other buildings burnt by the enemy in the haste of retreat, they being unable to remove the immense amount of provisions and clothing collected there. Smouldering ruins, wrecked cars and machinery, vast piles of flour, pork, beef, wagons, lumber, trunks, bottles, demijohns, tents, hides, tallow, bones, dismantled fortifications and rifle pits all mixed up together in inextricable confusion. Moving on, we entered a large open plain, surrounded by woods; and passing through a collection of deserted huts, we encamped in a pine forest on its border, in an old encampment of our skedaddling friends. The only thing of life left to welcome us was a pet turkey buzzard whose wings they had clipped to prevent its escape. What a fit emblem it would make for their bogus Government!

Near by, in a fine oak forest, were the ruins of the enemy's hospitals, which they burnt before leaving.

They were of boards, one story high and consisted of five rows, of ten buildings, each twenty-four by one hundred and twenty-eight feet, besides several detached houses and stables, all connected by broken sandstone walks, to protect the patient's feet from the damp earth. Near them was a large grave yard, and many clusters of graves were found in the neighborhood.

While here many of us visited the Bull Run battle field, situated about seven miles distant, finding but few occupied houses on the road, most of the inhabitants having left, they believing the stories so freely promulgated in the Southern papers of our monstrosities. Where they remained at home a guard was furnished for their houses and their property protected. Near the battle-field were a number of huts lately occupied by the enemy, and over the door of one was found nailed the cross bones and skull of a human being. Leg bones were also found with the marrow but partially dried up in them, from which finger rings had been sawed off. What singular and refined tastes the chivalry of the South have! It was noticed that while there were quite a number of bibles and tracts left in their cabins, there were no cards to be found, but whether this was to be accounted for by the fact of their being conscientiously opposed to gaming, or considered the cards the most valuable of the two, we cannot say. The field, of course, possessed much interest to all, and the important positions were carefully examined. The bones of men and horses lay scattered about unburied although the enemy laid in the immediate neighborhood for eight months. Near the water courses were found the skeletons of many of the wounded who had crawled to them to quench their thirst.

On the 12th the regiment was paid off by Major John M. Pomeroy, and soon after our sutler, Captain Knox, resigned and left us. Mr. Stokes was appointed in his place, but being unable to give satisfaction, soon after left. About this time Sergeant-Major Augustus T. Cross, was appointed adjutant of the regiment, vice Neide promoted.

Soon after our arrival, quite a number of sutler and other "shebangs," were opened in our neighborhood, which furnished us with an abundant supply of the various articles so necessary for the soldier's comfort. One individual was doing a thriving business, he having succeeded in smuggling through a barrel of cider, which delightful beverage he dispensed to his thirsty patrons at ten cents a glass. Some of the boys, however, conceived the idea of running opposition to him, and having succeeded through false pretence in borrowing an auger and spicket from him, cut a hole in the back of his tent, tapped his barrel, and commenced operations. As they charged but half price, and gave twice as much, they were liberally patronized, and after selling out in an incredibly short time, they decamped, when he was invited around to view the operation. He owned up he had been "sold" in the auger and spicket arrangement, but thought the joke a "little practical."

While here the Second and Third Brigades arrived, companies from our regiment were sent on picket, and frequent battalion drills were had.

At eight o'clock on the morning of the 17th, we formed and moved out on the open plain, where we laid until eleven o'clock, when we moved off to the south, soon striking the railroad, down which we marched, crossing Broad and Kettle runs on the new bridges that were being built to replace those destroyed by the enemy. Near the latter is Bristow Station, where Company A, Captain Neide, was detailed on guard duty. About a mile beyond this we filed into a woods, and encamped for the night near Brentsville. The next morning early we again moved down the railroad. The day was very warm, and many of the men threw away their overcoats to lighten their burdens. About noon we reached Catlett's Station, near Cedar Creek, a tributary of the Occoquan River, where we encamped. That night Companies

E and H, Captains Finnie and Mealey, were detailed for picket under Major Woodward, on the heights beyond Cedar creek. While we laid here, we found for the first time honest people, they acknowledging frankly they were secessionists at heart, but regretted secession since it was followed by war. It was much more satisfactory to talk to such than with hypocrites, who uttered sentiments of loyalty, while traitors at heart. Much rain fell while we laid here, which prevented our drilling.

While here our surgeon, Dr. Thomas B. Reed, of Washington county, Pennsylvania, was promoted brigade surgeon, and ordered to Yorktown. His departure from among us was regretted, as his eminent skill and ability, and fine intellectual qualities, caused his loss to be deeply felt.

On the 26th, about noon we marched off, crossing Cedar creek on falling trees, and passing over hills and dales, through the woods and fields, in a southeasterly direction and towards night bivouacked on the south bank of Elk creek, having marched six miles. On our route we passed several deserted houses and camps, also a number of newly made graves. The ground we laid upon was a gentle sloping hillside, admirably situated for our comfort, having an abundance of water and fence rails near by. What a sight it is to see a division bivouac for the night! The brigades and regiments as they march into the fields are assigned their positions, and no sooner have they stacked arms, than off goes their knapsacks, and the men rush for the nearest fences. In a few minutes they are torn down, and thousands of men, with several rails each upon their shoulders, are seen hurrying towards their stacks. Then another rush is made for water, and soon a thousand fires are brightly burning, with the busy blue coats around them cooking their coffee. Then the pipe, then the blanket, and soon all are lost in peaceful sleep, except the guard, who, through the lone hours of the night, keep watch and ward over their comrades.

The next morning was Sunday, a clear and beautiful day, and about six in the morning, after sounding the sick call, we marched off. On our march we passed two churches, one a Methodist and the other a Baptist, but in neither of them had service been held for eight months. Near one was collected a number of slaves, who told us they had been for sometime discussing the subject of moving North. They, however, were divided in their opinion, the old folks prefering to remain near their childhood's home, but the younger longing for the liberty they knew not of. We passed through a small village called White Ridge, near which, about noon, we encamped in a pine woods, having made eight miles. Near by was a pond of clear water with a spring in the middle of it, but without proper outlet. The men went to it to fill their canteens, but General Reynolds ordered his orderlies to ride in and muddy the water, which caused the men to seek other and purer water. On our route we were followed by many negroes and some whites, whose object, principally, was to get such clothes as the men would give them. At guard-mounting, an amusing scene took place. When the band commenced playing, the negroes involuntarily broke forth into a dance, clapping their hands and singing. After this was over, a grand butting match took place, their heads crushing together like rocks, but producing no effect upon them. After scrambling for a few handfuls of pennies thrown among them, they left for their homes, happy with their afternoon's sport. Companies B and K, Captains McDonough and Smith, were thrown out on picket for the night.

The next day was clear, pleasant, and cool for marching, and at six in the morning we moved off, following the fields along side of the roads. The country became more diversified and timber heavier. As we marched on we passed a large brick house, from a tree in front of which was flying the stars and stripes, and as the men caught sight of it, they rent the air with deafening cheers, which rolling down the line echoed through the woods. At noon a long halt was called, and then passing through Hartword, a small village, we bivouacked at three o'clock in a fine woods two miles from Falmouth, Stafford county, and although we made seventeen miles, the brigade came in in fine order with but few stragglers.

The next morning, the 29th, we marched early and passed by where our cavalry had a skirmish with the enemy on the 18th, and which was marked by a breastwork of rails, newly made graves, and dead horses. The enemy's force consisted of a regiment of infantry, one of cavalry, and a battery of artillery. They were charged by the First Reserve Cavalry under Colonel Bayard, and after being driven from their position were pushed to the Rappahannock, which they crossed on the upper bridge at Falmouth, which they burnt. Our loss was five men and fifteen horses killed, and sixteen men wounded. The enemy's loss was about equal to ours. Lieutenant-colonel Kilpatrick, Second New York (Ira Harris) Cavalry was wounded, and Lieutenant Decker killed. Colonel Bayard's horse was wounded in four places. Soon after we entered Falmouth, through which we passed with our banners unfurled and bands playing. The inhabitants flocked to the doors and windows to gaze at us, and a motley crowd of negroes followed, highly delighted at the music and sight. About a mile beyond, on the Aquia road we encamped in a fine wood, where we found an abundance of fuel and water. The same afternoon the Second Brigade, General Meade, arrived and encamped to our left.

The ground where our camp laid was once owned by Washington, he having inherited it from his father. Here he spent his youth between the age of ten and sixteen, during which time he obtained the principal portion of his education. Near the headquarters of General King, at the "Phillip's House," stood the old mansion, from the lawn in front of which, it is said, George threw a stone into the river, a feat which none of his companions were able to accomplish. We are not the least surprised at this, as the distance is about one mile! If this statement is true, the patriot in his youthful days must have been a powerful boy, and able to put in the shade the feats of David of old.

CHAPTER XI.

FALMOUTH. VISIT OF PRESIDENT LINCOLN. CROSSING THE RAPPAHANNOCK. GRAVE OF MARY WASHINGTON. LOVE BUBBLE. CEMETERY. MARCH TO GRAY'S LANDING. EMBARKATION FOR THE PENINSULA. VOYAGE TO THE WHITE HOUSE. MARCH TO DISPATCH STATION.

THE town of Falmouth is situated on the east bank of the Rappahannock, below the Falls, and nearly opposite Fredericksburg, with which it was connected by two bridges, one at the upper and one at the lower end of the town, the latter being used by the Aquia Creek Railroad, but both of which were burned by the enemy, with several steamboats and a number of sailing crafts upon our approach. A church in which several denominations formerly worshipped, a cotton factory, and several store houses constituted the brick portion of the town, and about eighty houses, mostly in a dilapidated condition, constituted the frame portion of it. Deep water gulleys were worn in the streets, and the whole place presented the appearance of decay. What few articles the inhabitants offered for sale commanded enormous prices, but soon the town was filled with our sutlers, storekeepers and photographers, who gave new life to it.

On the 1st of May, private E. M. Woodward, Company H, was appointed sergeant-major of the regiment, vice A. T. Cross, promoted adjutant. On the 3d, Easton's, Cooper's and Kern's batteries arrived. On the 4th, the

Third Brigade, General Ord, arrived, and on the 11th, Company A, Captain Neidé came in with the Fifth Reserve, Colonel Simmons, from Bristoe Station, where they lost William Holmes, the first one of the regiment that died. On the same afternoon, the enemy drove in our out-posts of the Second New York Cavalry, under Major Duffie, on the Bowling Green road, back of Fredericksburg, but coming upon the reserve, they were handsomely repulsed, with the loss of one lieutenant and ten men prisoners, one killed and several wounded; our loss being but one horse. The enemy in our front were under the command of General Anderson, and numbered about fifteen thousand men. On the 12th, there was great rejoicing in camp upon the reception of the news of the evacuation of Yorktown, and the destruction of the Merrimac by the enemy, in honor of which a salute was fired of forty-four guns. About the same time, William Goucher, of Easton Pennsylvania, was appointed sutler of the regiment, and soon after arrived with a good supply of stores. Lieutenant Robinson, with his recruiting party, also arrived from Philadelphia with a number of recruits.

At Falmouth a large bakery was established by Captain James B. Clow, division commissary, which was capable of turning out twenty-one thousand six hundred loaves of bread per day. The Reserves picketed as far as eight miles up the river, and in a circle around Falmouth, about two miles from camp. Several of the Eighth regiment were killed while on duty at the mines.

Near the upper end of the town, resided Mr. J. B. Fickner, a noted secessionist and a gentleman of great wealth, who owned large tracts of land on both sides of the river, the upper bridge and a factory. While we were on cattle guard at his farm, he frequently visited and conversed with us. He deeply lamented the war, not on account of the destruction of the Government, but of his property, but he consoled himself with the belief that the Government would have to pay for the damage done by the rebels. To this we fully agreed, and suggested to him the propriety of applying for a pension for his son, who was wounded while in the Confederate service. The old gentleman looked somewhat confused at this, he not being aware that we were acquainted with his own and his son's antecedents.

While we laid here Dr. Edward Donnelly, of Philadelphia, surgeon Fifth Reserve, was transferred to our regiment, vice Dr. Thomas B. Reed, promoted brigade surgeon.

On the 21st, at nine o'clock in the morning, we formed and marched about two miles to a large open field, where our brigade was reviewed and inspected by General Van Rensallaer, Inspector-General of our Corps. At the review, the bands of the five regiments numbering some eighty instruments were joined, producing the most soul-inspiring music. It was three o'clock in the afternoon before the inspection was got through with.

On the afternoon of the 23d, His Excellency the President of the United States, accompanied by the Honorable Secretary of War, and other members of the Cabinet, Major-General McDowell, staff and cavalry escort, reviewed the first corps about three miles from camp. As the President rode down the line on a fine spirited horse, the troops presented arms, the standards and colors drooped, officers saluted, drums beat, trumpets sounded, and a salute of twenty-one guns fired. Long and loud cheers for the honored chief, broke forth from the men, as he passed along the line.

As early as the 17th, General McDowell had been instructed to move upon Richmond by the general route of the Richmond and Fredericksburg railroad, as soon as joined by General Shield's division, which came in after long and fatiguing marches on the 22nd, and it was decided upon at a consultation between the President and the generals that the movement should commence on the morning of the 26th. But on account of the advance of the enemy under "Stonewall" Jackson down the valley of the Shenandoah, rendering the position of General Banks' force critical, General Shield's, King's and Ord's divisions and four companies of the "Bucktails" under Lieutenant-Colonel Kane were on the 25th dispatched to his relief.

Although this unforseen circumstance prevented the contemplated advance of McDowell, on the 26th, at eleven o'clock, A. M., we broke camp and marched toward Falmouth, halting at the abandoned camp of the Twenty-second New York, where we put up our tents, but had hardly got through with our work, when we were ordered to again move. Striking tents, we marched to the river and crossed over on a trestle bridge, and entered Fredericksburg. The day was drizzly and the streets muddy, but with our unfurled banners and martial music we marched merrily through the city. The houses of the rich were mostly closed; a few old folks and young children gazed out of the windows at us, and at the corners the negroes were collected in knots and appeared in a very happy mood. Passing through the city, we moved out William street about a half mile beyond the cemetery on the heights back of the city where we bivouacked in some scrub-oak brush to the right of the plank road, strict orders being given to avoid injuring the growing crops of the neighboring fields. Considerable rain fell during the night, and the next morning we moved to the left of the road, and encamped on a gently sloping hill commanding a fine view of the city.

Fredericksburg is an ancient city, situated on the western bank of the Rappahannock, and is principally noted for the refinement of its inhabitants, their aristocratic characteristics and the beauty of its women. Prior to the war it contained about five thousand inhabitants, and its exports amounted to some million of dollars yearly.

The first account we have of this locality is that given

by Captain John Smith who ascended the river in 1608, and fought the Indians on the present site of the town.

It was here that Mary, the mother of Washington resided for many years prior to her death, which occurred on the 25th of August, 1789. Her grave is near the outskirts of the town upon the edge of a pretty bluff near the cemetery. Some years ago an attempt was made to erect a suitable monument to the memory of this good and estimable lady, and the corner-stone was laid by President Jackson, but for want of public spirit the project fell through. Some years afterwards, a merchant from New York who was doing business there at the time, fell desperately in love with one of the Lewis branch of the family and her money, and to advance his suit determined to complete the monument, but before it was finished his firm collapsed and his bright visions of love and gold vanished like a soap-bubble. In the cemetery near by are several pretty monuments, and among them that of Hugh Mercer, M. D., a son of General Hugh Mercer, who fell so gloriously at Princeton. The general prior to the Revolution practised medicine here. There also, in newly-made graves, rested in quiet repose some three hundred Confederate soldiers, victims of the mad ambition of their reckless leaders. Though mostly strangers from the far South, the hand of sympathy had decked their graves with flowers, and already the "Love-entangled" and "Forget-me-not," had taken root in the new earth.

Soon after General McDowell arrived, work was commenced on the Aquia creek and Fredericksburg railroad, which was soon put in running order. The railroad bridge was also rebuilt across the river, a bridge of canal boats completed below it, a trestle one above, and a pontoon thrown over opposite Falmouth. Stockades and block houses were built to protect the approaches to these, and artillery commanded them on the eastern bluffs.

On the 9th of May, Mr. Hunnicutt commenced the reissue of his paper "*The Christian Banner*," which he was forced to suspend exactly one year before on account of its loyal sentiments. Until the retrograde movement of the enemy, three secession sheets were issued here. The advent of the northerners soon made a marked difference in the appearance of the town, they opening stores, restaurants, bakeries, etc.; in front of which were displayed numerous American flags. Although the streets were thronged with soldiers, we did not hear of any insult being offered to any of the inhabitants.

On the day of our crossing, General Reynolds was appointed Military Governor, and such was the course of his administration as not only to receive the warm thanks of the Mayor and Council, but when he was taken prisoner at the battle of Gaines Mill, they sent a deputation to Richmond to intercede for his release.

On the 26th, Henry Webb of "F," our detached battery company, was drowned.

On the same day our advance posts were eight miles from the town and on the 29th our cavalry advanced twenty miles beyond, skirmishing and driving the enemy. On the 30th, the regiment was paid off by Major Pomeroy, and the same night orders were received to have one day's cooked rations in haversacks. The next morning at eight o'clock the men were ordered to fall in without knapsacks, but at noon orders came to pack up all, and passing through Fredericksburg, crossed the river to the east side, where our artillery was posted upon the high banks, and we moved about a half mile back to the vacated camp of the Twenty-second New York.

The cause of this movement was: it being ascertained the enemy under General Anderson had moved toward Richmond, destroying the bridges in his rear, and on account of the weakening of our forces, by sending reënforcements to General Banks, we were unable to follow him, it was determined to place the Rappahannock between us and them, so as to spare reënforcements to McClellan.

About this time our brigade was furnished with white linen leggings and orders issued requiring the men to have two pairs of shoes.* The officers here took lessons in sword exercise from a Mr. O'Rouke, who was the only Irishman we ever met who was base enough to deny his nationality. On the 4th of June the river became so swollen from the effects of continued rains that fears were entertained for the safety of the bridges, and as a matter of precaution the pontoon was taken up, but in the afternoon the pile or trestle bridge being unable to resist the pressure, gave way, and was swept down the river, where its timbers coming in contact with the railroad bridge, carried it away also, and the wreck of both coming in contact with the canal boats, broke them from their moorings, destroying the bridge that rested upon them, sending them drifting down the river. The gunboats fortunately were enabled to get out of the way, and succeeded in recovering them all. As soon as it was known in the city that our bridges were in danger, the inhabitants of both sexes collected upon the shore, and as each structure gave way they demonstrated their joy by loud cheers and the waving of handkerchiefs.

On Sunday morning, the 8th, orders were received to prepare to march, and after spending the day in cooking rations and making other necessary arrangements, at sunset we struck tents, packed knapsacks and got into line. It was a clear and beautiful moonlight night, and as the brigade bands pealed forth their soul-inspiring airs we marched off, winding our way through the woods and over the hill to the Rappahannock, down which we marched the distance of seven miles, bivouacking at two o'clock that night in Cedar lane. The next morning after cooking breakfast we marched to Gray's landing,

* The object of this order was to decrease the transportation of the Division Quartermaster Department, and as Captain Hall did not carry a knapsack on the march he doubtless considered it a brilliant idea. Nine-tenths of the shoes were thrown away by the men on the march.

one mile distant, where were collected a fleet of steamboats to receive us. By four o'clock our wagons, baggage and supplies were embarked, and marching aboard we hauled out into the stream. Soon after General Reynolds pushed off in a skiff, and was received with loud cheers, when our bands striking up we steamed down the river, as happy a set of blue coats as ever trod this planet. At sundown we came to anchor off Port Royal, where we remained all night, as we had no pilot. The steamer Canonicus was a fine large boat, but as she had our regiment and five companies of the First and Eighth aboard, she was rather crowded, and by the time we all got ourselves laid out for the night, there was scarcely a square foot of deck unoccupied.

The next morning at five o'clock we weighed anchor, and again started on, accompanied by the ferry boat Chancellor Livingston, and about one P. M., came to anchor near the mouth of the river, where the rest of the flotilla soon afterwards arrived. The day had been a stormy one, but as the wind lulled in the course of a few hours, we again got under way, and passing into Chesapeake bay, headed to the south and at sunset entered the York river, passing by Yorktown and Gloucester City and coming to anchor during the night off West Point at the confluence of the Pamunkey and Mattapony rivers. Early on the 11th we again got under way and entering the Pamunkey, steamed rapidly up it. This river winds through a low, flat country, and on account of its exceedingly crooked course, it was interesting to watch our flotilla with their bows sometimes pointing in every direction. In fact when a strange steamer was discerned, it was impossible to tell whether she was going up or down the river, and when one was but a half mile from us in a direct line she was many times that distance off by the river. A "dark," who had resided in the neighborhood, it was said, answered that it was so crooked in some places that it was impossible to cross it, as no matter how often one rowed over, he would invariably find himself on the same side. We soon commenced meeting Government transports, mostly steamers and schooners laden with forage for the cavalry and artillery. The farther we ascended the more numerous they became, until they numbered hundreds lining the banks of the river for a long distance and obstructing the navigation. About nine o'clock we arrived at the White House, where we landed and stacked arms, awaiting orders.

White House is situated on the Pamunkey, where the Richmond and York River Railroad crosses, and was a position of great importance, being the depot of supplies for the army in front of Richmond. The house itself is an object of interest, being the spot where Washington met and loved Martha Custis in 1758. At the landing there was a forest of masts, and for a half mile the shore was covered with commissary stores and ammunition. There were thousands of tons on the wharf boats, and thousands more awaiting to be landed. There were many commissary, sutler, guard and other tents there, and many soldiers, sutlers, Government employees and contrabands, who, with innumerable wagons and orderlies, continually moving to and fro, and the arrival and departure of trains presented a scene of life and activity. Some distance back from the river was a canvas town, consisting of several hundred hospital tents, arranged in regular streets, with board floors and beds in them, and every thing prepared for the wounded of the coming battles.

The boys having had time to wash themselves and replenish their stock of tobacco, the brigade formed and marched up the railroad about two miles, passing an establishment "for the embalming the dead," whose proprietors distributed to their anticipated customers a bountiful supply of handbills. Moving into a field to the left, we bivouacked for the night. Here our baggage was reduced to the lowest possible amount, the officers being required to send to the landing all but a small valise or knapsack, and the companies being allowed their cooking utensils only. Orders were issued to cook three days' rations, we borrowing from the First and Fifth kettles for the purpose.

At nine o'clock the next morning, we formed and marched off up the railroad which runs nearly due west from here, passing Tunstall's Station. The country through which we moved was mostly low, heavily wooded, and interspersed with numerous swamps. In some places where there were deep cuts, there were large deposits of marine shells and corals that indicated that at one time this portion of the Peninsula had been the bed of the sea. The same formation was found in other portions of the Peninsula. The day being excessively warm many of the men threw away their overcoats and blankets to lighten their loads. About four o'clock we passed Dispatch Station and moved to the right of the road and encamped on the edge of a heavy wood near the Chickahominy river, we having marched ten miles. Through the day we heard the slow fire of heavy guns.

CHAPTER XII.

Siege of Yorktown. Battle of Williamsburg. Skirmishes at Seven Pines, Cold Harbor and Mechanicsville. Battle of Hanover Court House. Battle of Fair Oaks. Attack on Tunstall's Station. March to the Chickahominy. Nanaley's Mill. Shelling the Enemy. Battle of Oak Grove.

Before proceeding further, it will be necessary here to refer to the movements of the Army of the Potomac since its debarkation on the Peninsula. The presence of the enemy's steamer Merimac in the James river closed it to us, as a line of water communication between Fortress Monroe and the army operating against Richmond. To gain possession of the York river and its tributaries for that purpose, the reduction of Yorktown was necessary. Therefore, on the 4th of April, the army took up its line of march from the camping ground near Hampton to that point. At Big Bethel the enemy's pickets were encountered, but they fell back to Howard's creek, to which point they were followed by the main body of the army.

THE SIEGE OF YORKTOWN, APRIL 5TH TO MAY 4TH, 1862.—The next morning the column again advanced, and in a few hours was in front of the enemy's works at Yorktown. On examination of their position it proved to be one of the strongest that could be opposed to an invading force, and the delays thereby created occupied until the 1st of May, when our siege batteries opened fire on the enemy's works, which during the night of the 3d they evacuated, leaving two 3-inch rifled cannon, two 4½-inch rifled cannon, sixteen 32-pounders, six 42-pounders, nineteen 8-inch Columbiads, four 9-inch Dahlgrens, one 10-inch Columbiad, one 10-inch mortar, and one 8-inch siege howitzer, with carriages and implements complete, and seventy-six rounds of ammunition to each piece. Besides these there were a large number of guns left at Gloucester Point and other works on the left.

BATTLE OF WILLIAMSBURG, MAY 4TH, 5TH, 6TH, AND 7TH. —General McClellan immediately threw all his cavalry and horse-artillery in pursuit, under General Stoneman, Chief of Cavalry, supported by infantry under Generals Heintzelman, Hooker and Smith, who were followed by the divisions of Kearney, Couch and Casey, all under General Sumner, the second in command of the army Two miles east of Williamsburg, the advance came upon the enemy's works, four miles in extent, over two-thirds of their front being covered by the branches of College and Queen's Creeks. The principal works were Fort Magruder, and twelve other redoubts and epaulements for field guns. The woods in front of the fort were felled, and the open ground dotted with rifle pits. From this position the enemy opened fire upon the advance guard as it debouched from the woods, which being unsupported by infantry, was forced to retire, but held the enemy in check until the arrival of General Sumner with part of Smith's division, at half-past five P. M. Heintzelman and Keyes reached the ground during the afternoon. Early the next morning General Hooker came up, and began the attack on the enemy's works at seven and-a-half o'clock on the morning of the 6th, and for a time silenced Fort Magruder. Although the enemy was heavily reinforced, and attacked in turn, capturing five guns and inflicting heavy loss on Hooker, whose ammunition was nearly exhausted, he maintained his position until near four P. M., when Kearney arrived, and repulsing the enemy, held possession of the ground that night. The battle was renewed the next day, and about four P. M., General McClellan arriving from Yorktown, took command in person. Fearing there was no direct communication between the centre and left under Heintzelman, and hearing heavy firing in the direction of Hancock's command, he moved the centre forward, attempting to open communication with Heintzelman, and sent Smith and Naglee to the support of Hancock. Before these Generals reached Hancock, however, he was confronted by a superior force. Feigning to retreat slowly, he awaited the onset, and then turned upon them, and after some terrific volleys of musketry, he charged them with the bayonet, routing and dispersing their whole force, killing, wounding and capturing from five to six hundred men, himself losing only thirty-one men.

The enemy having fought to gain time to save their trains, abandoned their position during the night, leaving the town filled with their wounded in charge of eighteen surgeons. The official report of our loss is put down at two thousand two hundred and twenty-eight men killed, wounded and missing. The army was so much exhausted by the marches and conflicts which resulted in the victory at Williamsburg, as to render an immediate pursuit of the enemy impossible, in the condition of the country.

The divisions of Franklin, Sedgwick, Porter and Richardson, were sent from Yorktown by water to the vicinity of West Point, where, on the 7th, General Franklin handsomely repulsed the enemy under General Whiting, after a battle of nearly five hours duration.

Communication was soon opened between the two columns of the army, and headquarters was established at White House on the 16th, General Stoneman having occupied the place some days before. About the same time Generals Franklin, Smith and Porter, reached White House, the roads being in such a state as to require thirty-six hours for one train to move five miles.

A permanent depot for supplies being established at White House, the army was pushed forward along the York River and Richmond Railroad, and on the 20th the advance reached the banks of the Chickahominy River at Bottom's Bridge, which, as well as the railroad bridge about a mile above, they found destroyed. The operations of the army embraced that portion of the river between this point and Meadow Bridge, which covered the principal approaches to Richmond from the east, and over which it became necessary to construct eleven new bridges, all long and difficult, with extensive log-way approaches.

On the 22d, headquarters were removed to Cold Harbor, and on the 24th three important skirmishes took place. General Naglee made a reconnoissance in force, for the purpose of ascertaining the strength of the enemy, and dislodge them from a position in the vicinity of the "Seven Pines," eight miles from Richmond. Another portion of the army had a spirited engagement of two hours near Cold Harbor, and drove their assailants from the field. A third and brilliant little skirmish took place between the brigades of General Stoneman and Davidson, in which they drove the enemy out of Mechanicsville with their artillery, forcing them to seek safety on the opposite banks of the Chickahominy, they destroying the bridge in their retreat. General Stoneman also sent a portion of his cavalry three miles up the river, and destroyed the bridge of the Richmond and Fredericksburg Railroad.

THE BATTLE OF HANOVER COURT HOUSE, *May 27th.*—Having ascertained that the enemy were in force in the vicinity of Hanover Court House, threatening the right and rear of our army, General McClellan dispatched General Porter to dislodge them, for which purpose he moved at daybreak on the 27th. After a fatiguing march of fourteen miles through the mud and rain, General Emory arrived in position and opened the battle about noon, driving the enemy before him. The other columns soon after became engaged, and the enemy were defeated and routed with the loss of some two hundred killed, seven hundred and thirty prisoners, a 12-pound howitzer, a caisson, a large number of small arms, and two railroad trains. Our loss amounted to fifty-three killed, and three hundred and forty-four wounded and missing. The enemy's camp was also captured and destroyed. The next day detachments were sent out, which destroyed the railroad bridges over the Pamunky, the railroad bridges of the Virginia Central, and of the Fredericksburg and Richmond roads, and the country bridges over the South-Anna. These operations for a time cleared our right flank and rear, and cut off communication by rail with Fredericksburg, and with Jackson *via* Gordonsville, excepting by the circuitous route of Lynchburg.

On the 28th of May our troops were pushed forward to Fair Oaks, their advance being met with sharp opposition, and on the 30th their positions on the south side of the Chickahominy were as follows: Casey's division on the right of the Williamsburg road, at right-angles to it, the centre at Fair Oaks; Couch's division at the Seven Pines; Kearney's division on the railroad, from near Savage's Station towards the bridge; Hooker's division on the borders of White Oak Swamp. During the night of the 30th, a violent storm occurred, the rain falling in torrents, making the roads almost impassable, and threatening the destruction of the bridges over the Chickahominy.

THE BATTLE OF FAIR OAKS.—The enemy perceiving the unfavorable position in which our army was placed, and the possibility of destroying that part of it which was apparently cut off from the main body by the rapidly rising stream, the next day threw an overwhelming force upon the position occupied by Casey's division. The battle opened about one o'clock P. M., the attack being made simultaneously upon the front and both flanks. The unequal contest was maintained with great gallantry, the troops struggling against the overwhelming masses of the enemy, for the space of three hours, before reinforcements arrived, and were finally driven from the field with heavy loss, and the position occupied by Casey taken by the enemy. During this time the troops of Heintzelman, Kearney, Sumner, Keyes, Couch and Sedgwick, were engaged, and in a measure retrieved the disaster of the day, and when night closed the contest, the enemy fell back to their defensive line.

During the night our lines were newly formed, and artillery placed in position, and at five o'clock the next morning, June 1st, the battle was again renewed. The enemy boldly advanced without skirmishers, with two columns of attack supported by infantry in line of battle on each side, apparently determined to carry all before him by one crushing blow. He was met, however, with gallant resistance, and through the fierce battle he was driven back at every point, our troops pushing forward to the extreme lines held by them the day before, recovering their own wounded and capturing the enemy's. Our total loss was five thousand seven hundred and thirty-seven, and of the enemy, per their official report, six thousand seven hundred and eighty-three.

The only communication between the two banks of

the Chickahominy were Bottom's, New and Mechanicsville bridges, the two latter being completely enfiladed by the enemy's batteries upon the commanding heights opposite, supported by strong forces, having numerous rifle-pits in their front, which would have made it necessary to have fought a sanguinary battle, with not a certain prospect of success, before a passage could have been secured. Therefore, to have advanced on Richmond soon after the battle, it would have been necessary to march the troops from Mechanicsville and other points on the north bank of the Chickahominy down to Bottom's bridge and thence to Fair Oaks, a distance of twenty-three miles, which in the condition of the roads would have required two days to accomplish with artillery, by which time the enemy would have been secure within his entrenchments, but five miles distant.

On the 13th of June we rested. In the afternoon orders were received to be prepared to move at daylight the next morning. Soon after orders were issued to move immediately, then orders came to draw five days' rations, three of which were to be cooked and two put in the knapsacks. By the time we had got through, about eleven, news was received that an attack had been made upon "Tunstall's Station," in our rear, and our brigade was ordered out. The night was a beautiful moonlight one, and after a march of eight miles we reached there, but the enemy had left. The "Bucktails," Fifth and Eighth were posted on the different roads, and we ordered to occupy a commanding position and hold the station.

It appears that two squadrons of the Fifth United States Cavalry, under the command of Captain Royall, stationed near Hanover Old Church, were attacked and overpowered by a force of the enemy's cavalry, numbering about one thousand five hundred men, with four guns, who pushed on towards the White House in hopes of destroying the stores and shipping there, but the fortunate arrival of the Third Brigade of Reserves frustrated their design. Upon the enemy's arrival at the station a portion of them dismounted and awaited the arrival of the train, upon which they fired, killing one man and wounding several others. The engineer immediately put on steam and succeeded in running the train through. After this they set fire to the station-house and a car loaded with grain, and then tearing up a rail retired to a neighboring wood to await the arrival of another train now due. Upon the arrival of our brigade, however, they skedaddled.

The next morning a number of laborers, who had escaped and hid themselves in the woods came in, as also Colonel G. B. Hall, Second Excelsior Brigade, who fell from a platform car and was captured by the enemy. They bound his hands together and tied him to the stirrup of one of the men, but during the confusion of their skedaddle upon our arrival, he managed to give them the slip. The bodies of two or three poor laborers who had been wantonly killed were found and buried. Near the station they captured and burnt a number of Government and sutler wagons, from which they got considerable liquor, and some of them indulging rather freely, they were found lying around loose in the woods next morning and brought in. A Dutch butcher of Richmond came riding in, in a most glorious state of felicity, tickled half to death with the fun of the night before, which he related to us with great gusto, and proposed taking a drink with any one who had liquor, and shooting the Yankee prisoners. The terror of the poor devil upon discovering his mistake, almost instantly sobered him, and the boys, after frightening him to their hearts' content "bucked and gagged" him, and turned him over to the guard.

The day being excessively hot, we were moved across the railroad to a wood upon a hill, where we remained until the next morning. During the night companies K and H, Captain Smith and Lieutenant Kennedy were sent on picket, and Lieutenants Jack and Black were sent out with detachments to scour the woods, the latter returning with five prisoners.

On Sunday the 15th, the enemy having all disappeared, we returned to our former camping ground, the weather being oppressively hot and the men straggling much. The entire damage done by the enemy, besides that referred to above, was the killing of several of the guard and teamsters at Garlick's Landing, and the burning of two schooners laden with forage, they making the entire circuit of the army, repassing the Chickahominy at Long Bridge. It is somewhat remarkable that this raid was commanded by Fitz Hugh Lee, and executed a few days after the return of his mother to Richmond, from a visit to the White House, where she had been furnished with a pass and escort by General Fitz John Porter, who was a welcomed guest to her hospitalities prior to the war.

More effectually to conceal from the enemy our positions and numbers, orders were issued prohibiting the sounding of all calls, and ordering the tying to trees of any who discharged their pieces. Every morning early the enemy opened on our fatigue parties at work on the bridges, which the boys said was "Jeff calling the roll."

On the afternoon of the 16th the division was formed at five o'clock to receive General McClellan, but we were disappointed, and after waiting an hour we returned to our quarters. The next day we formed at nine, A. M., to receive the general, and remained in position until twelve, M., and reformed at six, when orders were read to us to march the next morning, which were received with enthusiasm. During the evening we were busy cooking rations, and at three the next morning, companies B and A, Captains McDonough and Neidé were recalled from picket. At five o'clock we moved off in a northwesterly direction parallel with the Chickahominy, and after marching eight miles encamped about noon near Gaines' House, and about three hundred yards from the river. Our bivouac was on an opening to the lef of the road, and between us and the river was a heavy woods, from the edge of which we could see the enemy on the other side busy at work. In the afternoon they opened with artillery on the workmen on the New bridge, to which the Reserve artillery responded, and with the exception of one man wounded and a gun dismounted, no damage was done our side. This artillery practice and skirmishing was of daily occurrence.

The next morning, the 19th, at day break we moved off to Ellerson's mills, on the river road where it crosses Beaver Dam creek, about one and a half miles distance, where we remained some time, and then counter-marching and moving to the left we bivouacked in an oat-field near a woods, where the Sixth Pennsylvania cavalry (Rush's Lancers) were encamped. The same afternoon Mr. Hall made an ascension in one of Professor Lowe's balloons near our camp, for the purpose of reconnoitering, but the enemy opening upon him from one of their batteries, he thought it prudent to postpone his aerial operations. Early the next morning we moved back about one mile to Nanaley's mill, where we encamped between the house and the road near a fine wood and a large mill-dam, where the boys enjoyed the luxury of bathing.

Our division upon its arrival was not attached to any Army Corps, but was assigned to the extreme right of the line, which was considered the post of honor.

On the 21st, orders were received to hold ourselves in readiness, to move night or day, at a moment's notice, and each morning to be under arms at three o'clock, and remain so until daylight. The same day, Lieutenant Fletcher and Sergeant Pidgeon arrived in camp from recruiting service. On the 23rd, we were under arms all the afternoon, and loaned our intrenching tools to the Fifth.

Early on the morning of the 24th, we started on picket to Mechanicsville, about one mile distant, where we found the Twelfth Reserves, Colonel John H. Taggart, four companies of Rush's Lancers and Cooper's Battery; Colonel Taggart, being in command of the line, he being the senior officer. Our regiment forming the Reserve, we laid in the grove back of Dr. Lumkin's house. Mechanicsville lies on the high ground, overlooking the Chickahominy on its north bank, from which it is about five hundred yards distance. It consists of a church and some fifteen houses, all of which were deserted and perforated by shot and shell. The south bank of the river rises gradually for about a half mile, where a long line of redoubts and rifle pits front a heavy wood. In the centre of the stream is an island, which is connected with either shore by a bridge, we holding one end of it, and the enemy the other, the island being neutral ground. The pickets at this point, although quite near one another, remained on good terms, the enemy's relief, upon one occasion, presenting arms to Lieutenant-Colonel McIntire, of the First Reserves, as he was visiting one of our posts. We were disposed, at this time, to show acts of courtesy to one another, as we daily expected to meet in battle. Richmond is but five miles distant from Mechanicsville, and from a shed near the road-side we could see its spires. One of our officers wagered a hundred segars he would be in the city in one week—he was, but as a prisoner.

During the night, the position of our guns were changed and General Reynolds required hourly reports to be made to him in writing. All passed quietly and the next morning we were up and in line at three o'clock. There being strong indications of a movement on the part of the enemy, about five, P. M., orders were received to feel them with our guns, to ascertain, if possible, what they were at, and accordingly Cooper's battery threw about twenty shells, but without eliciting any response. We subsequently ascertained, what we then suspected, that they were moving off to our right. The shells, however, dropped beautifully among them, and sent their wagons hurriedly down the pike.

BATTLE OF OAK GROVE, June 25th.—While this was transpiring on our extreme right, a more interesting scene was enacting on the left. The bridges and intrenchments being at last completed, an advance of our picket line on the left was ordered on the 25th, preparatory to a general forward movement. General Hooker's division of Heintzelman's corps, was pushed forward to occupy "Oak Grove," a new and important position in front of the most advanced redoubt on the Williamsburg road, and while advancing through a dense thicket and an almost impassable swamp, was suddenly attacked by the enemy, whom they repulsed and drove back. The fighting continued off and on during the day, and at sunset our object was accomplished, with the loss of fifty-one killed, four hundred and one wounded and sixty-four missing, making a total of five hundred and sixteen. The enemy's loss was about equal in number.

CHAPTER XIII.

STRENGTH OF THE OPPOSING ARMIES. OPENING OF THE SEVEN DAYS' BATTLES. BATTLE OF MECHANICSVILLE. BATTLE OF GAINES' MILLS. CROSSING THE CHICKAHOMINY.

IN anticipation of a speedy advance on Richmond, to provide for the contingency of our communications with the depot at the White House being severed by the enemy, and at the same time to prepare for a change of the base of our operations to James river, if circumstances should render it advisable, arrangements were made on the 18th of June to have transports with supplies of provisions and forage sent up the James river to Harrison's Landing.

By the report of the chief of the "secret service

corps," dated the 26th of June, the estimate strength of the enemy is put down at about one hundred and eighty thousand, and the specific information obtained regarding their organization, warrants the belief that this estimate did not exceed his actual strength. It is shown in the report that there were two hundred regiments of infantry and cavalry; including the forces of Jackson and Ewell, just arrived; eight battalions of independent troops, five battalions of artillery; twelve companies of infantry and independent cavalry, and forty-six companies of artillery· amounting in all, to from forty to fifty brigades. There were undoubtedly many others whose designations were not known.

The report also shows that numerous and heavy earthworks had been completed for the defence of Richmond, and that in thirty-six of these were mounted some two hundred guns.

On the 14th of May, General McClellan in his official report states "I cannot bring into actual battle against the enemy more than eighty thousand men at the utmost." Subsequent to that, he certainly did not receive reinforcements of more than ten thousand men, and deducting from this total of ninety thousand, the losses sustained in the three skirmishes of the 24th of May at Seven Pines, Cold Harbor and Mechanicsville, and at the battles of Hanover Court House and Fair Oaks and minor skirmishes, with the usual sickness attendant upon the unhealthy position of the army, it may be safely stated that the Army of the Potomac did not number over eighty thousand fighting men at the opening of the Seven Day's battles.

From information received from spies, contrabands and a deserter as early as the 24th, General McClellan had strong reasons to suppose the enemy meditated an attack upon his right and rear, and on the 26th of June, the day decided upon for the final advance on Richmond the enemy anticipated our movement by attacking our army.

THE BATTLE OF MECHANICSVILLE, June 26th.—Early that day our regiment was relieved by the Fifth Reserve, Colonel Simmons, and marched back to camp. At eleven o'clock we were ordered under arms, and at twelve, noon, just as our dinners were cooked, but before we could eat them, orders came to fall in with cartridge boxes and muskets. Marching up to Mechanicsville we turned to the right and moved up the river road to "Shady Grove Church," where we met the Eighth Illinois cavalry, Colonel Farnsworth, who were being driven in by the enemy who had crossed the Chickahominy at Meadow bridge. Colonel McCandless had some time before deployed Company B, Captain McDonough, as skirmishers, and learning that the enemy were approaching in overpowering force, he deployed the regiment across the road in connection with the Eighth Illinois to produce caution on their part, and thus gain time to withdraw to Mechanicsville, where General Reynolds with the rest of our brigade and General Meade with his, were drawn up. Three companies of the "Bucktails," under Major La Roy Stone, who were on our left, were surrounded by a heavy force of the enemy, but two of them cut their way through, company K, being captured. At Mechanicsville the line was again formed, and soon afterwards we withdrew to Beaver Dam Creek, where it was determined to give battle.

This position was naturally a strong one, the left resting on the Chickahominy and the right extending to dense woods (beyond the upper Mechanicsville road) which were occupied. The passage of the creek was difficult throughout the greater part of the front, and, with the exception of the roads crossing at Ellerson's Mill, near the left, and that near the right, above mentioned, impracticable for artillery. On the right of the last named road an *epaulement* calculated for four pieces of field artillery was thrown up, and rifle-pits constructed on the left of the road.

The line of battle was formed in the following order

from right to left: On the extreme right was the seven companies of the Second regiment, Lieutenant-colonel McCandless; then six companies of the "Bucktails," Major Stone with four guns of Cooper's battery in the *epaulement;* the Fifth regiment, Colonel Simmons in the rifle-pits on the left of the road; the First regiment, Colonel Roberts; the Eighth regiment, Colonel Hays; the Tenth regiment, Colonel Kirk; the Ninth regiment, Colonel Jackson; and the Twelfth regiment, Colonel Taggart, which occupied the extreme left. General Meade's brigade, which was in reserve, consisted of the Third regiment, Colonel Sickel; the Fourth regiment, Colonel Magilton; and the Seventh regiment, Colonel Harvey. Easton's battery of four twelve-pound Napoleon guns, and Kern's battery of six twelve pound howitzers, were also held in reserve. It should here be mentioned that the Sixth regiment, Lieutenant-colonel McKean, was detached at Tunstall's Station, and the Eleventh regiment, Colonel Gallagher, was on picket on the Chickahominy.

The position of the Second regiment, as before noticed, was on the extreme right, with a heavy wood in front and a ford near the right of it. Companies K and H, Captain Smith and Lieutenant Kennedy were detached under Major Woodward with orders to hold this ford at all hazards; and Company C, Captain Byrnes, was posted on the left in a dry swamp between us and the "Bucktails."

About three o'clock the enemy's lines were formed on the opposite side of the swamp and their skirmishers rapidly advanced, delivering their fire as they came forward. They were speedily driven back by the artillery and a rattling reply of musketry. In a short time the main body, who were commanded by General Robert E. Lee, in person, boldly advanced in force under cover of a heavy artillery fire, and attacked the whole front. It soon became apparent that the main point of their attack was the extreme right, upon which they opened a heavy fire of round shot and shell, and precipitated column after column of Georgian and Louisiana troops, who waded to their middle through the water, and boldly advanced up through the woods. They were received by the Second on their knees, with a withering fire, which they maintained without a moment's cessation for over three hours. During this time, assault after assault was made on the position, and upon three separate occasions the enemy succeeded in forcing themselves between us and the "Bucktails," and gaining the clear ground, but they were each time driven back at the point of the bayonet by charges led in person by Colonel McCandless.

At one time they charged the left and centre at the same time, boldly pressing on their flags until they nearly met ours, when the fighting became of the most desperate character, the flags rising and falling as they were surged to and fro by the contending parties, each struggling to defend its own, and capture its opponents'. Our left was driven back, the enemy at that point having passed the woods, bending our line into a convexed circle. But never for a moment were we broken. McCandless placing himself in front of the left, led it valiantly to the charge, hurling the brave Georgia boys back, and almost taking their flag. While this was going on in our front Major Woodward with his two companies was hotly engaged at the ford, the men delivering, from behind trees, a slow but destructive fire, or pouring in rapid volleys when hard pressed.

General Reynolds, whose ever-watchful eye was upon the regiments of his brigade, several times rode down to our position, at one time exclaiming, as he pointed with his sword, "Look at them, boys, in the swamp there, they are as thick as flies on a ginger bread; fire low, fire low." Just before dark, when we had driven back their last charge, knowing we had expended nearly all our ammunition, he ordered up the First Reserve, Colonel Roberts, who, in line of battle on our left and rear, opened fir but soon after forming in column of division and advancing deployed and opened again on the retreating masses. At the same time Kern's battery of six twelve-pounder howitzers supported by the Third Reserve, Colonel Sickel, took position some three hundred yards to our right, and we moved to the right to give play to the guns, which opened a most terrible fire of shell upon the confused and broken masses of the enemy on the opposite side of the swamp. Colonel McCandless here offered to storm a battery posted opposite to us across the swamp, if support was given to him, which being promised, we moved down the road on our right to the ford held by Major Woodward, but the promised support luckily failing to come, the attempt was abandoned, and the regiment was deployed on the edge of the swamp and again opened fire. The musketry soon after ceased, but the artillery fire was continued until nine o'clock at night when the battle ceased, and the Reserves slept on the field of victory. Griffin's brigade and Edward's battery were also sent to the right to our support, but they with the Third regiment did not become engaged.

About five o'clock a most determined attempt was made by the enemy to force the left at Ellerson's Mill, but they were gallantly repulsed by General Seymour, who drove back column after column that was hurled against him.

The prisoners taken by our regiment, mostly by companies H and K, numbered fifteen, and were utterly surprised at the smallness of the force that was opposed to them, and expressed their full confidence, if permitted to rejoin their comrades, that they could return and drive us from our position.

It was here that the most desperate fighting was done, our regiment which numbered but three hundred and seventy-one, officers and men, losing nearly one-half of the number killed, and one-fourth of the killed and wounded of the whole division, which numbered about seven thousand, including officers. The enemy acknowledged the loss of over five hundred men at this point, and General McCall puts down their whole strength as twenty thousand; and states, in his report, that he "learned from official authority, while a prisoner in Richmond, that General Lee's loss, in killed and wounded, did not fall short of two thousand; and that the Forty-fourth Georgia lost nearly two-thirds." The loss of the division is officially reported at thirty-three killed and one hundred and fifty wounded. The great disproportion in the losses must be attributed to the nature of the ground.

But while we rejoiced at the laurels entwined around our banners, our hearts were saddened at the fall of our comrades whose life blood gushed out upon the field of victory.*

General McCall, in his official report, honorably mentions the conduct of Lieutenant-colonel McCandless and the regiment during the battle.

During the night ammunition was sent for and distributed to the men. Companies H, and K, remained at the ford; B, Lieutenant Jack, was thrown out on picket to the right, and the rest slept on the field all night. All was the stillness of death, not a voice being heard save the moaning of the enemy's wounded that came up out of the swamp and woods beyond.

The next morning, long before daybreak, we were in line, and the enemy during the night having received heavy reinforcements, the attack was again commenced, but principally upon the left. The position of Beaver Dam Creek, although so successfully defended, had its extreme right flank too much exposed, and was too far from the main army to make it available to retain it longer, therefore, just before daybreak orders were received from General McClellan for us to fall back to the rear of Gaines' Mills. To withdraw a large force in broad daylight, while under fire, is one of the most deli-

---

* See Appendix, A.

cate and difficult movements in war, particularly in presence of a greatly superior force. It, nevertheless, was most successfully accomplished, great caution and deliberation being used to screen the movement, and the troops being withdrawn slowly and at intervals. Meade's brigade was the first to move; then came Griffin's brigade and battery, next Reynold's under cover of the Bucktails and Cooper's guns, and last Seymour's.

During these movements a scattering fire of artillery and musketry was kept up and continued until all was brought out. So coolly and deliberately was the movement accomplished that the regiments as they filed past, marched as steadily as if coming from the parade ground, we burying all our killed and sending off our wounded, not leaving a man, gun or musket on the field.

The retrograde movement at this time was not comprehended by us, and we slowly fell back in good order, but in any thing but a good humor, to the point designated in rear of Gaines' Mills, where we arrived at ten o'clock in the forenoon. On our route we met Cooper's battery which we saved the day before from being flanked, and the men freely distributed coffee, bread and tobacco to our hungry boys who had fasted for twenty-four hours.

THE BATTLE OF GAINES' MILLS, JUNE 27TH.—It having been ascertained on the preceding night that the enemy was approaching in full force with the intention of cutting off our communication with the White House, General McClellan determined to carry out his intentions of changing his base from the Pamunkey to the James Rivers, for which purpose he withdrew the troops on the left bank of the Chickahominy to a position around the bridge heads where its flanks were reasonably secure, and it was within supporting distance of the main army. This movement secured the withdrawal of all the heavy guns, wagons and stores to the right bank of the river, and afforded time to perfect arrangements to secure the adoption of the new base. To General Fitz John Porter with the Fifth Corps and all the disposable reinforcements, was assigned the task of resisting the enemy.

The line of battle was about an arc of a circle formed on the interior edge of the dense woods bounding the extensive plain of cleared lands stretching some twelve or fifteen hundred yards back of the river. Morell's division held the left of the line in a strip of woods on the left bank of the Gaines' Mill stream, resting its left flank on the descent to the Chickahominy, which was swept by our artillery on both sides of the river, and extending into open ground on the right towards Cold Harbor. In this line General Butterfield's brigade held the extreme left, General Martindale's joined his right, and General Griffin, still further to the right, joined the left of General Sykes' division, which, partly in woods and partly in open ground, extended in the rear of Cold Harbor.

Each brigade held in reserve two of its own regiments. General McCall was informed by General Porter, that as his division had been engaged till late the previous night, and suffered from loss of sleep, and had been under fire for some hours in the morning it would be held in reserve. It therefore formed the second line, occupying the ground some six hundred yards in the rear of the first. Meade's brigade on the left near the Chickahominy. Reynold's brigade on the right covering the approaches from Cold Harbor and Despatch Station to Sumner's Bridge, and Seymour's in reserve to the second line, still further in rear. The artillery occupied the space between the lines and the cavalry of the division, the Fourth Pennsylvania, was placed under cover of a slope in the rear. General P. St. George Cooke, with five companies of the Fifth Regular Cavalry, two squadrons of the First Regular, and three squadrons of the Sixth Pennsylvania Cavalry, (Rush's Lancers,) was posted behind a hill in rear of the position, and near the Chickahominy, to aid in watching the left flank and defending the slope of the river.

The troops were all in position by noon, with the artillery on the commanding ground, and in the intervals between the divisions and brigades. Besides these division batteries, there was from the artillery reserve Tidball's horse battery, posted on the right of Syke's division, and Robertson's on the extreme left of the line, in the valley of the Chickahominy. Shortly after noon the enemy were discovered approaching in force, and it soon became evident that the entire position was to be attacked. His skirmishers advanced rapidly, and soon the firing became heavy along the whole front. At two o'clock P. M., General Porter asked for reinforcements. By three P. M., the engagement had become so severe, and the enemy were so greatly superior in numbers, that the entire second line and reserves were moved forward to sustain the first line against repeated and desperate assaults along the whole front.

The Second and Third brigades of the Reserye were ordered forward and were soon under fire, in some instances the regiments going at once into line where intervals had been left, while in others they halted directly in rear of the line already formed. Our brigade, which had laid in a sheltered position behind a hill for five hours, with round shot and shell continually whizzing and bursting over head, was soon after ordered to advance. Once more the boys prepared for battle, their brave hearts beating with high hopes of victory, and on double quick they moved to the edge of a heavy swampy woods, where they were halted for a few moments.

General Reynolds soon rode up, and ordered our regiment to advance through the wood, clear it out and take up a position on its extreme edge. Colonel McCandless not entirely liking the order, asked the General's permission to move in at right angles to the position assigned to us, on the left of it. The General was silent for a moment, his face bearing the expression of great perplexity and dissatisfaction, when he replied, "Colonel, General Porter is fighting the battle on certain parallels, and his orders will have to be obeyed." "I would to God," remarked the Colonel afterwards, "I had not asked him the question, but had taken my regiment in by mistake." "Forward," passed down the line, and moving on we advanced into the wood, strewed as it was with the dead and the dying, and reaching its outer edge, laid down to await the coming storm.

The First Reserve lay on our right, the Sixth Regulars in our rear, and several other regiments near by. A regiment of New York Zouaves were posted in an open field about five hundred yards in our front and facing us. Easton's battery of Reserves to our front and right were firing in the opening between us and parallel to our front. The enemy, as we well knew before we entered, were on our left flank. We may have been judiciously posted, and good soldiers should not think, but we could not help noticing that we were in a better position to attack our own troops than to inflict damage upon the enemy.

Steadily the solid columns of the foe were advancing on our left, their leading lines dressed in our uniform, showing no flag and treacherously crying out they were our friends, and not to fire upon them. But we were not deceived, and poured into them a left oblique fire with good effect. But onward they pressed until almost upon us, when they poured into us a deafening roar of musketry, above which the artillery fire at times could scarcely be distinguished. Line after line delivered their fire, and falling to the ground gave range to those behind them. It sounded like one long continuous roar, not a susceptible interval being perceived for several minutes. Overpowered, flanked, and with the enemy in our rear, with scattered remnants of other regiments in the excitement of the moment firing into us, we broke and were scattered through the woods, fighting the best we could from behind trees, until finally we were driven headlong out, with our muskets thoroughly heated, and our ammunition almost exhausted.

We were driven from the woods to the right and parallel with the line we entered on, but did not retire more than three hundred yards, before we came to a depressed road, where once more we raised our banner to the storm and rallied the boys around it. Cut off from our brigade and division, we laid here, and with Easton's battery, which was directly on our right, held the foe at bay, who seeing reinforcements coming up, dared not advance into the open field.

Soon a gallant brigade passed by, with their arms at a right shoulder and lines dressed with the precision of a parade. Steadily, silently and firm paced, they advanced with their glorious banners and glittering bayonets gleaming in the sun, and like a mass of living valor entered the woods and disappeared from sight. Soon their loud cheers and volleys told they had met the foe. If our brigade had entered the woods as they did, we would have met the enemy on our front and not our flank.

At this time we were ordered into a low woods in the rear of Easton's battery, but had not remained there long before we were moved to the left on an open field. Soon afterwards we were ordered to the right, and further to the rear of the battery. An hour had now passed by, and soon a few stragglers were seen flying from the woods, and in a few moments the foe burst upon us in overwhelming numbers. The guns of Easton's battery vomited forth their hail of double-shotted canister against which it appeared impossible for men to stand, yet onward with undaunted bravery the enemy pressed, closing up their vast gaps and sweeping everything before them. The gallant Easton was killed, his brave cannoniers bayoneted at their guns, the majority of the horses disabled, and, despite the most heroic resistance, the battery was taken. A dozen or fifteen horses cut loose from the battery, dashed through our line followed closely by the enemy, and again driven, we slowly and sullenly, but in good order retreated down over the fields, under a murderous fire that brought many a brave man to the ground.

Having reached a position whose sloping ground afforded some slight protection, Colonel McCandless rallied the men and reformed the line, collecting a large number of stragglers from different regiment, and soon after Colonel Simmons of the Fifth Reserve appeared and took charge. A squadron of Rush's Lancers and a squadron of Indiana cavalry, now came up and formed in our rear, and General McCall stopped two batteries that were in retreat and bringing them into battery opened upon the enemy, who just then appeared on the opposite hillside, and checked their advance at this point.

Soon after French's and Meagher's brigades came up, and the fire of the batteries was stopped as they passed down the hill in front, but upon their reaching the foot of it, they were met by General Porter, who halted them, as the enemy had retired from view and the sun was setting.

The other regiments and brigades of the Reserve fought with great gallantry, the First and Eighth being relieved and brought out by General Reynolds, and the Fifth retiring only when their ammunition was exhausted. The Eleventh, Colonel Gallagher, having relieved the Fourth New Jersey, Colonel Simpson, while engaged by the enemy became so completely enveloped in the smoke of the battle as not to observe the rest of the line had retired, and being completely surrounded by a vastly superior force of the enemy, the major part of them and the Fourth New Jersey were captured, but no censure whatever, was attached to either of the gallant commanders of the regiments.

About eight o'clock, the battle ceased and we were moved some distance towards the rear, near a field hospital where the wounded were being continually brought in for surgical treatment, after which they were laid upon the grass, a blanket thrown over them, and a canteen of water put by their side, where some slept and others died. The poor fellows displayed most heroic fortitude, and though many of them were horribly mangled and suffering intense pain, only suppressed murmurs escaped their lips. All of our regiment were collected and laid together, and were cared for by their comrades until we moved. While the surgeons were at work by the flickering light of candles, the ruthless enemy opened fire upon them with shell, but they continued, hiding the lights as best they could with their caps and bodies.

Through the night General Reynolds was surprised, with Captain Charles Kingbury, his Assistant Adjutant-general, and taken prisoner by the enemy. The command of our brigade, therefore, devolved upon Colonel Simmons of the Fifth Reserve.

The number of troops engaged on our side was not more than thirty-five thousand men, and that of the enemy has been computed to be from seventy to seventy-five thousand men. The loss on our side was heavy, but as no general returns were made until after the Seven Days' battle, the losses during the series of battles were estimated together. The number of guns captured by the enemy on the field were nineteen, and three were lost by being run off the bridge during the final withdrawal.

Although we were finally forced from the first line after the enemy had been repeatedly driven back, yet the object sought for had been attained. The enemy was held at bay, our siege guns and material were saved, and the right wing could now be withdrawn and joined to the main body of the army.*

The wearied and exhausted men who had fought for two days, and many of them without a mouthful to eat, threw themselves upon the ground and sank to sleep with their cartridge boxes strapped upon them and their muskets in their hands. But their slumbers were of short duration, as soon orders came to wake them up and get into line without noise. It was hard work to rouse the sleepy boys, it being necessary to roll some of them over, shake them, pound them, and even to lift

---

* See Appendix A.

them upon their feet. Having got the men in line, our division waited here until near morning to cover the withdrawal of the army from the left bank of the Chickahominy, and then crossing the bridge opposite Trent's Hill about seven o'clock we blew it up; moving on about a mile and a half we halted on Trent's Hill, where we laid during the 28th.

CHAPTER XIV.

CHANGE OF BASE. MARCH TO THE JAMES RIVER. BATTLE OF ALLEN'S FARM. BATTLE OF SAVAGE'S STATION. A NIGHT ON PICKET. THE BATTLE OF GLENDALE. THE RIVER REACHED.

WHILE the battle of Gaines' Mills or Chickahominy was progressing on the left bank of the river, the enemy were not idle on the right bank, they having a large force between our left wing and Richmond showing their numerical superiority. Sharp musketry and artillery fighting took place there, along nearly the whole of the line, which was threatened by such heavy masses that the corps commanders deemed their forces were smaller than were adequate to the emergency. Therefore, to have sent more reinforcements to Porter would have imperilled the movement across the Peninsula. After the battle it was necessary to unite the two wings of the army which could have been done on either bank of the river, but if it had been on the left bank, although our united force could have defeated the enemy and have marched to the White House, as they held the roads leading there, our supply trains could not have been sent in advance of the army, but would have had to follow us, and the guarding of these trains would have seriously embarrassed our operations in battle. We would have been immediately followed by the enemy on the Richmond side of the river, who would have operated on our rear, and if we had been defeated, we would have been forced to fall back to the White House and probably to Fort Monroe; and, as both our flanks and rear would then have been entirely exposed, our entire supply train, if not the greater part of the army, might have been lost. The enemy anticipated this movement on our part and were prepared to take advantage of it, but they were disappointed.

When our army was concentrated on the Richmond side of the Chickahominy, and a large portion of the enemy were drawn away and separated from them by the river, we could have marched directly upon the city with very reasonable hopes of capturing it, but as the amount of rations we had with us was very limited and the enemy could at any time have severed our communications with the supply depot at the White House, our victory might have been turned into disaster. It is therefore clear that the movements of General McClellan were dictated by sound military judgment.

During the day, rations, of which we were greatly in need, as some of the men had been forty-eight hours without food, were received and issued, but as we had left every thing in our camp near Mechanicsville, which was subsequently burnt by order of General McCall, we had no haversacks. However, as soldiers are never at a loss for ways and means, they substituted the extremities of their shirts which answered most admirably. The same day our most efficient Quartermaster, Dr. Chas. F. Hoyt, was promoted Captain and Commissary of Subsistence of the brigade *vice* Captain Jas. B. Clow.

We remained on an open field under a broiling sun during the 28th, which really afforded but indifferent rest, as we could not sleep, except as Montezuma on his bed of roses, and at nine o'clock that night, during a drenching rain, we moved off towards White Oak Creek. Our division took with it Hunt's Reserve Artillery, consisting of thirteen batteries, which with our own trains extended the column many miles in length, and as our flanks were constantly exposed to attacks, the Third Brigade was placed by regiments between the batteries, to afford them support.

Our movement, owing to narrow and bad roads, was necessarily slow, and all night long we toiled through dark woods and swamps unable to see but a few feet on either side of us. While thus moving, one of the wagon guard of the Fourth Reserve, stepped into the woods a little way and his musket being accidentally discharged he was mistaken for a foe, and a number of shots fired at him. This frightening some of the teams, they dashed in among us, which, with the unexplained firing, for a time created considerable excitement.

About daybreak we reached Savage's Station, on the York River and Richmond Railroad, where we found hundreds of wagons and ambulances almost choking the roads and covering the fields in every direction. Here were collected vast piles of commissary and quartermaster's stores, which were opened and the men allowed to take whatever they wanted. We also found here a large number of wounded of the preceding battles, and among them were our own, many of whom were subsequently taken prisoners. The boys went to see them and did all they could for them, improvising crutches for such as could hobble off, and giving water and money to those who had to remain. There was also a large amount of ammunition here which was later in the day loaded on twelve cars and with an engine run into the Chickahominy, a fuse being attached, and so well timed as to blow the whole up at the proper instant. Moving on past the station, we met a large number of prisoners captured during the battles, and about noon we crossed White Oak Creek Bridge, some distance beyond which General McCall was ordered to place his division in position to repel any attack by the enemy from the direction of Richmond. It was here we learned that General McClellan had caused to be read to the army a complimentary return of thanks to the Pennsylvania Reserves for their conduct at Mechanicsville, in defeating and holding a vastly superior force in check, until he could perfect his arrangements for the withdrawal from the left bank of the river.

Before proceeding further, we will detail the general events of the day. The essential operation was the passage of our trains across the swamp, and their protection against attack from the direction of Richmond, and the establishment of our communication with the gunboats on James river. For this purpose the corps of Sumner and Heintzelman, and the division of Smith were ordered to an interior line, with their right resting on Savage's Station.

BATTLE OF ALLEN'S FARM, JUNE 29TH.—General Sumner evacuated his works at Fair Oaks at daylight, and marched his command to Orchard Station, halting at Allen's field, between Orchard and Savage Stations. The divisions of Richardson and Sedgwick were formed on the right of the railroad, facing towards Richmond, Richardson holding the right, and Sedgwick joining the right of Heintzelman's corps. The first line of Richardson's division was held by General French; General Caldwell supporting the second. A log building in front of Richardson's division was held by Colonel Brook with the Fifty-third Pennsylvania volunteers, with Hazard's battery on an elevated piece of ground, a little in the rear.

At nine o'clock, A. M., the enemy commenced a furious attack on the right of General Sedgwick, but were repulsed. The left of General Richardson was next attacked, the enemy attempting in vain to carry the position of Colonel Brooks. Captain Hazard's battery, and Pettit's battery, which afterwards replaced it, were served with great effect, while the Fifty-third Pennsylvania Volunteers kept up a steady fire on the advancing enemy, compelling them at last to retire in disorder. The enemy renewed the attack three times, but were as often repulsed.

BATTLE OF SAVAGE'S STATION, JUNE 29TH.—During the morning, General Franklin hearing that the enemy, after having repaired the bridges, was crossing the Chickahominy in large force, and advancing towards Savage's Station, moved Smith's division to that point, and communicated the intelligence to General Sumner. A little after noon, General Sumner reached the station, and united his troops with those of Franklin, and assumed command. The troops were posted in line of battle, in the large open field to the left of the railroad, fronting Richmond, the left resting on the edge of the woods, and the right extending down to the railroad. General Brooks, with his brigade, held the wood to the left of the field, where he did excellent service. General Hancock's brigade was thrown into the woods on the right and front. About four in the afternoon, the enemy advanced upon the Williamsburgh road and commenced the attack in large force. They were gallantly met by General Burns' brigade, supported and reinforced by the reserve, and the Sixty-ninth New York Volunteers and Hazard's and Pettit's batteries. The other batteries were also brought into play, and the battle, which was fought with great obstinacy until nearly nine o'clock at night, terminated in the enemy being driven from the field.

Our division remained in its position on high open ground in the hot sun until four o'clock, when we were ordered to proceed to the Quaker road crossing of the New Market road, and take a position to repel any attack from Richmond. The object of this movement was to cover the Turkey Bridge road, leading to the James river, along which trains were moving all night. On our march the road was nearly blocked up with innumerable wagon trains and artillery, besides a drove of twenty-five hundred cattle, through which we wound our way, and arrived at the designated point about six o'clock. We halted on Nelson's farm, the battle-field of the next day, and where a sharp skirmish had taken place with the enemy's cavalry early in the morning, showing that their efforts were about to be directed towards impeding our progress to the river. General McCall made his headquarters at the farm house during the night.

Leaving the Second and Third Brigades in reserve, at dark our brigade and a battery of artillery, under the command of Colonel Simmons, silently moved off to the front, about a mile, crossing a small creek and turning to the left through a deep woods, where we were posted on picket, on a by-road. The night was intensely dark, and we were unable to see but a short distance from us. The men were laid down on the edge of the road with orders for no one to speak or sleep, but to be ready to spring into line at an instant's notice. In front of us, at the distance of fifty paces, pickets were posted under command of Lieutenant Clendining. The countersign was—to bare the right arm and raise and lower it twice. When all was the stillness of death, a rapid fire of musketry opened a few hundred yards in our rear, and we were unable to tell whether it was an attack of the foe, or our friends firing upon one another. We found out afterwards it was our own men.

About the middle of the night, a number of the battery horses got loose, and came dashing down the rear of our line, like a charge of cavalry, and several shots were fired into them in rapid succession. One of the horses being wounded, kept up a most unearthly cry through the night, making the most distressing noise possible to imagine, and the farm dogs far and near were continually barking, indicating the proximity of the foe. In fact, and we strongly suspected it at the time, we were surrounded on all sides by the enemy, who knew our exact position, and had it in their power to cut in pieces or capture us, but they wished to bag the whole division, and were waiting for the arrival of one of their columns in the position assigned to it. Fortunately it was delayed on its march, for which the general commanding was severely censured by his Government. The tedious hours of watching at last passed away, and the welcomed light of day broke in upon us, and with it, we withdrew our line and returned to the field where we halted the preceding afternoon, and which before the setting sun was drenched with our blood.

During the night all the troops fell back and crossed White Oak swamp, and by five A. M. on the 30th, General French commanding the rear-guard, crossed the bridge over the creek and destroyed it. General Keyes having been ordered to move to the James river, and occupy a defensive position near Malvern Hill, to secure out extreme left flank, arrived there in safety early in the morning with all his artillery and baggage. Other troops and long trains had also passed to the left.

BATTLE OF CHARLES CITY CROSS-ROADS OR GLENDALE, June 30th.—It being the 30th of June, the regiments were formed for muster, and while this was being gone through with, the pickets commenced exchanging shots, and so close were they to us, that Corporal John Collins, Company H, received a bone wound in his arm, and we had hardly time to get through with the muster before the division was moved a short distance, and assigned its position for the battle.

General McCall was ordered to take up a position on the left of the New Market or Long Bridge road, near its crossing with the Charles City road, in front of the Quaker road leading to Malvern Hill and Turkey bridge, and to maintain it until the whole of the immense supply trains of the army, then slowly advancing from White Oak creek, had passed towards James river, and to repel any attack on it. For this purpose General Meade's brigade was posted on the right, General Seymour's on the left, and Reynold's, now Colonel Simmons', held in reserve. The artillery was placed in front of the line, Randall's on the right, Cooper's and Kern's opposite the centre, and Dietrich and Kennerheim's, German batteries, accidentally with the division, on the left of the line. The Fourth Pennsylvania Cavalry, Colonel Childs, was drawn up on the left and rear, but not being called into action, were subsequently ordered to fall back.

The field was a large open plain, with a front of about eight hundred yards, and depth of one thousand yards, intersected on the right by the New Market road and a narrow strip of timber, parallel to it, and on the left, near the centre, with a marshy woods, near which was Nelson's small farm house. In the rear of the plain was a steep wooded hill running to a broad plateau or table land, across which run the Quaker road leading to the river. Upon the upper edge of the woods laid the First Brigade in reserve.

On the right of the Reserves was posted Kearney's division, and on the left and somewhat retired was Sumner, and further to the left, and slightly advanced, was Hooker.

About half past two o'clock, P. M., the cavalry and infantry pickets of the Reserve were driven in, and soon after the enemy opened a heavy fire of shell upon our centre, under cover of which they sent forward two regiments at different points to feel the line. These were driven back, one by the Third regiment, Colonel Sickel, and the other by the Seventh regiment, Colonel Harvey.

Our division being too small to occupy the plain, both our flanks were exposed, and soon after a furious attack was made on the left by a heavy column of infantry. This advance was made under cover of a terrific artillery fire, and was gallantly met and driven back with great slaughter, and over two hundred prisoners taken. The "Bucktails," Major Stone, at this time were sent to the left and posted in the marsh woods, the First, Colonel Roberts, was sent to support Kern's battery, the Fifth, Lieutenant-colonel Fisher, and the Eighth, Colonel Hays, were ordered forward to the support of the left centre, and the last regiment of the reserve, the Second, Lieutenant-colonel McCandless, was ordered to the left front.

In anticipation of this order we had been advanced down the hill to near the edge of the woods, where the cannoniers of a section of a Dutch battery belonging to Porter's corps and assigned that day to the Reserves, having cut their traces, came dashing through our regiment, trampling several men to the ground and breaking the line. Their guns were abandoned in the plain before us, but the regiment advanced with loud cheers and swept across the field under a murderous fire of round shot and shell, and reaching a point near Nelson's house, and immediately on the right of the marsh woods, were laid down under a slight elevation of the ground. Here we were joined by a detachment of the Twelfth, under Adjutant McMurtrie, who were placed on our left.

The battle was now raging with terrific fury, a perfect storm of shot and shell passing harmlessly over our heads. As the gallant Seymour sat unmoved upon his horse in our rear, and saw the restiveness of the boys to advance, he said to them, "lay down Second, lay down and go to sleep, I will wake you up when I want you." "Come and take a nap with us, General," replied the boys. The foe being heavily reinforced, were steadily adavncing, and the regiments that had driven them back with such gallantry had become somewhat disordered by the very impetuosity of the charge, and had not time fully to reform, and they in their turn were forced back, passing to our right. The Fifth and Eighth in the mean time had joined us on the right, and when the foe had arrived within fifty yards of us, Seymour cried out, "Up and at them," and rising we poured in a murderous fire that caused them to stagger and reel. With loud cheers we rushed upon them with the bayonet, and one of those desperate hand-to-hand struggles ensued that are seldom witnessed in war. The two hostile flags were surging over the struggling mass a few feet from each other, and around them was poured out the best blood of Pennsylvania and Virginia. The struggle was a short but desperate one. Already had Major Woodward, Captains Smith and Neidé, and Lieutenants Fletcher and Nightingale, and many other gallant spirits fallen, and the ground was crimsoned with their blood. In vain the wounded boys, who laid thick and near, urged on their comrades, but the enemy in crushing masses poured in around us, and with impetuous fury charged, to wrench from our hands the glorious banner that flaunted over our heads.

Overpowered, but with our banner and our honor unsullied, we were swept from the field. General Meade was borne off wounded, the heroic Simmons, who commanded our brigade, and Biddle, the Adjutant-general of the division, were mortally wounded, and a host of brave officers and men of the brigade laid around them. As we retreated across the plain before us and up through the woods, the fire of hell was let loose upon us, the shells and canister tearing up the ground in deep furrows, or rushing, shrieking and hissing through the air, rending the very vault of heaven.

On the plateau in the rear of the woods, the "Bucktails," Second, Fifth and Tenth regiments were rallied by their respective commanders, and formed in line to the right of Sumner, and with the artillery that was playing over their heads succeeded in checking the further progress of the foe, and advancing, drove them back and recovered the ground lost. Meanwhile a portion of the Twelfth regiment, with detachments of the Fifth, Eighth and Tenth, who were carrying prisoners to the rear, retreated to the left on a by-road between Sumner and Hooker, followed closely by the enemy, who suddenly and unexpectedly coming upon these fresh troops, for neither had hitherto been engaged, soon recoiled, and were driven over upon our centre.

While this was going on on the left, the centre and right of the Reserve were also hotly engaged, and so graphically is the operations of these portions of the line described by General McCall, in his official report of the battle, that we copy it verbatim.

"It must not be imagined that the enemy was inactive along the centre and right of my line during all this time. Cooper's and Kern's batteries, in front of the centre, were boldly charged upon, each time a regiment dashing up to within forty or fifty yards. They were then hurled back by a storm of canister and the deliberate fire of the First regiment, Colonel Roberts, whom I had placed immediately in the rear of Kern's, and the Ninth regiment, Colonel Jackson, in the rear of Cooper's. The contest was severe, and put the steadiness of these regiments to the test; both suffered heavy loss, but particularly the First regiment, whose gallant Lieutenant-colonel (McIntire) was severely wounded.

"Some time after this, the most determined charge of the day was made upon Randall's battery, by a full brigade, advancing in wedge-shape, without order, but with a wild recklessness that I never saw equalled. Somewhat similar charges had, as I have stated, been previously made on Cooper's and on Kern's batteries by single regiments without success, the Confederates having been driven back with heavy loss. A like result appears to have been anticipated by Randall's company; and the Fourth regiment (as was subsequently reported to me) was requested not to advance between the guns as I had ordered, as it interfered with the cannoniers, but to let the battery deal with them. Its gallant commander did not doubt, I am satisfied, his ability to repel the attack, and his guns fairly opened lanes in the advancing host. These gaps were, however, immediately closed, and the enemy came on, with arms trailed, at a run, to the very muzzles of his guns, where they pistoled or bayoneted the cannoniers. Two guns were limbered, and were in the act of wheeling to the rear when the horses were shot, the guns were both overturned, and presented one confused heap of men, horses and carriages. Over all these the men of the Eleventh Alabama regiment dashed in, a perfect torrent of men, and I am sorry to say, the greater part of the Fourth regiment gave way. The left company (Captain Conrad) of that regimet, however, stood its ground, and with some fifty or eighty men of other companies met the Alabamians.

"I had ridden into the regiment and endeavored to check them; but, as is seen, with only partial success. It was here, however, my fortune to witness between those of my men who stood their ground and the Rebels who advanced, one of the fiercest bayonet fights that perhaps ever occurred on this continent. Bayonets were crossed and locked in the struggle; bayonet wounds were freely given and received. I saw skulls crushed by the heavy blow of the butt of the musket, and, in short, the desperate thrusts and parries of a life and death encounter, proving indeed that Greek had met Greek when the Alabama boys fell upon the sons of Pennsylvania.

"My last reserve regiment I had previously sent to support Cooper, and I had not now a man to bring forward. My men were bodily borne off the ground by superior numbers. A thick wood was immediately in the rear, and the Confederates did not follow my men into the thicket. It was at this moment, on witnessing the scene I have described that I bitterly felt that my division ought to have been reinforced.

"My force had been reduced, by the battles of the 26th and 27th, to less than six thousand, and on this occasion I had to contend with the divisions of Longstreet and A. P. Hill, estimated among the strongest and best of the Confederate army, and numbering that day from eighteen to twenty thousand.

"The centre was at this time still engaged and I could not withdraw any troops from it.

"The Alabama troops did not attempt to enfilade my line, and leaving the guns on the ground, (the horses having, during the fight, been either killed or dispersed.) they retired to the woods on my right.

"It was now near sunset and the heat of battle had greatly subsided. I now rode to the rear to rally and collect the stragglers. At a short distance I came upon two regiments of Kearney's division. I requested them to move forward, but was informed their orders were to await the arrival of General Kearney. I moved on and set some officers at work to form the stragglers of my own regiments into line. On my return I found General Kearney. He put his regiments in motion and moved to the front and on the right of my line.

"As he rode away he said to me, 'If you can bring forward another line in a few minutes we can stop them.' By this time the sun had set, and the desultory firing was confined to the extreme right.

"In a short time Lieutenant-colonel Thompson, Third regiment, came up and reported to me that he had collected about five hundred men, with whom he was then advancing. I rode on with him at the head of the column in a direction to bring this force up on Kearney's left.

"On arriving near the ground where Randall's battery stood, I halted Thompson's command, wishing to ascertain whether any of my men were still in front of me. I had left Captain Conrad's company about one hundred yards in advance, but it was now so dark I could scarcely distinguish a man at ten paces. The battle, in fact, was now over; the firing on the left and centre had ceased, and there was only a desultory firing between Kearney's men and the enemy, some distance to the right. I rode forward to look for Conrad, and on the ground where I left him I rode into the enemy's picket, the Forty-seventh Virginia, Colonel Mayo, resting under some trees, and before I knew in whose presence I was, I was taken prisoner. Unfortunately for myself I had no staff officer with me, or I should have sent him forward to examine the ground, instead of going myself; but my Adjutant-general, the valiant Captain Henry J. Biddle, had been mortally wounded; Lieutenant Scheetz had his horse killed, and was injured by the fall; my Chief of Ordnance, the gallant Beatty, had been severely wounded at my side, and only left me when I had insisted on his doing so; my excellent Orderly, Sergeant Simeon Dunn,

Fourth Pennsylvania Cavalry, was also fatally wounded at my side, and out of my escort of a captain and twenty men of the Fourth Cavalry, but one corporal (the brave King) and one private remained with me; these two men were made prisoners with myself. About the time I was taken prisoner the desultory firing on my right died away."

The Reserves remained on the field during the night, and the rear guard withdrew from it about three o'clock the next morning, rejoining McClellan at Malvern Hill, after every gun and wagon of the Army of the Potomac had passed safely to the river.*

The loss of the division in killed, wounded and prisoners, in the three battles of the 26th, 27th and 30th of June, was three thousand one hundred and eighty, out of about seven thousand who went into the battle of Mechanicsville. The trophies of the day were three stands of colors captured and nearly three hundred prisoners.

The command of the division now devolved upon General Seymour, and of our brigade upon Colonel Hays, of the Eighth Reserve.

In regard to this battle, justice and truth requires that notice be taken of the report of General Hooker, of the part taken by his division in it, as published in "*Wilkes' Spirit of the Times*," of November 1st, 1862. In this report that officer states, "the whole of McCall's division was completely routed," &c. This sweeping assertion has always been regarded by every officer and man of the division as exhibiting a misapprehension of facts that was perfectly incomprehensible, and evidence has since been produced to show that it was not in accordance with facts.

Besides the official report of General McCall, which is a sufficient refutation of the charge, we have his testimony before "the Joint Committee of the Conduct on the War," in which he states:

---

* See Appendix A.

"I have no desire to treat lightly the reverses on both flanks oi my division in this hard-fought field; they were the almost inevitable results of greatly superior numbers, impelled on those points with great impetuosity; but the Pennsylvania Reserves as a division, although terribly shattered, were never "routed"; they maintained their ground with these exceptions, for three hours against thrice their numbers, in, I believe, the hardest fought and bloodiest battle in which they ever have been engaged, and in this opinion I am sustained by most of those officers, if not all, with whom I have conversed on the subject.

Had my division been routed, the march of the Federal army would certainly have been seriously interrupted by Lee forcing his masses into the interval. (See General Porter's statement herewith.) When I was surrounded and taken prisoner, I was conducted at once to Lee's headquarters. Here Longstreet told me they had seventy thousand men bearing on that point, all of whom would arrive before midnight; and had he succeeded in forcing McClellan's column of march, they would have been thrust in between the right and left wings of the Federal army. Now, under this very probable contingency had I not held my position (see General Porter's report herewith) the state of affairs in the left wing of McClellan's army would have been critical indeed; but Lee was checked (as Longstreet admitted) by my division (see Surgeon Marsh's report herewith), and the divisions in the rear, together with the Pennsylvania Reserves and others, moved on during the night, and joined McClellan at Malvern Hill before daylight. What share my division had in effecting this happy result let the country judge."

General Porter writing to General McCall from Washington, October 20th, 1862, says: "Had not McCall held his place on New Market road, June 20th, that line of march of the (Federal) army would have been cut by the enemy."

General Meade, to the same, from camp, near Warrenton, Virginia, under date of November 7th, 1862, writes: * * * "It was only the stubborn resistance offered by our division (the Pennsylvania Reserves), prolonging the contest till after dark, and checking till that time the advance of the enemy, that enabled the concentration, during the night, of the whole army on James river, *which saved it.*"

Colonel Roy Stone, one hundred and forty-ninth regiment, Pennsylvania volunteers, who commanded the "Bucktails," at New Market cross-roads, writes:

"Meantime the enemy (recoiling from Sumner and Hooker) turned to the left and was repulsed by your centre. About sunset I was ordered to the right, and went directly to the ground occupied by me when the action commenced, and I can bear witness that the ground held by the centre of your division when the battle opened, was held by your troops in the face of a large force of the enemy long after dark; and so far as my observation extended, the only regiments that broke in the early part of the fight were those that had become disordered by their own charge into the enemy's line."

Colonel Hays, Eighth Reserves, writes: * * * "I ordered the line to advance and take a position in a field immediately in front of where General Seymour had been in the commencement of the action. We lay till four o'clock, the next morning, and so near the enemy that we could hear the voices of officers giving orders."

Lieutenant-colonel Warner, commanding Tenth Reserves, writes: * * * "The enemy being checked in these woods, the regiment again formed in line, with others of the Reserves who were rallied at this point, and moved forward to within a hundred yards of the ground it held at the beginning of the battle. Here it remained in line of battle, till 11 o'clock at night, when it was ordered to move to Malvern Hill."

Surgeon N. F. Marsh, Fourth Pennsylvania cavalry, writes:

"WASHINGTON, *November 25th,* 1862.—General:—After the battle of the 30th of June, I remained at 'Willis' Church, with a large number of our wounded. The next morning I was directed by General Jackson (Stonewall) to report to General Lee. I found General Lee in company with General Longstreet, Magruder and Hill, on the New Market road. I addressed General Lee and informed him that I was a Federal surgeon, and had remained to care for our wounded, and wished protection and supplies for our men. He promised supplies, and directed General Longstreet to write the necessary permit. At the time I approached they were discussing the battle of the previous day, being then on the ground. General Longstreet asked me if I was present. I replied I was. He asked what troops were engaged. I replied I only knew the division I was connected with—McCall's—which fought just where we then were. General Longstreet said, 'Well, McCall is safe in Richmond; but if his division had not offered the stubborn resistance it did on this road, we would have captured your whole army. Never mind, we'll do it yet.'

"On Thursday, 3d July, General Roger A. Pryor came into the Church (hospital,) and we had a long conversation. He repeated in substance what General Longstreet said, and spoke in the highest terms of the 'pluck dis played by McCall's Pennsylvania troops.'

"The interest I felt in the Reserve Corps made me careful to remember these acknowledgments of the rebel generals."

Surgeon James R. Riley, of the One hundred and twenty-seventh Penna. Vols. writes:

"Washington, January 16, 1864.—General:—On the 18th of December, 1862, I was engaged dressing the stump, having previously amputated the leg of Captain —— (name not recollected,) of the Twelfth Mississippi regiment, who had been wounded at the battle of Fredericksburg, when he asked me what corps I belonged to, I replied the Pennsylvania Reserves. He said he had been in seventeen battles, and in all those on the Peninsula; that if the Pennsylvania Reserves had not fought so well at Mechanicsville, where they had their best troops, and again at New Market cross-roads, the Confederates would have captured McClellan's army."

It is not necessary to dwell longer upon this subject, as the above adduced testimony sets at rest the matter beyond all controversy.

While the battle of Charles City cross-roads was progressing, the enemy were attempting to force a passage of White Oak swamp which was held by General Franklin. Between twelve and one o'clock they opened a fierce cannonade upon the divisions of Smith and Richardson, and Naglee's brigades at this bridge. This artillery fire was continued by the enemy through the day, and he crossed some infantry below our position. Richardson's division suffered severely. Captain Ayres directed the artillery with great effect. Captain Hazzard's battery, after losing many cannoniers, and the Captain being mortally wounded, was compelled to retire. It was replaced by Pettit's battery, which partially silenced the enemy's guns.

General Franklin held his position until after dark, repeatedly driving back the enemy in their attempts to cross the White Oak swamp.

The rear of the supply trains and the reserve artillery of the army reached Malvern Hill about four o'clock that afternoon. About this time the enemy began to appear in General Porter's front, which was posted on the left, holding the river road to Richmond, and at five o'clock advanced in large force against his left flank, posting artillery under cover of a skirt of timber, with a view to engage our force on Malvern Hill, while with his infantry and some artillery he attacked Colonel Warren's brigade. A concentrated fire of about thirty guns was brought to bear on the enemy, which, with the infantry fire of Colonel Warren's command, compelled him to retreat, leaving two guns in the hands of Colonel Warren. The gunboats rendered most efficient aid during the attack.

CHAPTER XV.

Battle of Malvern Hill. March to Harrison's Landing. Cruelty to our Wounded. Hunting Greybacks. White Gloves and Ragged Clothes. Visit of President Lincoln.

Battle of Malvern Hill, July 1st.—At Malvern Hill was collected the whole Army of the Potomac with all its artillery, to give battle once more to the vigilant foe, who, though defeated in every battle of the seven days' fight except one, (Gaines' Mills,) were victorious in the campaign. Flushed with the knowledge of our retreating, the sight of our dead, the capture of many of our wounded, and the spoils of the field, they in spite of their terrible losses, almost looked upon it as a triumphant march, and believing they had driven us to the water's edge, they considered our capture or annihilation as certain, and so confident were they of this, that Jefferson Davis, accompanied by the officials of his Government, visited the army to receive the sword of McClellan.

Malvern Hill is an elevated plateau, about a mile and a half by three-fourths of a mile in area, mostly clear of timber, and with several converging roads crossing it. In front were numerous ravines, and the ground sloped gradually towards the north and east to a heavy woods, giving clear range for artillery in those directions. Towards the northwest the plateau falls off more abruptly into a ravine, which extends to James river. Upon this hill the left and centre of our line rested, while the right curved backwards through a wooded country towards a point below Haxall's on the James river.

The left of the line was held by the Fifth Corps, General Porter, consisting of the divisions of Sykes and Morell, of Warren's, Buchanan's and Chapman's brigades, and Griffin's, Martindale's and Butterfield's brigades. The artillery of the two divisions was advantageously posted, and the artillery of the reserve so disposed on the high ground that a concentrated fire of some sixty guns could be brought to bear on any point in its front or left. Colonel Tyler had also succeeded in getting ten of his siege guns in position on the highest point of the hill. Couch's division was placed on the right of Porter; next came Kearney and Hooker; next Sedgwick and Richardson; next Smith and Slocum; then the remainder of Keyes' corps, extended by a backward curve nearly to the river. The Pennsylvania Reserves were held in reserve, and stationed behind Porter's and Couch's position. One brigade of Porter's was thrown to the left on the low ground to protect that flank from any movement direct from the Richmond road. The line was very strong along the whole front of the open plateau, but from thence to the extreme right, the troops were more deployed. This formation was imperative, as from the position of the enemy his most obvious line of attack would come from the direction of Richmond and White Oak swamp, and would almost necessarily strike upon the left wing. Commodore Rogers, commanding the flotilla on James river, placed his gunboats so as to protect this flank, and to command the approaches from Richmond. The right wing was rendered as secure as possible by slashing the timber and by barricading the roads. There was posted upon different parts of the field, and in some places tier above tier, about two hundred and fifty pieces of artillery.

About ten o'clock A. M., the enemy emerged from the woods on the opposite side of the plain and commenced feeling along the whole left wing, with his artillery and skirmishers, which was promptly responded to by our artillery, and in about one hour the firing on both sides nearly ceased. An ominous stillness, indicating the manœuvring and placing in position of troops, now followed, preparatory to the terrific struggle that was soon to take place. About two o'clock a column of the enemy was observed moving towards our right, within the skirt of woods in front beyond the range of our artillery. Although the column was long, occupying more than two hours in passing, it disappeared, and was not again heard of. It probably returned by the rear, and participated in the attack afterwards made on the left.

During this long silence, our troops lay quietly upon the field, eating their scanty rations, and enjoying the rest they had not known for so long. Thus the day wore on with but little animation until about three o'clock, when a heavy fire of artillery was opened on Kearney's left and Couch's division, near the centre of the line, followed by a brisk attack of infantry on Couch's front. This was immediately responded to by our artillery, but Couch's infantry remained lying on the ground until the enemy had advanced within musketry range, when they sprang to their feet and poured in a deadly volley that broke and drove them back with considerable slaughter. They were followed for nearly half a mile, where our line halted and occupied a much stronger position, resting upon a thick clump of trees.

This affair occupied about one hour, when the fire ceased over the whole field, and the enemy evinced neither a disposition to attack or withdraw. About six o'clock, the enemy suddenly opened upon Couch and Porter with the whole strength of his artillery, and at once began pushing forward his columns of attack to carry the hill. Now opened one of the most desperate and sanguinary battles ever fought upon this continent. Brigade after brigade, formed under cover of the woods, started at a run to cross the open space and charge our batteries, but the heavy fire of our guns, with the cool and steady volleys of the infantry, in every case sent them reeling back to shelter, and covered the ground with their dead and wounded. But fresh lines were again hurled forward with a desperation and recklessness seldom witnessed before. No troops ever acted with more desperate courage than the enemy did upon that occasion, but like the storm-lashed ocean, madly dashing its billows against a rock-bound shore, they were hurled back broken and confused, but to unite and return again to the assault. From batteries upon batteries were vomited forth sheets of flame and smoke, whose storms of grape and canister mowed down the columns of advancing valor, leaving vast gaps, that were filled up by the mad and infuriated masses. To add to the terror of the slaughter, the gun-boats in the river opened with their 11-inch guns throwing their elongated shells into the woods which were densely packed with the enemy, tearing into splinters the largest trees, and destroying whole companies at once.

About seven o'clock, as fresh troops were being pushed in by the enemy, Meagher and Sickles were sent in with their brigades to relieve such regiments as had expended their ammunition, and batteries from the reserve were pushed forward to replace those whose boxes were empty. Until dark the enemy persisted in his efforts to take the positions so tenaciously defended; but despite his vastly superior numbers, his repeated and desperate attacks were repulsed with fearful loss. The sun went down, but the carnage did not cease, for though the musketry closed, the fiery messengers of death coursed their swift-winged path through the skies, dealing destruction among the enemy, who but feebly replied. It was after nine o'clock before all firing ceased. Never was a repulse more signal, the confused masses of the enemy's infantry, artillery, and cavalry, all struggling together, choking the roads and crossing the fields in every direction. So complete was the confusion, that one or two days elapsed before the men of the different regiments and commands could be collected together and put in shape, and it has been ascertained upon competent authority, that with twenty thousand fresh troops McClellan could have marched into Richmond.

As the army in its movement from the Chickahominy to Harrison's Landing was continually occupied in marching by night and fighting by day, its commanders found no time or opportunity for collecting data, which could enable them to give exact returns of casualties in each engagement. The aggregate of our entire losses, from the 26th of June to the 1st of July, inclusive, was ascertained, after arrival at Harrison's Landing, to be as follows:

Return of the killed, wounded, and missing in the Army of the Potomac, from the 26th day of June to the 1st of July, 1862, inclusive.

	Killed.	Wounded.	Missing.	Aggregate.
First, McCall's division	253	1240	1581	3,074*
Second, Sumner's	187	1076	848	2,111
Third, Heintzelman's	189	1051	833	2,073
Fourth, Keyes'	69	507	201	777
Fifth, Porter's	620	2460	1198	4,278
Sixth, Franklin's	245	1313	1179	2,737
Engineers	....	2	21	23
Cavalry	19	60	97	176
Total	1582	7709	5958	15,249

* General McCall in his official report states the loss of the Reserves to be 3,180

It will be observed that the division of Pennsylvania Reserves lost more than any corps, excepting the Fifth, and more than Sumner's and Keyes' or Heintzelman's and Keyes' combined.

Although the result of the battle of Malvern Hill was a complete victory, it was, nevertheless, necessary to fall back to a position below City Point, as the channel there was so near the southern shore that it would not be possible to bring up the transports, should the enemy occupy it. Besides, the line of defence was too extended to be maintained by our weakened forces, and the supplies of food, forage and ammunition, being exhausted it was imperatively necessary to reach the transports immediately.

The greater portion of the transportation of the army having been started for Harrison's Landing during the night of the 30th of June and the 1st of July, the order for the movement of the troops was at once issued upon the final repulse of the enemy at Malvern Hill. About eleven o'clock that night the sleepy boys were woke up and put in motion, and passing by Haxall's house we slowly wound our way down the hill to the river road, along which we marched, passing over Turkey bridge. The night was extremely dark, but the road, which for a long distance was exceedingly bad, was lit up by thousands of candles placed in the trees, and bright fires burning upon the wayside which were continually replenished by the guard stationed at them. At daybreak we entered a fine field of standing wheat, where we laid down and rested for an hour and then moved on. It soon commenced raining, turning the deep dust into heavy mud, and in an incredible short time the artillery, wagons, cavalry and infantry rendered the road almost impassable. But onward the column pressed until it crossed Herring run and debouched into the open plain of Harrison Landing.

The Reserves were here put into a heavy pine woods to the right of the road, and by building bough arbours somewhat sheltered themselves. During the day and night, the rain descended in torrents, rendering the kindling of fires almost impossible, but, as the boys had but little to cook, it did not matter much. The withdrawal which was conducted by General Keyes was most skilfully effected, and with no other loss than the few wagons that broke down upon the road. The rear guard, consisting of the Third Pennsylvania cavalry, a brigade of infantry and one battery, under the command of Colonel Averill, did not leave the field until ten o'clock on the 2nd of July, and the last of the wagons reached Harrison's Landing on the 3rd.

On the morning of the 3rd a small force of the enemy having followed up the rear guard and taken an advantageous position, opened with shell, to which our guns responded. The Reserves were drawn up about nine o'clock in an open field where they stood in the mud up to their knees with shells bursting and round shot whistling over their heads until three in the afternoon, when they were marched to a neighboring field, and bivouacked on the banks of Herring creek.

While this change of base from the Pamunky to the James river was progressing, the White House was successfully evacuated with comparatively a trifling loss of stores, etc. No less than seven hundred vessels were in the river at the time, all of which were successfully removed. The last of our wagons left under guard of General Stoneman's cavalry, not a man or contraband being left behind, and the telegraphic communication with General McClellan was not severed till one o'clock, P. M., on the 28th, and at seven o'clock the enemy made their appearance in the neighborhood of the White House, where they were welcomed with shell and grape from three gunboats in the river.

Thus ended the "Seven Day's Battles," which will ever be viewed by military men, as one of the greatest feats of the war. Never did such a change of base, involving a retrograde movement, and under incessant attacks from a most determined and vastly more numerous foe, partake so little of disorder. The immense artillery and wagon train, the latter if stretched out in one line, extending nearly forty miles, the Commissary and Quartermaster's stores, the ammunition, a drove of twenty-five hundred cattle; in fact, the army and its entire material, horse, foot and dragoon, bag and baggage, was transferred successfully with an incredibly small loss of material. The movement was conducted with perfect order.

There was no trepidation or haste, no smashing up of wagons by careless or fast driving, yet there was no moment for repose, no opportunity scarcely to properly care for the wounded; and the dead, excepting at Mechanicsville, were left unburied. The enemy closely watched every movement, and with an army more than double that of our own, had the ability to constantly launch fresh troops upon our rear, an advantage which they were quick to discover, and remorseless in improving. Their perfect knowledge of the roads, paths and bridges, the topography of the country which took us time to learn, placed an immense advantage in their hands, yet they were, excepting in one instance, unable by their utmost efforts to drive us from any field.

Our army regarded the movement as the carrying out of a necessary plan, and the only dissatisfaction expressed being at the leaving behind of so many of the wounded. We have no hesitation in asserting, and without the least fear of contradiction, that upon the arrival of the army at Harrison's Landing, the *morale* of it was almost as good as ever, and that the men had such unbounded confidence in McClellan that they would fearlessly have followed him at any time if he had assumed the aggressive.

While an advancing army loses nothing in men and material by capture, it is necessarily the reverse with a retreating one, besides, though it may be successful in every battle, it loses the advantages of following up its victories, which are transferred to the enemy. Though this naturally has the tendency of weakening the *morale* of an army, such did not appear to be the case with ours, for the men went into every one of the many and protracted battles in most excellent spirits, and with full confidence of victory.

Throughout the whole struggle the Union and Confederate troops displayed upon every field the most desperate bravery and indomitable courage, and learned by the noble qualities they discovered, to respect each other. Never upon the field did we see an act of cruelty done, and the testimony of our wounded, and the surgeons who remained with them, was to the universally kind treatment they received from the privates of the enemy. It is to be regretted that the same cannot be said of their officers, and all unite in attesting to the bitter animosity and heartlessness shown by the non-combatants and civilians.

After the battle of Glendale, Doctor E. Donnelly, the surgeon of our regiment, among others, volunteered to remain behind and take charge of our wounded, and from him we subsequently learned many interesting facts in regard to their treatment and condition. He was placed in charge of a hospital improvised upon the battle-field near Nelson's house, where were collected our wounded in the outbuildings and on the surrounding lawn. The only assistance he had was from young Hartman, Company K, and some Confederate privates, who volunteered to help. These men carried in the wounded, or moved them into the shade, brought them water, and divided their scanty rations among them. They spoke and acted towards them with the greatest kindness, but the sufferings of the poor boys were great. With no medicine or stimulants, with a scanty supply of rags and water, and the help of Hartman and these men, the doctor amputated the limbs and dressed the wounds of hundreds, who were sinking from the loss of blood, and the want of food. But no medicine, liquor, food or assistance could be obtained from the officials, one of whom deliberately stole the doctor's case of instruments while he was performing an operation.

On the day of the battle of Malvern Hill a large number of citizens from Richmond visited the battle-field of New Market cross-roads, anticipating the pleasure of seeing our army surrender. None of them, however, showed the least disposition to assist our wounded, though to satisfy their curiosity they walked among them, and were very inquisitive and rude in their inquiries, and some of them were shameless enough even to steal their canteens and cups—articles that then were worth more than gold to the helpless fellows, who laid for days afterwards upon the field, burning with fever and without a mouthful of water to quench their thirst. One man, and we are sorry to say that he was a minister of the Gospel, so far forgot the precepts of his Master, the Prince of Mercy, and the better feelings of his heart—if he ever had any—in his bitter hatred of Union soldiers, as to commence upbraiding as "mercenaries" and "hirelings," the poor wounded sufferers, some of whom had lost their limbs, and others, from whose wounds maggots were crawling. When suffering all the anguish that mortals are heir to, when faint with the loss of blood and nervous excitement, this paroled prisoner of h—l, clothed in the sacred garb of religion, taunted and denounced these poor creatures over whom the guardian angels of heaven were weeping. It is, though with unfeigned pleasure, that we contrast with this the conduct of Doctor Hill Carter, a most worthy and estimable gentleman, whose house was also used as a hospital for our wounded. Doctor Carter, though a secessionist, not only put all he had at the disposal of our surgeons, but he and his family assisted, to the utmost of their ability, to alleviate the sufferings of the wounded, and their kindness will ever be remembered with gratitude by those whose sufferings they alleviated. All the wounded were subsequently removed to Richmond, though some of them not until a week afterwards, they lying upon the field during that time exposed to the burning rays of the sun of the day, and the cold dews of the night. Some of these, whose wounds were undressed, died on the road, and one relates the fiendish expression of an ambulance driver, "that corduroy roads were bully to haul wounded Yankees over."

Upon their arrival they were stowed away in Libby prison, a loathesome hole, foul with the stench of two water closets and the putrefaction of the bodies in the dead house underneath, which were exposed to their sight through a large open grating in the floor of their apartment. A little medicine, and that stolen from our surgeons, was doled out to them. A pittance of tainted beef and hard crackers was given each day, without a change of clothing, or blankets to cover themselves with at night, or water to wash with in the morning, they were huddled together by hundreds, and this was the treatment they received from the Government. But the treatment they received from the soldiers was universally kind. When we say soldiers, we do not mean the guards around the prison, who had never been upon the field, but the men who had fought them, and had learned to respect a brave foe. With these they were all right. On the field, when we drove them from positions formerly held by us, we found in many cases our wounded had been supplied with water and sometimes placed behind logs or trees in sheltered positions, and at Glendale, when several of the enemy were taken prisoners and were being sent to the rear, although they were under a heavy fire, they picked up and carried off a wounded Union soldier. Many other acts of kindness were frequently displayed upon the field, that showed there was not felt the bitter animosity and vindictiveness shown by civilians and politicians.

At Malvern Hill, the morning after the battle, both parties had pickets stationed upon the field, and the enemy were permitted to remove their wounded, but they fired upon our men when they approached for the same purpose. This may have seemed cruel, but it was a military precaution on their part, that doubtless was deemed justifiable, as it was of vital importance to them to conceal from us the extent of their disaster, the demoralization and position of their troops.

The position now occupied by our army was a line of heights, some three miles long and about two miles from the James, and the plain extended from them to the river. As these heights commanded the whole position, it would have been necessary to have maintained them to the last. Both flanks were well supported by the gun boats. The position though remarkably strong, and one that could only be carried by overwhelming numbers, was by no means impregnable, especially as a morass extended between the heights and the river, from the centre to our right. In the broad area or plain of Harrison's Landing, Evelington Heights, or West Over, were collected an immense amount of army stores and ammunition, and vast numbers of siege guns, mortars, etc.; removed from the former line occupied by the army Here also was encamped a considerable portion of the army, while the balance occupied the heights. The Landing presented a most interesting scene, the river bank, for a long distance, being lined with canal boats and barges from three to ten and twelve deep, most of which, having been emptied of their vast amount of stores, served as wharves for the large transports to unload at. Schooners, brigs, and ships innumerable, were here at anchor, through which steamers of all sizes and descriptions were continually winding their way, presenting a scene of animation and life seldom witnessed.

Colonel Hays, Eighth Reserves, being the senior officer of the brigade, assumed command of it, upon the death of Colonel Simmons, of the Fifth, but on account of indisposition he turned it over to Colonel McNeill, of the "Bucktails." On the 4th, the Eighth regiment was transferred to the Second Brigade, and the Sixth regiment transferred to ours, which placed Colonel Sinclair in command of it.

The anniversary of our national birthday was duly celebrated, by the firing of salutes and the display of flags, among the most conspicuous of which were those captured from the enemy by the different regiments. On dress-parade the following address was read at the head of each regiment, which was received with the most enthusiastic cheering from the men:

"HEAD-QUARTERS, ARMY OF THE POTOMAC,
CAMP NEAR HARRISON'S LANDING,
July 4th, 1862.

"SOLDIERS OF THE ARMY OF THE POTOMAC:—Your achievements of the last ten days have illustrated the valor and endurance of the American soldier. Attacked by superior forces, and without hope of reinforcements, you have succeeded in changing your base of operations by a flank movement, always regarded as the most hazardous of military expedients. You have saved all your material, all your trains, and all your guns, except a few lost in battle, taking in return guns and colors from the enemy. Upon your march, you have been assailed day after day with desperate fury, by men of the same race and nation, skilfully massed and led. Under every disadvantage of number, and necessarily of position also, you have in every conflict beaten back your foes with enormous slaughter. Your conduct ranks you among the celebrated armies of history. No one will now question that each of you may always with pride say: 'I belong to the Army of the Potomac.' You have reached the new base, complete in organization and unimpaired in spirit. The enemy may at any moment attack you. We are prepared to meet them. I have personally established your lines. Let them come, and we will convert their repulse into a final defeat. Your Government is strengthening you with the resources of a great people. On this our Nation's birthday, we declare to our foes, who are rebels against the best interests of mankind, that this army shall enter the capital of the so-called Confederacy; that our national Constitution shall prevail, and that the Union, which can alone insure internal peace and external security to each State, 'must and shall be preserved,' cost what it may in time, treasure, and blood.

"GEORGE B. McCLELLAN."

As soon as circumstances permitted after our arrival, means were taken to reorganize, equip and put the army into fighting order again. The stragglers soon found their regiments. Upon inspecting the arms, it was found that in the various regiments were collected every calibre and pattern known in the service, the Harper's Ferry, Springfield, Sharpe's, Maynard's, Burnside, Enfeld, Tower, Belgium, Richmond, Palmetto, etc.; all mixed promiscuously together among the men, who having lost their own, appropriated their neighbors'. These when not of the calibre of the regiment, were turned in, assorted and re-issued, so that each regiment, brigade and division, if possible, would be armed alike. Accoutrements, ammunition and clothing were likewise distributed, as fast as received, and in an incredibly short time the whole army was in as good condition as ever it was to meet the foe, and their *morale* increased by the consciousness of what they had achieved. To General Seymour was accorded the honor of being the first to get his division into proper trim.

While these matters were occupying the serious attention of the general officers of the army, the great question that agitated the public mind, was the getting rid of the "greybacks," whom, there was every reason to suppose, had domiciled themselves upon the persons of the patriots and held them in a ticklish position. As we had destroyed all our clothing except what we stood in, and as soap was an article that could neither be procured "for love or money," and as clothing was issued by piece meal, it was a task easier undertaken than accomplished. But by dint of washing, scrubbing, scouring and constant vigilance, the feat was accomplished, and the boys came out in their new uniforms as clean and bright as new dollars. It is a matter of impossibility for an army to pass through what we did in the summer without being overrun with vermin, and among soldiers one is not blamed for having them on, but for keeping them. So universal were they at that time, that no one thought of being ashamed of them, and we have even heard the boys declare that they knew all the bugle calls, and had become so expert in drill as to go through the battalion movements quite accurately, and to have their regular guard mountings and dress parades. If any of our delicate readers should feel shocked at this exposure of our private affairs, we must remind them that part of our task is to show up soldier life in its true light.

A rather amusing incident occurred about this time, that was in strange contrast with the foregoing. Some months previous white gloves had been ordered for the men, out of the regimental fund, and when the boys were in the greatest need of underclothing, and even shoes and blouses, they arrived, and just in time to be distributed prior to the regiment going out on a general review of the division. The remarks of our friends of the other regiments in regard to the strange contrast in our clothing was quite amusing.

On the 8th, His Excellency Abraham Lincoln, arrived from Washington on a visit to the army, and in the afternoon he rode along the lines of the different divisions who were drawn up to receive him. He was most enthusiastically received by the troops, who honored and respected the chief who had sworn to preserve and perpetuate the nation, at any cost or sacrifice.

On the 10th, Captain William D. Reitzel's new company, raised in Lancaster county and Philadelphia, arrived in camp and was assigned letter "G." They were a fine set of young men and numbered sixty-eight rank and file. The Lieutenants were, First John L. Rhoads, and Second, Max Wimpfheimer. This made our ninth company, though one was detached from us. On the same day the promotion of Lieutenant-colonel William McCandless to a full colonelcy, to date from November 1st, 1861, was received. This was in acknowledgment of his gallantry during the late battles, more particularly at Mechanicsville, where he was honorably mentioned in the official report of General McCall.

On the morning of the 14th, we moved our camp

about two miles down the creek to Evlington Heights on the right of our line. Here we occupied a broad open plain near the creek where the men could enjoy most excellent bathing. As good water was scarce, every regiment dug a fine deep well, from which they obtained a bountiful supply of good water. Sibley tents were issued, and our rations brought up to the full standard, with cabbage, beets, onions and other vegetables in addition. Division guard mountings, company and battalion drills, and dress parades were ordered. Several reviews by Generals McClellan and Seymour took place. The sutlers also arrived, and letters and newspapers were received daily.

While here the United States truce steamer Louisiana came down the river with a load of paroled Union prisoners from Richmond, among whom were Major Woodward, Captains J. Orr Finnie, P. I. Smith, and Horace Neidé, and Lieutenant Hugh P. Kennedy, of our regiment, all wounded. Also a large number of our boys, most of whom were sent north to the hospitals. Doctor Donnelly, our efficient surgeon, who had remained with the wounded, also came and was welcomed. All bore testimony to the kindness of the privates and cruelty of the officials of the Confederate Government. Towards the latter part of the month orders were issued to hold ourselves in readiness to march at a moment's notice, with arms, accoutrements and blankets only. The balloons made daily reconnoissances. This was probably occasioned by Generals Hill and Longstreet crossing the Chickahominy at Long Bridge on a reconnoissance in force.

CHAPTER XVI.

MIDNIGHT SHELLING. A SPY. PROMOTIONS. RETURN OF GENERALS McCALL AND REYNOLDS. WITHDRAWAL FROM THE PENINSULA. VOYAGE ON THE JAMES AND POTOMAC. GENERAL POPE'S MOVEMENTS. HUNTING OUR DIVISION. RUNNING THE GAUNTLET.

A LITTLE after midnight, on the 1st of August, the enemy brought some light batteries to Coggin's Point and the Coles House, on the right bank of the James river, directly opposite Harrison's Landing, and opened a heavy fire upon our shipping and encampments. The shot and shell flew around our camp in the most lively manner, which occasioned a grand stampede among the "darks," who took to the swamps and hid themselves. The majority of the boys taking a philosophical view of the matter considered themselves about as safe in one place as another, and did not disturb themselves from their blankets, while others of a more excitable nature, after admiring the pyrotechnical display for a time, lit their candles and went to playing cards. In about thirty minutes our guns silenced their fire, and the next morning, three of their dead, a disabled caisson and flag were found. Our loss was ten killed and fifteen wounded. No harm of the slightest consequence was done to the shipping, although several of the vessels were struck. One of the dead had no wound or mark upon him whatever, which was probably occasioned by a ball rolling over his chest and pressing the breath out of him. The popular opinion that a cannon ball passing near one's mouth may take away the breath and produce death is erroneous.

The next morning, the Coles House, which had been a rendezvous for the enemy, was destroyed, and four hundred men of our brigade were sent over the river under command of Colonel McNeill, of the "Bucktails," to fell the timber, and a picket guard of four hundred of the First Michigan were thrown out to protect them. They returned at night with an abundance of fruit, vegetables and berries. These details were continued daily, entrenchments were thrown up by contrabands, and some heavy guns put in position, giving us a safe debouche and securing us from further midnight cannonading.

One day our detail brought in a man who attempted to run through our pickets. He was an intelligent young Virginian, who crossed the river with them in the morning, representing himself as being connected with the commissary department, and appearing perfectly at home th the men. When taken he was on horseback, and tried hard to escape. He showed considerable bitterness against the "Yankees," appeared indifferent as to what they might do with him, and although annoyed at his capture, an expression of concealed fun was, in unguarded moments, caught lurking in his bright eyes. He was turned over to the provost-marshal. The next day he crossed again with a squad of cavalry, from whom he managed to slip, and despite their efforts could not be recaptured. We afterwards learned that he was a spy in the employment of General McClellan.

On the 3d, Colonel Averill, with three hundred men of the Third Pennsylvania and Fifth regular cavalry, marched to Sycamore Church, some five miles from Coles House, where they found and attacked a cavalry force of the enemy five hundred and fifty strong, whom they routed, and burned their entire camp and commissary and quartermaster's stores.

On the 4th the following promotions were read out on dress parade: Major G. A. Woodward to be lieutenant-colonel, *vice* McCandless, promoted; Captain Horace Neidé, Company A, to be major, *vice* Woodward, promoted; First Lieutenant Daniel H. Connor, Company A, to be captain, *vice* Neidé, promoted; Second Lieutenant John J. Ross, Company A to be first lieuteuant, *vice* Connor .

promoted; First Lieutenant John M. Clark, Company F to be captain, *vice* John E. Barnacle, resigned. The same day Dr. A. G. Coleman, of Schuylkill county, Pennsylvania, reported for duty as assistant-surgeon; each regiment being now allowed two assistant-surgeons. About this time Captain P. McDonough and Lieutenant John Curley, Sergeants John Cullin, Company B; Andrew Casey, Company C; Edward Cherry, Company D; George H. Morrow, Company E; H. C. Hostetter, Company G; William McGlenn, Company H; Peter Gillis, Company K, and private William Aiken, Company A, were detailed to proceed to Philadelphia on recruiting service. About this time James Harbison, Company D, died, and was buried in the Fifth Corps' ground, in a pretty woods near the banks of Herring Landing. His death was hastened by the recent loss of almost all his relatives. While here we were paid off by Major Pomeroy up to the 1st of July.

Deserters having reported the enemy were moving south of James river, and that the force in Richmond was small, General Hooker with his division, and Pleasanton's cavalry was sent to feel in that direction, on the 2d, and having been joined by General Sedgwick's division, he succeeded in turning Malvern Hill on the morning of the 5th, and driving the enemy back toward Richmond. The enemy's force consisted of a very considerable body of infantry and artillery, and over one hundred prisoners were captured and a number killed and wounded, with a loss on our side of three killed and eleven wounded. Colonel Averill pushed a reconnoissance in the direction of Savage Station and near White Oak Bridge he encountered the Eighteenth Virginia cavalry, whom he drove, capturing twenty-eight men and horses, and killing and wounding several. Hooker encamped that night on Malvern Hill, and on the morning of the 7th returned to camp. While this movement was being made orders were issued to hold our division in readiness to move with two days' cooked rations. General McClellan at one time intended to have supported him with the whole army, but the receipt of advices from Washington induced him not to do so.

On the 10th all the regimental bands were mustered out of service, brigade bands only being provided for by the late act of Congress. The same day, orders were received to pack our knapsacks, and label each with the owner's name, and send them down to the landing to be shipped in charge of the quartermaster-sergeant. Orders were also received to have three days' cooked rations in haversacks and five in bulk. At dark we were got into line and marched to the upper landing and then to the lower one, and after waiting there until eleven o'clock, we returned to our camp.

On the 13th, Generals McCall and Reynolds arrived from Richmond, and the Reserves paraded to receive them. The reception was most enthusiastic, the boys cheering and throwing their hats in the air. General McCall having not yet recovered from the effect of his sickness and imprisonment, did not assume command but went north. This separation was final between the general and the division, every officer and man of which respected, honored and loved him. It was he who organized, disciplined, and brought to that high state of efficiency the division, which rendered them so efficient in the field and won for them a proud and glorious name.

General Reynolds succeeded to the command of the division. The same night the sergeants of the old First Brigade met and resolved to raise a subscription among the men to present to General Reynolds a magnificent sword, belt and sash. The same day General Meade arrived from Philadelphia and took command of his brigade, which was now the First, and General Seymour assumed the command of our brigade which was now the Second.

On the 30th of July Major-general Halleck, commanding United States Army, issued orders for the shipment of all the sick from Harrison's Landing to the north, which at that time amounted to about twelve thousand five hundred, which was immediately commenced.

It having been determined to withdraw the Army of the Potomac from the Peninsula to Aquia creek, orders for the same were issued on the 3d of August. The reasons that led to this determination were, that at that time General McClellan's army numbered but ninety thousand effective men, and the army of General Pope, charged with the covering of Washington, numbered but thirty-eight thousand. The former was twenty-five miles from Richmond and the latter about eighty or ninety miles from Washington, while between them were the enemy, numbering over two hundred thousand men. This would enable the enemy to fall with his superior numbers upon one or the other as he might elect, without either being able to reinforce the other in case of attack. It was in the enemy's power at any time to exchange Richmond for Washington, and while the loss of their capital would be but trifling to them, the loss of Washington to us would be conclusive, or nearly so, in its results upon the war. General McClellan most earnestly protested against the withdrawal of his army, he contending that the true defence of Washington was on the banks of the James river; that the heart of the rebellion laid directly in front of his army, and that a decided victory there would crush the military strength of the rebellion. He asked for reinforcements to the extent of thirty-five thousand men, and as the Government had no disposable troops to send him, he pointed to Burnside and Pope's forces from which they could be drawn. Without attempting to criticize the military opinions of either General McClellan or Halleck, we think that subsequent events showed the absolute necessity of withdrawing the army from the Peninsula.

It having been ascertained that "Stonewall" Jackson was moving north, General McClellan, in compliance with orders from Washington, embarked five batteries for Aquia creek, where General Burnside had landed with infantry only.

On the 13th, the enemy anticipating an advance on Richmond, burnt the wharves at City Point.

On the 14th,* General Heintzelman's corps marched for Yorktown *via* Jones' bridge, and General Porter's *via* Barrett's Ferry, near the mouth of the Chickahominy, where a pontoon-bridge, about two thousand feet long, had been laid. On the morning of the 16th, when the last man and last wagon had left, General McClellan bid farewell to the scenes of his glory and disappointment, and followed in the track of the grand Army of the Potomac down the Peninsula. On the morning of the 18th the rear guard crossed the river; and on the 20th the greater portion of the army was ready to embark at Yorktown, Fortress Monroe and Newport News. Thus terminated the ever memorable campaign of the Peninsula, in which ten severely contested and sanguinary battles had been fought, besides numerous smaller engagements, in all of which the troops exhibited the most determined enthusiasm and bravery. They submitted to exposure, sickness, and even death, without a murmur, and never was a Government more cheerfully or devotedly served than our own was by the Army of the Potomac.

But to return to the movements of our regiment. At dark on the 14th we formed and marched to the ordnance wharf and bivouacked for the night on the banks of the river, where we laid until sunset the next afternoon, when we embarked aboard a steamer and schooner and bidding farewell to the scenes of our glory and sadness, we steamed down the river. During the night the steamer run aground, and the next morning at high tide the little Schuylkill steamer "Reindeer," came along side and lightened her by taking the men on board until a tug could haul her off.

---

* General Lee was at Gordonsville at this time.

On the voyage down we passed many gunboats and transports, and at eight o'clock at night we came to anchor about ten miles above Newport News. Early in the night one of the staff horses got loose and running aft among the sleeping men created great excitement, during which Samuel McGarvey, of company E, fell overboard and was drowned. Hamilton, of the same company, who also got overboard, was rescued with considerable difficulty. The next day we weighed anchor, and got under way at eleven in the morning, passing the sunken frigates Congress and Cumberland, and running down to Hampton Roads, where we came to anchor.

While here Captain Reitzel, of company G, which had been detailed as wagon-guard, came aboard for the mail, and reported having a pleasant and quiet march down the Peninsula. Bread, cakes, watermelons, oranges, cocoanuts, etc., were brought aboard for sale. The boys also enjoyed good fishing and luxurious bathing. We were detained here by head winds until early on the morning of the 20th, when we got under way, passing through a forest of masts and entering the Chesapeake bay, when, heading northward, we continued on, entering the Potomac, and passing up to Aquia creek, where we came to anchor about four o'clock on the afternoon of the 21st, after a passage of six days, the distance being two hundred and fifteen miles. The vessels were hauled into the landing, and about eleven o'clock at night we embarked aboard the cars, and proceeded to near Falmouth, where we slept under a commissary shed on piles of oats and corn, protected from the rain which was then falling.

For an intelligent understanding of subsequent events it is necessary to take a summary review of General Pope's movements. On the 26th of June, the day of the battle of Mechanicsville, General Pope was assigned to the command of the Army of Virginia, consisting of Major-Generals McDowell's, Banks' and Fremont's army corps, numbering thirty-eight thousand men. The duties assigned to him was the covering of Washington, the safety of the valley of the Shenandoah, and the operating upon the enemy's lines in the direction of Gordonsville and Charlottesville to draw off, if possible, a portion of the enemy from Richmond. As early as the 16th of July, Jackson's advance force under Ewell reached Gordonsville, and on the 7th of August all the infantry and artillery forces of Pope's army, amounting to twenty-eight thousand and five hundred men, were assembled along the turnpike from Sperryville to Culpeper, excepting King's division, which was opposite Fredericksburg. The cavalry pickets extending on the right from the Blue Ridge on the Rapidan, down the same until they joined King's, at its junction with the Rappahannock.

On the 9th, General Banks was ordered to move forward to Cedar or Slaughter Mountains, and to take up a strong position occupied by Crawford's brigade, and hold the enemy in check. General Banks, however, left his strong position late in the day, and advanced at least a mile, throwing his whole corps into action against a superior force of the enemy strongly posted and sheltered by woods and ridges. This advance led him over open ground, which was everywhere swept by the fire of the enemy concealed in the woods and ravines beyond. The battle lasted about an hour and a half, during which time our forces were driven back to their former position with heavy loss. At this point Rickett's division came up and joined in the engagement, and General Pope, at he same time arriving, drew in General Bank's too much extended line, and the enemy were driven back. An artillery fight was kept up until midnight. Both sides suffered severely during the action, and the estimate loss of our army was one thousand eight hundred in killed, wounded and prisoners.

General Pope, in his official report, states: "The consolidated report of General Bank's corps, received some days previously (to the battle), exhibited an effective force of something over fourteen thousand men. It appeared subsequently, however, that General Bank's force at that time did not exceed eight thousand men!" Under such a display of military genius, as shown upon this occasion, we would prefer not to serve under General Banks.

Before daylight the next morning Jackson withdrew his forces two miles and during the night of the 11th, he fell back across the Rapidan, in the direction of Gordonsville leaving many of his dead and wounded on the field. General Pope being subsequently reinforced by General King's and Reno's division advanced again to the Rapidan. Having captured a letter from General Lee to General Stuart, dated Gordonsville, August 15th, General Pope was apprised of the position of the enemy and their intention to overwhelm him, before the arrival of reinforcements from the Army of the Potomac. He therefore on the 18th, retired behind the Rappahannock and occupied that line from three miles above Rappahannock station to Kelly's ford. On the 20th, the enemy drove in his pickets in front of Rappahannock station and Kelly's ford and during the next three days made strong efforts to cross at various points, but was repulsed.

On the 22nd, the Pennsylvania Reserves under General Reynolds, with the exception of the second regiment, joined the Army of Virginia, at Kelly's ford, and was attached to the Third corps, General McDowell, they being among the very last to leave Harrison's Landing and the first to join General Pope.

Early on the morning of the 22d, our regiment moved into a field near by and had three days' rations served out, and, although, we had had no meat for six days, we were forced to leave this behind as we had no kettles to boil it in, and salt beef roasted creates too great thirst for men to march with during hot weather. That day, at noon, we commenced our march through Falmouth, and moved up the river on the Bealton road. The weather was oppressively hot, and the men suffered much. During the march, for the first time this season, we met with fruit, and although it was green and the men were suffering much from the diarrhœa, they could not restrain their appetites from enjoying the delicacies, and, contrary to all expectations, it proved a most effectual remedy for the disease; their systems being disposed to the scurvy, the acids of the apples acting as an antidote. At dark we bivouacked in a wood by a roadside.

Early the next morning we marched to the tune of the booming gun that came rolling down the river, passing by Hartwood and halting at the Grove churches during the heat of the day. About a mile beyond there we turned to the left passing Crittenden's mills where Morell's division was encamped. Pushing on towards Rappahannock station, which laid eight miles beyond, and where we knew the Reserves were engaged with the enemy, we marched four miles, when about dark we met two cavalrymen, who informed us our division had abandoned the station, at two o'clock that afternoon, and fallen back towards Warrenton. Under these circumstances, Colonel McCandless fell back to the mills, where we reported to, and bivouacked with, General Morell. A heavy rain had fallen through the afternoon and continued through the night. That day we marched seventeen miles, though we made but nine.

The next morning some of the boys discovering a number of sheep running around loose in the woods, shot several of them and brought them into camp, which General Morell hearing of, was shocked beyond measure at the impropriety of the act, and ordered them to be buried near his tent, that he could see it done with his own eyes. But while the culprits were digging the grave, another party were tunneling from the side of the bank, and drew the sheep out, which soon became part and parcel of the Second Reserves.

That afternoon, General Morell marched with his whole force to the northeast where we took up a strong position at the gold mines near Morrisville and laid during the night. Here we remained until the next afternoon, when our Colonel, anxious to join the division, solicited and obtained permission to attempt the hazardous task of running the gauntlet outside our picket line, and General Morell taking compassion on our craven stomachs, gave us a fine ox and his blessing, with which we departed on our way rejoicing. In a few miles we were outside the picket lines, pushing direct for our forces, through a section of country continually scoured by the enemy's cavalry. About dark we passed Bealton station, which is four miles from Rappahannock station, and moving one mile beyond bivouacked in a wood, and killing our ox, we enjoyed a hearty meal to which we had been strangers for some time past. That night we posted strong guards and pickets under Captain Connor and sleeping soundly were up before daybreak the next morning and off.

Being in entire ignorance of the country excepting the general directions, and the unreliable information we gathered from the few inhabitants we met, and having no knowledge of the location of our forces except that they were falling back, and that the rear guard of cavalry and artillery were engaged with the enemy in the direction of Warrenton, Sulphur Springs and Waterloo bridge, the booming of whose guns we could plainly hear, we felt exceedingly anxious to find our division. A regiment lost from its division, is like a soldier lost from his regiment, or a child from his home. Though it was excessively hot, and we had added to the length of our wearied march by a long detour in the early part of the day, the boys steadily pressed on over the hilly roads, with but few and short halts for rest or water. About four o'clock the spires of Warrenton were seen, and soon afterwards we passed through the town and moved about two miles down the Waterloo road, where we at length found our division, and bivouacked in a woods near the road, having marched twenty miles.

The next morning, the 27th, our wagons arrived, and

rations were again served out to us, but the heads of the beef barrels had hardly been stove in before we received orders to march. This was rather hard for the boys, as they had had but one ration of meat since the morning of the 16th. But there was no remedy, so the meat was packed in the wagons again, and we took up the line of march through Warrenton, past New Baltimore, and bivouacked at Buckland Mills, where Broad Run crosses the Alexandria and Warrenton turnpike.

The enemy during the preceding night having passed through Thoroughfare Gap, and cut the railroad in the neighborhood of Kettle Run, about six miles east of Warrenton Junction, were attacked on the afternoon of the 27th, by Hooker's division, about four miles west of Bristoe Station, and driven back along the railroad to Broad Run, where, at dark, he still confronted Hooker. The loss on each side was about three hundred killed and wounded, the enemy leaving his wounded, and much of his baggage on the battle-field. During the night Ewell retired to Manassas Junction.

CHAPTER XVII.

Second Battle of Bull Run. Conduct of General Fitz-John Porter. The Army falls back. Battle of Chantilly. Arlington Heights. Upton's Hill.

Second Battle of Bull Run, on the Plains of Manassas, July 28th, 29th, and 30th,—The next morning, the 28th, we commenced our march at three o'clock, and upon arriving at Gainesville about ten, the head of the column was fired upon by a battery of artillery posted on an elevation to our front and left. The whole column was marvellously soon unwoven, and formed into line of battle and skirmishers advanced, but upon Cooper's rifled guns being brought to bear upon them, they withdrew, but not, however, before some loss had been sustained on our side; the adjutant of the Eighth Reserve losing a leg, and one man being killed and five wounded. This was supposed to be merely a demonstration by the enemy to save a wagon train, which was seen moving off on the Sudley Springs road. We then resumed our march, striking across the country towards Manassas Junction, in the neighborhood of which a portion of the enemy's forces, under Generals Jackson, Ewell, and A. P. Hill, were posted, the object being to cut off this force to the east, from the main body under General Lee, who were advancing from the west, through Thoroughfare Gap.

About five o'clock in the afternoon, it being ascertained the enemy had moved from Manassas towards Centreville early in the day, we turned off to the left, near Bethlehem Church, and took the Sudley Spring road towards the Warrenton pike. About this time a heavy cannonading was heard, which continued until it grew into the thunder of a desperate battle. We had already marched many long and weary hours and miles, but tired and exhausted we pressed on until the musketry firing became distinct, the flashing was seen and the mingling voices of the combatants were heard. It was after nine o'clock that night, after a march of eighteen hours and twenty-eight miles, with many of the men without any thing to eat, that we arrived upon the battle-field, and stretched our wearied limbs upon the grass to sleep.

King's division of our Corps had encountered, near Groveton, Jackson's force, whom Kearney had in the afternoon driven out of Centreville, and who were retreating towards Thoroughfare Gap, to form a junction with the main army. About the same time Rickett's division became engaged with Longstreet's Corps, near Thoroughfare Gap, about eight miles further west. Both actions were severe, but not decisive for either side.

Early the next morning, the 29th, the Reserves were

formed and moved forward to meet the enemy. We advanced some distance and passed through a woods into an open plain, where we were drawn up on the left of a vast mass of troops and pushed into a woods beyond. Soon we were ordered back, and then commenced a series of marches and countermarches through the hot sun and under a never-ceasing fire of shot and shell, until late in the afternoon, without pulling a trigger. The day was extraordinarily hard on the men of our regiment, who were worn out and weak, they having had but one ration of meat in thirteen days, and but little to eat the day before, and nothing this day.

The day was opened by Sigel attacking the enemy early in the morning, a mile or two east of Groveton. Jackson fell back several miles, but was so closely pressed, that he was compelled to make a stand. He accordingly took up a position with his left in the neighborhood of Sudley Springs, his right a little to the south of Warrenton turnpike, and his line covered by an old railroad grade which leads from Gainesville in the direction of Leesburg. His batteries, which were numerous, and some of them of heavy calibre, were posted behind the ridges, in the open ground on both sides of Warrenton turnpike, whilst the mass of his troops was sheltered in dense woods behind the railroad embankment. Heintzelman's corps occupied the right of our line, General Sigel the centre, and the Pennsylvania Reserves, under Reynolds, the extreme left, south of the Warrenton turnpike. A portion of Reno's force was in the line, and a portion held in reserve, in the rear of the centre.

Up to four o'clock very severe skirmishes occurred constantly at various points on our line, being brought on at every indication that the enemy made of a disposition to retreat, the object being to hold them until Porter and McDowell with the rest of his corps could turn their right and rear, when it was confidently expected we would be able to overwhelm or capture the larger portion of Jackson's forces before he could be reinforced. At two o'clock, when Porter and McDowell should have been in the positions assigned them, they had not arrived, and peremptory orders were sent by General Pope to Porter, to advance and attack the enemy. At half-past five o'clock, when it was confidently expected that Porter was coming into action in compliance with orders, Generals Heintzelman and Reno, on the right, commenced an assault upon the enemy's left. The attack was made with great gallantry, and the whole of the left of the enemy was doubled back towards his centre, and our forces, after a sharp conflict of an hour and a half, occupied the field of battle, with the dead and wounded of the enemy. In this attack Grover's brigade broke through two of the enemy's lines and penetrated to the third before it could be checked. By this time General McDowell arrived on the field with the balance of his corps, which was pushed to the front along the Warrenton turnpike to fall upon the enemy, who was retreating towards the pike from the direction of Sudley Springs.

This attack was made by King's division at about sunset, but by that time the advance of the main body of the enemy, under Longstreet, had begun to reach the field, and he encountered a stubborn and determined resistance at a point about three-fourths of a mile in front of our line of battle.

While the attack was being made on the enemy's left, General Reynolds was ordered to threaten their right and rear, which he proceeded to do under a heavy fire of artillery from the ridge to the left of the pike. This battery of heavy guns it was determined to attempt to capture, for which purpose the First Reserves, Colonel Roberts, and our regiment, Colonel McCandless, were sent into a dense woods to the right from which we soon drove the enemy's skirmishers without any loss. Having advanced through the woods to the opening upon the opposite side, we displayed ourselves to attract the attention of the enemy, who soon opened upon us a most terrific fire of shell and grape, to which we could give no response. Having succeeded, however, in drawing the fire from the storming party, we laid down quietly and watched our comrades on the left. Generals Seymour and Jackson, at the head of their brigades, most gallantly led them to the charge, but notwithstanding the steadiness and courage shown by the men, they were compelled to fall back before the heavy artillery and musketry fire which met them both on the front and left flank.

The fire for a time was drawn from us, but soon again it returned, the iron hail whistling and bursting over our heads through the woods, tearing the branches from the trees and scattering the bark in every direction. It was here that young Poulson of Company K was killed. As the storming party had been driven back and as there was no further use of our maintaining the position, Colonel McCandless withdrew the regiment in good order from the woods, and we fell back over the fields with the round shot and shell plowing up the ground and bursting over us. If we had had a battery of rifled guns, the result would probably have been different, but Ramson's being smooth-bored, their range was too short. We withdrew to the position we moved from in the morning, the enemy occasionally sending round shot at long range among us.

Whilst this attack was going on, the forces under Heintzelman and Reno continued to push the left of the enemy in the direction of the Warrenton turnpike, so that about eight o'clock in the evening, the greater portion of the field of battle was in our possession. Bayard's cavalry also made an attack on the extreme left, which ended the fighting for the day, which we could safely now claim as ours.

In regard to the conduct of General Fitz John Porter, the following is extracted from the official report of General Pope:

"Nothing was heard of General Porter up to that time,

(eight, P. M.,) and his force took no part whatever in the action, but were suffered by him to lie idle on their arms within sight and sound of the battle during the whole day. So far as I know, he made no effort whatever to comply with my orders nor to take any part in the action. I do not hesitate to say, that if he had discharged his duty, as became a soldier under the circumstances, and had made a vigorous attack on the enemy, as he was expected and directed to do, at any time up to eight o'clock that night, we should have utterly crushed or captured the larger portion of Jackson's force before he could have been by any possibility sufficiently reinforced to have made any effective resistance. I did not myself feel for a moment that it was necessary for me, having given General Porter an order to march towards the enemy in a particular direction, to send him in addition specific orders to attack, it being his clear duty, and in accordance with every military precept, to have brought his forces into action wherever he encountered the enemy, when a furious battle with that enemy was raging during the whole day in his immediate presence. I believe—in fact, I am positive—that at five o'clock in the afternoon of the 29th, General Porter had in his front no considerable body of the enemy. I believed then, as I am very sure now, that it was easily practicable for him to have turned the right flank of Jackson, and to have fallen upon his rear; that if he had done so, we should have gained a decisive victory over the army under Jackson, before he could have been joined by any of the forces of Longstreet; and that the army of General Lee would have been so crippled and checked by the destruction of this large force as to have been no longer in condition to prosecute further operations of an aggressive character. I speak thus freely of the strange failure of General Porter, not because I am more convinced of its unfortunate results now than I was at that time, but because a full investigation of the whole subject, made by a court-martial has fully justified and confirmed that opinion."

Our loss during the day was estimated by General Pope at from six to eight thousand killed and wounded, and Generals Hooker and Kearney, who had been over the whole field, separately estimated the loss of the enemy at from two to one, and from three to one of our own.

The weary and hungry boys had just thrown themselves upon the ground to sleep, when orders came for our brigade to go on picket. Picket on the battle-field means to be in line of battle within a short distance of the enemy, and to be prepared at any moment for an attack in force. We silently moved off to a woods on the edge of which we were concealed, with pickets about twenty yards in advance of us. In our front, and within hearing of their voices, were the foe reposing on their arms. A sleepless night was passed, but at last dawn came, and we were relieved and marched back to the division.

The men of our regiment were now absolutely suffering for food, and were worn down by constant marching, fighting and loss of sleep, and unfit for the battle-field, until they had rest and rations. Many of them were so utterly exhausted that it was necessary to send them to the rear, as they could not continue with us. The brave boys who had been without food for two days, and had hardly murmured before, now commenced complaining, and four of them came to appeal to the Colonel. McCandless heard their story, which he knew was too true, and turning to his saddle-bags, drew forth two buns which he had just received from an aid, and breaking them in half, distributed them, remarking, "Now, I have fed the regiment." The men seeing this, complained no more.

Soon after we marched to the right of the Warrenton pike, and a few boxes of crackers were distributed among us, giving to each man about five. We then hurried into line and moved forward, crossing Young's creek, where we found a number of wounded men who were collected and sent to the rear. Moving forward, we were deployed as skirmishers to the left of the "Bucktails," over a rising piece of ground flanked on either side by heavy woods. As we advanced a pretty but sad sight presented itself. It was the dead of the preceding day, most of whom at this point were the Fourteenth Brooklyn, dressed in their large flowing red trousers and blue jackets. Through the gray of the morning they resembled Zouaves sleeping peacefully upon the ground, and interspersed with them as we approached nearer, we could see the blue coats and gray jackets taking their last sleep also. This was the pretty sight, but when we crept up stealthily among them on our bellies watching for the foe, it was sad to gaze upon their cold pale faces, and think of the happy ones at home that would soon be steeped in anguish for the loss of the brave but still hearts that laid around us.

After feeling for the enemy for some time they were found occupying a store and some out-buildings about three hundred yards in advance of us, from which they kept up a brisk fire. Leaving a portion of the skirmishers to occupy their attention, McCandless moved with the balance to the left, and under cover of the woods crept up upon them, but the scamps were too wide-awake to be caught, they skedaddling before we could flank them. Taking up a position in the buildings and the extreme edge of the woods, a sharp fire was opened by both sides across a broad field, beyond which the enemy were posted in a woods, with their sharp-shooters in the trees, from which they were dropped in a lively manner by volleys from squads of our men who marked every tree from which smoke issued. While at this work Captain Connors received a severe wound from a rifle-ball passing through his right breast. At the same time a brave little "Bucktail," who was going "'to try my luck," got knocked over.

As it was desirable to ascertain more fully the strength

of the enemy in our front, we were ordered to advance, and with loud cheers we crossed the field that intervened between us and the foe, driving them before us, and pressing on about four hundred yards when we halted. In the meantime a masked battery was discovered to our right and front about three hundred yards, and a large force of infantry and artillery on our left and rear about twelve hundred yards distant. By this time the Third Reserve, Colonel Sickel, come to our support, but McCandless seeing the critical position we were in, ordered us to retire, which we did with the utmost deliberation and order, some of the men stopping to destroy muskets left upon the field by the enemy. A fine brass howitzer was also found in the road, which would have been brought off had not the spokes of its wheels been cut. Taking up our former position we laid down and were quiet for about an hour without the enemy molesting us in the least.

It was now near two o'clock and the day thus far had been remarkably quiet, nothing but a little skirmishing going on. Up to ten o'clock in the morning every indication pointed to the retreat of the enemy from our front along the Warrenton pike in the direction of Gainesville. Our line was formed with Heintzelman's Corps on the right, Reno's next, Sigel's next, and Porter's on the left and the Warrenton pike, and the Reserves on the extreme left, south of the turnpike, they being the pivot in the attack which Porter's Corps was to make on the enemy's right wing, then supposed to be on the pike and in retreat. About this time, two o'clock, Porter's Corps supported by King's division of McDowell's Corps, attacked the enemy along the pike, and at the same time, Heintzelman and Reno on the right were ordered to push forward to the left and front towards the pike, and attack the enemy's flank.

It was soon after this attack, that our line of skirmishers fell back over the field, and when General Reynolds saw it he inquired of Colonel McCandless why he had withdrawn, and upon being informed the enemy were on our left, he replied it was impossible. Putting spurs to his horse he boldly dashed through our skirmishers to the left and passing into the open ground beyond, he found a line of skirmishers of the enemy nearly parallel to our line covering the left flank, with cavalry formed behind them, perfectly stationary, evidently masking a column of infantry, formed for attack on our left flank when our line should be sufficiently advanced. The skirmishers hoping for a rich prize opened fire upon him, but he run the gauntlet and gained the division, losing an orderly who followed him.

It was now apparent that the enemy was not falling back, but massing his troops on the south of the pike to turn our left flank, and General Reynolds upon communicating the fact to General McDowell was directed by him to form his division to resist this attack, the dispositions for which were rapidly completed. Our line fell back over the same ground we advanced on in the morning, crossing the creek, and joining our division which was drawn up on the Ball Hill in rear of a heavy woods. Our guns to the right of us were soon engaged with a battery, whose range they soon got, and forced to withdraw.

Farther to our right and front, in the woods covering the right of the field we first skirmished over in the morning, Porter's Corps was hotly engaged with the enemy, and from the number of brigades we saw going into the woods some hours before we had strong hope they would be able at least to hold their ground, as they were fresh troops, having arrived upon the field that day. But Porter's attack was not with the vigor or persistency it should have been, and soon it retired in considerable confusion.

The Reserves were then ordered across the field to the rear of Porter, to form a line, behind which his troops might be rallied, but before the rear of our column had left the position the threatened attack by the enemy's right began to be felt, and the rear brigade, under Colonel Anderson of the Ninth Reserve (the gallant Colonel Jackson having been taken sick on the field early in the day), with three batteries of artillery, were obliged to form on the ground on which they found themselves to oppose it. With the remaining two brigades we hurried on across the field to the right under a heavy fire of round shot and shell, passing by the Robinson house across a road, our course being diverted by the difficult nature of the ground, and the retreating masses of the broken columns, among the troops of Heintzelman's Corps already formed, by which much time was lost and confusion created, which allowed the enemy to sweep up with his right, so far as almost to cut us off from the pike, leaving nothing but the Third brigade, the three batteries of artillery of the Reserves, Tower's two Brigades and McLean's to resist the advance of the enemy on our left. This attack on the Ball Hill was too severe for the troops to hold it long under the hot fire the enemy maintained upon it, and after heavy loss, little by little they were compelled to yield it. It was here that the most severe loss of the Reserves was sustained, both in men and material; Kern losing his four guns, but not until wounded and left on the field; Cooper, his caissons. Colonel Harding, Twelfth Reserve, was here severely wounded. The brigade sustained itself most gallantly, and though severely pushed on both front and flank maintained its position until overwhelmed by numbers, when it fell back, taking up new positions wherever the advantages of ground permitted.

Our two brigades and battery took up a position on the brow of a hill, near a road, from which we overlooked a large portion of the field, and Porter's troops commenced forming behind us, but on account of the position at the Ball house being forced by the enemy, we were ordered over to the extreme left, and took up a position on the Henry House Hill. There we were formed in column of brigade, with Ransom's battery of

Napoleons in our front, who were throwing their shells at long range upon the heavy masses of the enemy, who were advancing upon us. Here, under a most terrific shower of shell we remained for nearly an hour, with the brave boys falling around us, but all in good heart, hoping yet to gain the day. While here, an act of heroism was performed that has seldom been surpassed upon any field. A shell dropped a few feet in front of the left of our regiment, which naturally recoiled from it, when the fiery missile was seized by a non-commissioned officer and hurled into a hole.

At last we saw line after line of our troops giving way, as the enemy came sweeping on in dense columns, shouting their victorious huzzahs as they advanced. If this position was lost, our left wing would be turned and the enemy would interpose his force between the main body of our army and Centreville, on the Warrenton pike, at the crossing of Bull Run creek, and the result would be fearful. Therefore it was necessary for us to maintain it at all hazards. Onward the well-dressed lines of the enemy advanced, when, "forward Reserves!" shouted the gallant Reynolds, as he dashed the spurs into his horse's sides, and led the charge, followed by a mass of living valor, whose loud cheers drowned the roar of battle. The columns met, like the meeting of contending waves of the ocean, bubbling up and foaming over—but the rear ranks pressed on, trampling the wounded and the dead under their feet, till faltering and trembling, the gallant enemy were hurled back upon the denser masses that supported them, and were advancing through the woods. The scene at this moment was the most magnificently grand man ever beheld. In the van, towering above the masses, rode the gallant Reynolds, waving aloft a standard shot from its staff. Near him was the cool-headed Meade, who in the heat of battle almost became excited as he urged the men forward, and next followed Seymour with his brigade, who by the gentle waving of his hand restrained the ardor of his men and preserved the distinctness of the lines.

Onward we pressed, pushing the enemy into the woods, when their reserve of five or six lines deep opened upon us a withering fire, while several batteries of artillery that had obtained our exact range, poured into us their flaming missiles, which bursting in our midst, produced fearful havoc. At the same time, the enemy from their vastly superior numbers were able to turn our left flank into which they poured a rapid and destructive fire of musketry. The struggle here became most fearful, and it was a long while before our lines could be forced back. But at last, slowly and in good order we yielded the ground, and fell back to our original position, near which we reformed and again held the foe at bay, reinforced by a brigade of regulars, under Lieutenant-colonel Buchanan. After dark, having been forced back about three-quarters of a mile, but still covering the turnpike, we withdrew, but not until our ammunition had become almost exhausted, and almost the whole army had been withdrawn from the field. The Third brigade soon afterwards rejoined us, and in the early part of the night we marched toward Centreville, and bivouacked with Sykes' division upon the east bank of Cub Run.

When we were forced to yield the ground to the enemy, Colonel McCandless, whilst most gallantly urging the men on, received a severe wound in the right thigh, near the groin, and seizing the flag he attempted to push on with it, but was taken from the field by main force, by Captain Mealey, and the flag saved.*

Lieutenant James C. Justus, who, though sick, had continued with the regiment from Harrison's Landing, was taken from the field utterly prostrated, and sent to Washington.

On account of Company G being detached, and the

---

* See Appendix A.

number of sick and those who had given out from exhaustion and want of food, we entered that day's battle with but one hundred men.

In the official report of General Reynolds, the loss of our division is put down at six hundred and fifty-three men, and the conduct of our regiment and Colonel McCandless is complimentarily noticed, as also in the reports of Generals Seymour and McDowell.

Of our Generals and Division, General Pope says: "Brigadier-General John F. Reynolds, commanding the Pennsylvania Reserves, merits the highest commendation at my hands. Prompt, active, and energetic, he commanded his division with distinguished ability throughout the operations, and performed his duties in all situations with zeal and fidelity. Generals Seymour and Meade, of that division, in like manner, performed their duties with ability and gallantry and in all fidelity to the Government and to the army."

Early on the 31st, our division marched to Centreville and halted on the right of the road. It had been raining through the night and during the morning until ten o'clock, it was very heavy. The houses in the town were crowded with our wounded, and the road thronged with soldiers of every arm of the service, trying to find their respective commands. Wagons were moving to and fro, generals, aids, and orderlies were galloping about, and squads of prisoners sent to the rear, and long trains of ambulances were pushing towards Washington. Omnibusses, carriages and other vehicles lined the roads and covered the fields in every direction, the Government having impressed all they could find in Washington, Georgetown, and Alexandria, and sent them out for the wounded. Large droves of horses, tied to long ropes were also sent from the Government corals at Washington. Almost all the Government employees, and many citizens also came out, and emptied their pockets of all the tobacco and post stamps they had, as those articles were in great demand among the soldiers.

About eleven o'clock the division was marched about two miles down the pike and halted, when coffee and crackers were issued, and we soon got our fires burning. This was a perfect god-send to us, every mouthful of coffee we drank seeming like so much life passing into us. We remained here a couple of hours, when we marched back to Centreville, and halted until near dark, and had salt beef served up to us, it being the second time we had meat during sixteen days. Just before dark our division was sent out to relieve General Reno, who occupied the position of Cub Run, our artillery shelling the woods as we advanced. Our position was on a range of high hills, covered with heavy woods and dense undergrowth, in which we rested on our arms all night, the enemy not disturbing us, excepting for a while when we were taking our position, when they sent their little bees humming around our ears. It was a long night of watching for our wearied men, through the rain, but at last the welcomed morning came and we were relieved and marched back beyond Centreville. As we came in we passed hundreds of ambulances and army wagons going to the field after the wounded, a flag of truce being arranged for that purpose.

That morning, September the 1st, we were mustered for pay by Captain James N. Byrnes, upon whom the command of the regiment devolved, he being the senior officer; all our field officers being wounded. The day before was the proper day, but it was impracticable.

It having been ascertained that the enemy were attempting to turn our right, and cut off our communications with Washington, by moving a large force on the Little river or Aldie turnpike, towards Fairfax Court House, our army was stretched along the Warrenton and Alexandria pike, from Centreville to beyond the Court House. At noon we moved off down the pike, marching on the fields along the sides of the road which was filled with continuous strings of wagons, moving both ways. A little before sunset, just as our division had passed in front of Chantilly, an attack was made by the enemy on the troops in our rear, and we were put in position in a large open field in reserve. The battle raged furiously for some time, the shot and shell falling among us, but doing little damage to our division. In the midst of it a terrific thunder storm occurred, and it appeared as if heaven and earth were contending for the mastery. But the darkness of night terminated the conflict, the enemy was driven entirely back from our front, but the gallant Generals Kearney and Stevens fell. We then moved off, a short distance and bivouacked on the outskirts of Fairfax Court House, it continuing to rain all night.

The next morning our appetites were sharpened by the sight of several beeves driven in to our butchers, but before the hides were fairly taken off of them orders were received to march, but the boys cut some good slices from them and took along. Marching down the road, we passed through Fairfax to Anandale, where we turned to the left, and after a halt of an hour we moved on past Ball's cross roads to near Arlington Heights, where we bivouacked for the night. On the road we passed large numbers of wagons, artillery and fresh troops. The new regiments were easily distinguished by their white faces and full knapsacks, the one of which Old Sol had tanned for us, and the other we had learned to do without.

During the day there was some artillery fighting in the direction of Vienna, but before nine o'clock at night, all the command was inside the intrenchments of Washington, excepting three corps on the Vienna and Chain Bridge roads, that did not arrive until the next day.

It may as well be stated here that General Banks was stationed along the railroad, charged with the safety of the wagon and railroad trains, and as during no time on the 28th, 29th, 30th and 31st of August, the road was interrupted between Bristoe Station and Alexandria they were withdrawn with very little loss.

The next morning, the 3d, we moved about three miles to near the Arlington House, the late residence of the Confederate General, Robert E. Lee, where we laid in the woods until four o'clock the next afternoon, when we marched to Upton's Hill.

Here terminated our campaign with the army of Virginia, under General Pope, which, though short, was arduous and severe, and its failure is not to be attributed to the want of generalship on the part of the commanding general or his subordinates. The conduct of General Fitz John Porter, on the 29th, when the golden opportunity of crushing a divided foe was lost, proved fatal to the army the next day, and so clear a case was made out against him, by General Pope in his report, as to leave no doubt upon the subject. He was subsequently dismissed from the service by a court-martial, and disqualified from ever holding any office of honor or trust under the Government.

It may seem impossible to some that General Porter could be guilty of so dark a crime, but it must be remembered that the heart of man is now governed by the same impulses it ever has been from the earliest record, and that history furnishes many instances of men sacrificing their fortunes, lives, souls and even country, to avenge an insult their pride could not brook, and the only explanation we know, of the conduct of Porter, was the unfortunate address to the Army of Virginia, issued by General Pope upon assuming command of it, in which he indirectly insulted General McClellan and his counsellors of the Army of the Potomac.

General Pope estimated his forces on the morning of the 30th as follows: "McDowell's corps, including Reynold's division, twelve thousand men; Sigel's corps, seven thousand men; Reno's corps, seven thousand; Heintzelmen's corps, seven thousand men; Porter's corps, which had been in no engagements, and was, or ought to have been, perfectly fresh, I estimated at about twelve thousand men, including the brigade of Piatt, which formed a part of Sturgis' division, and the only portion that ever joined me. But of this force the brigades of Piatt and of Griffin, numbering, as I understood, about five thousand men, had been suffered to march off at daylight on the 30th to Centreville, and were not available for operations on that day This reduced Porter's effective force on the field to about seven thousand men, which gave me a total force of forty thousand men. Banks' corps, about five thousand strong, was at Bristow Station, in charge of the railroad trains, and of a portion of the wagon trains of the army still at that place."

Of these the general says: "As may be supposed, our troops, who had been so continually marching and fighting for so many days, were in a state of great exhaustion. They had had little to eat for two days previous, and the artillery and cavalry horses had been in harness and saddled continually for ten days, and had had no forage for two days previous. It may easily be imagined how little these troops, after such severe labor, and after undergoing such hardships and privations, were in condition for active and efficient service."

In our regiment early on the 29th, it was well known that some trouble existed between Generals Pope and Porter, and that the latter would not render a cordial cooperation. This was the common conversation among the officers and men, who had gathered it upon the field, and we may here remark that among old troops it is almost a matter of impossibility to conceal the object of any extraordinary movements from them. There are always among the many thousand eyes that are watching, some who can divine the truth.

CHAPTER XVIII.

CROSSING THE POTOMAC. MARCH THROUGH MARYLAND. BATTLE OF SOUTH MOUNTAIN. REMARKABLE INCIDENT.

THE army having been withdrawn to the defences of Washinton, General McClellan was assigned to the command of it on the 2d of September. It soon after being ascertained that the enemy intended to cross the Upper Potomac into Maryland, our army was put in motion to again meet them.

On the 6th, company G, Captain Reitzel, rejoined us, they having marched down the Peninsula with the wagon trains, and the same night about nine o'clock we fell in and marched off through the woods to the pike, passing a long line of ambulances, carriages and wagons filled with our wounded from the late field, and passing over to Washington on the Long Bridge, we proceeded through the city to its outskirts on the Leesboro road where we laid down about two o'clock A. M. After a short repose, we were up and moved soon after light to Leesboro, ten miles distance, where we laid in a scrub woods until noon on the 9th, when we marched through Mechanicsville to near Brookville, and bivouacked about sunset. We were forced to leave at Leesboro, under charge of a guard, all our ammunition, rations and baggage, as our wagons were unloaded and taken to Washington, ostensibly for clothing, and did not rejoin the regiment until after Antietam.

About noon the next day we moved to the head waters of the Patuxent river and bivouacked, and the next day to near Poplar springs. We were now approaching the neighborhood of the enemy, a company of whom were at the springs the night before. There, and all through Maryland where they had been, we found they had taken whatever they wanted, leaving the farmers almost destitute, paying for the articles in Confederate money and quartermaster's orders that were not worth the paper they were written on.

On the 12th, at the urgent request of His Excellency Governor Curtin, General Reynolds was detached from the command of the Reserves, and ordered to Pennsylvania for the purpose of organizing the militia of the State and preparing them for armed resistance to the enemy, and General Meade was ordered to assume his position. On the morning of the same day we marched, and striking the Baltimore and Frederick turnpike passed through Ridgeville and New Market, bivouacking about four miles beyond the latter place. All along the route we heard the complaints of the inhabitants of the plundering operations of the "Liberating Army," that came to free "My Maryland" from the "oppressor's heel," and bring back into "their" old Union all the States. Their liberating operations, however, seemed to partake much of the nature of the vultures, coveting and devouring.

The next morning we marched about four miles, crossing the Monocacy and halting for the day and night on its banks. A brisk artillery skirmish took place during the day about eight miles from here on the side of the mountains, where we could plainly see the smoke of the guns. The day before a skirmish took place here, the enemy trying to blow up the turnpike bridge over the Monocacy, but were frustrated in their design by our cavalry. They were also driven out of Frederick, where there was a smart little street fight. While in possession of the city, the "Liberators" ordered all the stores to be opened, which they soon emptied of their contents, paying for the same in their worthless trash. They also opened a recruiting office, but did not do a very thriving business.

On our march from Washington, Lieutenants Black, Company E, and Manton, Company B, were taken sick, and with others of the regiment were sent back to the hospitals.

Our army, which had been slowly moving through Maryland in five columns between the Potomac river and the Baltimore and Ohio Railroad, covering both Washington and Baltimore, was now concentrated near Frederick following closely the retiring foe. During the march the progress of reorganization, rendered necessary after the demoralizing effects of the disastrous campaign upon the Virginia side of the Potomac, rapidly progressed, the troops regaining their confidence and spirit, and being anxious to again meet the enemy.

BATTLE OF SOUTH MOUNTAIN, SEPTEMBER 14TH.—On Sunday, the 14th of September, the reveille was sounded at three o'clock, and after coffee and crackers we took up our march, passing through Frederick, whose inhabitants were hardly up, yet we found many flags waving and bright eyes peering from the windows. We moved on the National road winding up the Catoctin Mountains past Fairview to Jerusalem on the summit, where the day before an artillery fight had taken place much to the discomfort of the enemy, one of whose caissons was exploded. This mountain separates the valley of the Monocacy from that of Catoctin, and the scenery on both sides is magnificent, equalling almost any of the kind we ever saw. Beyond was the South Mountains from whose side issued puffs of smoke from guns of the enemy, whose reports came booming over the valley. About noon we marched through Middletown, a pretty and thriving place, whose inhabitants turned out *en masse* to welcome us and cheer us on our way to battle. Never was a more cordial welcome given to troops than was given to us. Bread, cakes, milk, water, fruit and tobacco, were freely given by the good people who crowded the doors and windows and lined the pavements, and flags and handkerchiefs were waved and flowers thrown as we passed. We felt then, for the first time during the war, we were fighting among friends.

Marching on with happy hearts we crossed the Catoctin where the enemy had burned the bridge, mill and surrounding houses, and halted near its banks to make coffee.

During the morning General Pleasanton, with his cavalry and horse artillery, had been skirmishing with the enemy, and had at last driven them to Turner's Gap, of the South Mountains, where they determined to make a stand. The mountain at this point is about one thousand feet high, and there are two country roads, one to the north and the other to the south of the turnpike or National road, which gave access to the crests overlooking the main road. The one on the north is called the "Old Hagerstown road," and the one on the south the "Old Sharpsburg road."

General Cox's division was sent to support Pleasanton, and the First brigade arrived about nine A. M., and was sent up the old Sharpsburgh road to feel the enemy and ascertain if he held the crest on that side in force. Such being found to be the case, upon the arrival of the other brigade, General Cox, being assured by Reno he would be supported by the whole of his corps, advanced to the assault. Two twenty-pound Parrots and four light guns were put in position near the pike, where they did good execution against the enemy's batteries in the gap. Colonel Scammon's brigade was deployed, and well covered with skirmishers, it moved up the slope to the left of the road to turn the enemy's right. It succeeded in gaining the crest in spite of the vigorous efforts of the enemy, who was posted behind stone walls and in the edge of timber, with a battery which poured into them canister and case shot. Colonel Cooke's brigade followed at supporting distance. A section of a battery was moved up with great difficulty and opened with canister at very short range on the enemy's infantry, but was forced to withdraw.

The enemy several times attempted to retake the crest, but were each time repulsed. They then withdrew their battery to a point more to the right, and formed columns on both our flanks. It was now about noon; and a lull occurred in the contest, which lasted until about two P. M., during which time the rest of the corps came up. Upon the arrival of General Wilcox's division, General Reno ordered him to move up the old Sharpsburgh road and take a position to its right, overlooking the turnpike. Two regiments were detached to support General Cox, and a section of Captain Cook's battery was placed in position near the turn of the road, on the crest, and opened fire on the enemy's batteries across the gap. As the division was deploying, the enemy suddenly opened with a battery at short range, and drove Cook's cannoniers with their limbers from their guns and caused a temporary panic, in which the guns were nearly lost. But the Seventy-Ninth New York, and the Seventeenth Michigan rallied, and advancing soon restored order, and the division was formed in line on the right of Cox, and was kept concealed as much as possible under the hill side, until the whole line advanced. It lost heavily from the fire of the battery in front, and those on the other side of the turnpike.

Shortly before this, Generals Burnside and Reno arrived at the base of the mountains, and the latter was directed to move up the divisions of Sturgis and Rodman to the crest by Cox and Wilcox, and to attack the enemy with his whole force as soon as Hooker, on the right, was well up the mountains. General Sturgis reached the scene of action about half-past three o'clock, and Clark's battery was sent to assist General Cox's left. and the Second Maryland and Sixth New Hampshire were detached and sent forward a short distance to the left of the turnpike. The balance of the division was formed in rear of Wilcox's, and Rodman's division was divided; Colonel Fairchild's brigade being placed on the extreme left, and Colonel Harland's on the right.

General McClellan ordered the whole line to move forward and take or silence the enemy's batteries in front, which was executed with enthusiasm. The enemy made desperate resistance, charging our advancing lines with firmness, but they were every where routed and fled.

The chief loss was in Wilcox's division. The enemy made an effort to turn our left about dark, but were repulsed, as also in their efforts to regain the lost ground in front of Sturgis and Cox. A lively fire was kept up until nearly nine o'clock, several charges being made by the enemy, and repulsed with slaughter, and we finally occupied the highest part of the mountains. General Reno, a brave and skilful soldier, was killed just before sunset.

While these operations were progressing on the left. the right, under General Hooker, was actively engaged, About two o'clock we moved forward from the Catoctin, on the main road, and turned off to the right, on the old Hagerstown road, passing through the woods and over the fields, along the base of the mountains about one mile and a half, where we rested. While moving to this position, the enemy opened upon us with several pieces of artillery, throwing their shell in close proximity, which caused great consternation among the citizens, who accompanied us to see the fun. The children laid down upon the ground, the women shrieked, and the men displayed wondrous agility in leaping the fences, which caused considerable amusement among us.

General Seymour, whose brigade occupied the extreme right, deployed the "Bucktails" as skirmishers to feel the enemy, with our regiment about fifty yards in their rear, as a support. Advancing up the foot hills, we soon became engaged, and drove them from a farm house, where they made considerable resistance, during which the lines of the two regiment became mixed and were not again fully separated. We drove the enemy a long distance, with the left wing of our regiment acting as a support, when coming to a stone wall, at the immediate base of the mountains, they rallied and made a stubborn resistance, but the impetuosity of the boys carried them over it, when one of the most exciting and spirited fights took place we ever witnessed. The ground was of the most difficult character for the movement of troops, the mountain side being very steep and rocky, and obstructed by stone walls, rocks and timber, from behind which the enemy, in lines and squads kept up an incessant fire, as also from their guns posted upon the mountain tops. All order and regularity of the lines were soon destroyed, and the battle partook of the nature of a free fight, every one going in "on his own hook," as it suited his fancy. From wall after wall, and rock after rock, the enemy were driven until our glorious banners caught the gleam of the setting sun, that had been hid from our sight by the mountain tops. Our loud cheers of victory arose from the crest, and was rolled down the mountain side. It was dark before the battle was over, and a desultory fire was continued until near nine o'clock. Towards the close of the battle, General Hooker ordered up General Duryea's brigade of Rickett's division, but they did not arrive until after the action closed, and upon their reaching the crest, they lustily cheered the Reserves.

In his official report General McClellan says, "General Meade speaks highly of General Seymour's skill in handling his brigade on the extreme right, securing by his manœuvres the great object of the movement, the outflanking of the enemy."

While the Reserves were at work on the extreme right, General Hatch's division was engaged in a severe contest for the crest to our left, which they carried soon after dusk with considerable loss. General Gibbon with his brigade late in the afternoon moved up the turnpike and attacked the enemy's centre, and after a severe engagement which lasted until nine o'clock entirely defeated and drove him away.*

Just before the battle opened our Adjutant, A. T.

* See Appendix A.

Cross was detailed as an Aid to General Seymour and acted with conspicuous bravery.

The troops we fought consisted of D. H. Hill's Corps, our old friend Longstreet's, and a portion of Jackson's, numbering about thirty thousand men. Our force was about the same, and our loss was three hundred and twelve killed, one thousand two hundred and thirty-four wounded and twenty-two missing, making an aggregate of one thousand, five hundred and sixty-eight. About fifteen hundred prisoners were taken by us during the battle, and the loss to the enemy in killed was much greater than our own, and probably also in wounded.

That night we slept on the mountain, and found the heavy dews chilling and damp. To the west in the valley below us the enemy's camp-fires burnt brightly all night. Through the night ammunition was received and distributed to the men. About one o'clock, the Adjutant of the Fifth Alabama who was probably waking up the men of his regiment to withdraw them, got among our boys in mistake, who not admiring the rough shaking he gave them, coupled with the information that the "Yanks" were near, one of them got up and knocked him down, and took him prisoner.

In the morning we were up early, and buried the dead. Among the enemy's was Colonel Gale of the Twelfth Alabama, a very gentlemanly looking fellow. Our pity was excited by a young Alabamian who had a musket ball through the forehead. He was unconscious, yet vitality in him was strong and he swallowed water freely.

A rather remarkable incident occurred in this battle. In the ——— regiment there was a man who had been through the Mexican and this war, but who had never been in a battle, he always shirking, and neither the threats of his officers or ridicule of his comrades could induce him to go into danger, as he declared he had a presentiment when a boy that he would be killed the first fight he went into. Some of his comrades, however, determined he should go into this battle, and threatened to shoot him if he did not. Soon after his regiment got under fire he laid down behind a trunk of a tree where he was perfectly safe, but seeing a large rock a few feet from him, he got up to go to it, and the instant he rose he fell dead with nine of the enemy's balls in him. What ever could have induced him to go a soldiering a second time after he had discovered his failing we cannot imagine.*

Before we left the field, General Seymour thanked Captain Byrnes and the regiment for their conduct during the battle.

The Reserves moved off about nine A. M., but we were detained on the mountain until noon, when we marched to the turnpike along which we moved to Boonsboro', where we found the churches and buildings filled with the enemy's wounded. Large numbers of prisoners were also there under guard, and further on we passed many more, the most of whom had voluntarily come in and given themselves up to the citizens. Here early in the day our cavalry overtook the enemy's and charging them, killed and wounded a number and captured two hundred and fifty prisoners and two guns.

At Boonsboro' we turned to the left, and marched to Keedysville, where we halted for several hours. Here the boys were most liberally supplied with hot cakes and bread by Mr. John Cost, a good Union citizen of that place, and from whom Captain Byrnes got liquor enough to give the men a ration. Just before dark we moved off and bivouacked in an orchard.

---

* Bravery is born in us and not acquired. It lies in the blood and is a species of instinct. It is involuntary, and depends not upon ourselves. It is always thoughtlessly impetuous and is inspired by the impulse of example, the blindness arising from common danger, and the heat of battle.

Courage, which is generally confounded with bravery, is not always united with it. It is in the soul, and is a real virtue, a sublime and noble sentiment. It is the result of reflection, of education and sometimes of misfortune. It is animated by patriotism, self-respect and a zeal for the cause engaged in. It is not inaccessible to fear; but it overcomes it. Bravery in the hour of danger is sometimes weakened by reflection; courage is always strengthened by it.

CHAPTER XIX.

THE BATTLE OF ANTIETAM. FIELD HOSPITALS. THE ENEMY WITHDRAWN TO VIRGINIA. PORTER'S RECONNOISSANCE. VISIT OF PRESIDENT LINCOLN.

DURING the day the army under McClellan had been concentrated in the neighborhood of Antietam creek, where the enemy was found occupying a strong position on the heights to the westward of it. Some artillery firing had taken place between our advance and the enemy, but it amounted to little on either side.

BATTLE OF ANTIETAM, SEPTEMBER 16TH AND 17TH.—Antietam creek, in this vicinity, is crossed by four stone bridges—the upper one on the Keedysville and Williamsport road; the second on the Keedysville and Sharpsburg turnpike, some two and a half miles below; the third about a mile below the second, on the Rhorerville and Sharpsburg; and the fourth near the mouth of Antietam creek, on the road leading from Harper's Ferry to Sharpsburg, some three miles below the third. The stream is sluggish, with few and difficult fords.

The enemy had the mass of his troops concealed behind the heights to the west of the creek. Their left and centre were upon and in front of the Sharpsburg and Hagerstown turnpike, hidden by woods and irregularities of the ground; their extreme left resting upon a wooded eminence near the cross roads to the north of J. Miller's farm, their left resting upon the Potomac. Their line extending south, the right resting upon the hills to the south of Sharpsburg, near Sheavely's farm. On all favorable points the enemy's artillery was posted, and their reserves hidden from view by the hills, on which their line of battle was formed, could manœuvre unobserved by our army, and from the shortness of their line could rapidly reinforce any point threatened by our attack. Their position, stretching across the angle formed by the Potomac and Antietam, their flanks and rear protected by these streams, was one of the strongest to be found in this region of country, which is well adapted to defensive warfare.

On the right, near Keedysville, on both sides of the Sharpsburg turnpike, were Sumner's and Hooker's corps. In advance, on the right of the turnpike and near Antietam creek, General Richardson's division of Sumner's corps was posted. General Sykes' division of General Porter's corps was on the left of the turnpike and in line with General Richardson's, protecting the bridge on the Keedysville and Sharpsburg pike. The left of the line, opposite to and some distance from the bridge on the Rohrersville and Sharpsburg road, was occupied by General Burnside's corps. In front of General Sumner's and Hooker's corps, near Keedysville, and on the ridge of the first line of hills overlooking the Antietam, and between the pike and Fry's house on the right of the road were placed Captains Taft's, Von Kleiser's, and Lieutenant Weaver's batteries of 20-pounder Parrott guns. On the crest of the hill in the rear and right of the bridge on the Rohrersville and Sharpsburg road; Captain Weed's 3-inch and Lieutenant Benjamin's 20-pounder batteries, General Franklin's corps and Couch's division held a position in Pleasant valley in front of Brownsville, with a strong force of the enemy in their front.

The enemy was commanded by General R. E. Lee. and their force was composed of General Jackson's, Longstreet's, D. H. Hill, Stuart, Ransom's, Jenkins', and other troops, and from information obtained by the examination of prisoners, deserters, spies, etc., previous to the battle, they were estimated to number ninety-seven thousand four hundred and forty-five men for duty, and four hundred guns. Our own force, composed of the corps of General Hooker, Sumner, Porter, Franklin, Burnside, Banks; the divisions of Couch and Pleasanton numbered eighty-seven thousand one hundred and sixty-four.

About daylight on the 16th the enemy opened a heavy fire of artillery on our guns in position, which was promptly returned; their fire being silenced for the time, but was frequently renewed during the day. Early in the morning our division moved off to the right of the Keedysville and Williamsport road, where it laid until near three o'clock in the afternoon, during which time we received sugar, coffee, and a few crackers, the roads from Frederick being so crowded with masses of infantry, cavalry and artillery, as to delay the arrival of the supply trains.

At this time our regiment numbered one hundred and seventy-one, rank and file, and four commissioned officers present for duty. Colonel McCandless, Lieutenant-colonel Woodward, and Major Neidé being absent wounded, the command devolved upon Captain Byrnes. Adjutant Cross was acting as an aid to General Seymour. Captain Connors being wounded, the command of Company A devolved on Lieutenant Ross. Captain McDonough being on recruiting service, Lieutenant Jack absent wounded, and Lieutenant Manton absent sick, that of Company B, on Sergeant Cullen. Captain Byrnes being in command of the regiment, Lieutenant Robinson absent wounded, and Lieutenant Nightingale dead, that of Company C, on Sergeant Michael Crowley; Captain Ellis having left his company, Lieutenant Curley being on recruiting service, and Lieutenant Young being absent sick, that of Company D, on Orderly Sergeant Thomas Canavan. Captain Finnie being wounded, Lieutenant Black absent sick, and Lieutenant Fletcher dead, that of Company E, on Orderly Sergeant John Taylor. Captain Reitzel and Lieutenant Rhoads being sick, that of Company G, on Lieutenant Wimpfheimer. Captain Mealey was the only officer present in Company H. Lieutenants Kennedy and Clendinning being absent wounded, and Captain Smith being wounded, Lieutenant Harvey detached to the

Signal Corps, and Lieutenant Justus being absent sick, Company K was commanded by Sergeant Thomas May. Companies C and K, jointly, were under the command of Sergeant-major Woodward.

It was near three o'clock in the afternoon, when our division, followed by Rickett's and Doubleday's, which comprised Hooker's corps, crossed the Antietam at a ford and the upper bridge, and advanced to attack and, if possible, to turn the enemy's left. Some cavalry and Cooper's battery accompanied us, and after moving about a mile, we turned off into the fields to the left of the road, near the house of D. Miller, advancing slowly in columns of divisions, ready to form to resist cavalry, which threatened our flanks and front. Soon the enemy opened, sending their round shot and shell singing in among us, to which Cooper briskly replied, while the infantry advanced, and a severe contest commenced, in which we drove the enemy from the first strip of woods over the fields to the second, the battle lasting until eight o'clock, and the Reserves resting upon their arms on the ground won from the enemy, unassisted by the other divisions of the corps. During the battle, our most estimable and gallant adjutant, Augustus T. Cross, who, at the request of General Seymour, was acting on his staff, was killed, as was also Colonel McNeil, of the "Bucktails."

During the night, we laid in support of Cooper's battery, which continued firing until after nine o'clock. Through the night, shots were continually exchanged between ours and the enemy's pickets, who laid within a short distance of each other in the second woods, and about two o'clock in the morning, the "Bucktails," who were determined the Reserves should have the honor of opening the second day's fight, as they had the first, opened a brisk fire, but they getting short of ammunition, we were sent to relieve them, arriving there just at the grey of the morning. Deploying, we crept on our bellies to our position, and opened a heavy fire upon the enemy, both parties keeping the ground and maintaining their positions. Sometime afterwards the whole of our corps came up, and the battle opened in earnest, the enemy being driven into the woods and pressed hard upon the right of our line. The contest now became obstinate, and as the troops advanced the opposition became more determined and the number of the enemy greater. General Hooker then ordered up General Mansfield's corps, which had crossed the Antietam during the night, and bivouacked about a mile in our rear. General Williams' division was deployed to the right, with its right brigade under General Crawford, right resting on the Hagerstown pike. The second division, under General Green, joining Williams' left. During the deployment, the gallant veteran Mansfield fell mortally woundea, while examining the ground in front of his troops.

The One-hundred-and-twenty-fourth Pennsylvania Volunteers were pushed across the turnpike into the woods, beyond J. Miller's house, with orders to hold the position as long as possible.

The command of this corps now devolved upon General Williams, and its line of battle was formed, and it became engaged about seven A. M., the attack being opened by Knap's and Hampton's Pennsylvania, and Cothran's New York batteries. To meet this attack, the enemy had pushed a strong column of troops into the open fields in front of the turnpike, while he occupied the woods on the west of the pike in strong force. The woods were traversed by out-cropping ledges of rock. Several hundred yards to the right and rear was a hill, which commanded the debouche of the woods, and in the fields between was a long line of stone fences, continued by breastworks or rails, which covered the enemy's infantry from our musketry. The same woods formed a screen, behind which his movements were concealed, and his batteries on the hill, and the rifle-works covered from the fire of our artillery in front.

For about two hours the battle raged with varied success, the enemy endeavoring to drive our troops into the second line of woods, and ours in turn to get possession of the line in front.

Our troops ultimately succeeded in forcing the enemy back into the woods, near the pike, General Green, with his two brigades, crossing into the woods to the left of the Dunker Church. During this conflict, General Crawford was seriously wounded and taken from the field.

General Green being much exposed, the Thirteenth New Jersey, Twenty-seventh Indiana, and the Third Maryland were sent to his support, with a section of Knap's battery.

About nine o'clock, A. M., General Sedgwick's division of General Sumner's corps arrived. On nearing the scene of action, the column was formed in three parallel lines by brigade, and moved upon the field of battle, under fire from the enemy's concealed batteries. Passing diagonally to the front across the open space and to the front of the first division of General Williams' Corps, this latter division withdrew.

Entering the woods on the west of the pike, and driving the enemy before them, the first line was met by a heavy fire of musketry and shell from the enemy's breastworks and batteries; meantime a heavy column of the enemy had succeeded in crowding back the troops of General Green's division, and appeared in rear of the left of Sedgwick's division. General Howard faced the third line to the rear, preparatory to a change of front, to meet the column advancing on the left; but this line suffered so severely from a destructive fire, both in front and on its left, which it was unable to return, gave way towards the right and rear in considerable confusion, and was soon followed by the first and second lines.

General Gorman's brigade, which constituted the first line, and one of General Dana's, soon rallied and checked the advance of the enemy on the right. The second and third lines now formed on the left of Gorman's brigade, and poured a destructive fire upon the enemy.

During Sedgwick's attack, General Sumner ordered General Williams to support him. General Gordon, with a portion of his brigade, moved forward, but when he reached the woods, the left of General Sedgwick's division had given way; and finding himself opposed to a superior force, he withdrew to the rear of the batteries, at the second line of woods. As Gordon's troops unmasked our batteries on the left, they opened with canister, and the enemy unable to withstand their deadly fire in front, and the musketry fire from the right, they were driven back with great slaughter, behind the woods and rocks beyond the turnpike.

During this assault, Generals Sedgwick and Dana were seriously wounded and taken from the field. General Howard assumed command of Sedgwick's division.

About the time of General Sedgwick's advance, General Hooker, while gallantly urging on his men, was severely wounded in the foot, and General Meade was placed in command of our corps.

Upon the repulse of Sedgwick, on our right, the battle in our front became more desperate, the woods resounding with one continuous roar of musketry, and the line of flame and smoke swaying to and fro. Already had Captain Mealey been taken from the field, severely wounded, and the gallant Lieutenant Wimpfheimer fallen. The regiment on our right had given way, the enemy were pressing us hard, forcing back our right flank and curving us into a semi-circle, but steadily our boys stood their ground, pouring into the enemy a constant fire, before which their advance withered away. General Seymour was there cheering us on, and General Hartsuff, of our corps, was wounded in our ranks, but notwithstanding the gallant efforts of the officers and heroically brave conduct of the men, we were overpowered by superior numbers and forced back. But no rout—no precipitate retreat—but steadily and in good order, the brave men delivered their fire upon the advancing foe; and though we were retiring, our flag flaunted proudly over our heads. At this time, unexpectedly, a column of the enemy suddenly opened upon us, from the right, a deafening crash of musketry, before which our little band was swept away, and breaking, we were driven over the field in confusion, but reaching a favorable position, Captain Byrnes, who had acted throughout with conspicuous bravery, rallied the men once more around the standard and reformed the regiment. Though weakened and exhausted with over six hours hard fighting, the wearied limbs and brave hearts of the men sought not repose. The Reserves had not yet been defeated, nor did they intend to be, for as long as there are brave men to stand by the colors, there is hope of victory.

The batteries of the Reserves were pushed forward in front of the first line of woods to our right, and opened a murderous fire of case-shot and canister that swept the advancing foe back. and again the Reserves charged with loud cheers over the ploughed field into the cornfield and the woods beyond, where the hardest and deadliest struggles of the day took place. Some times pressed hard, we were forced back, and at others the foe yielded to our charge. But as the battle wore on, out of the woods came sudden heavy and terrible volleys from fresh troops, that with their weight of fire bent and bore down to the ground the front, forcing back our shattered lines, that slowly and sullenly retired to the woods where our lines were formed to meet the foe, whom we again hurled back.

While the conflict was so obstinately raging in our front and on the right, General French was engaged with the enemy further to the left. His division was formed in three columns, General Max Weber's brigade in front, Colonel Dwight Morris' of raw troops next, and General Kimball's brigade last. The division advanced under a heavy artillery fire, and driving in the enemy's skirmishers, encountered their infantry at the group of houses on Roulette's farm, and drove them from their position.

While General Weber was hotly engaged with his brigade, General French ordered the brigade of Kimball to the front, and passing to the left of Weber, they drove the enemy back to near the crest of a hill, where he was encountered in greater strength in a sunken road, forming a natural rifle-pit. In a cornfield in rear of this road were also strong bodies of the enemy. As Kimball's line reached the crest of the hill, a galling fire was opened on it from the sunken road and cornfield. Here a terrible fire of musketry burst from both lines, and the battle raged with great slaughter.

The enemy attempted to turn the left of the line, but were gallantly repulsed by the One hundred and thirty-second Pennsylvania and Seventh Virginia Volunteers. Foiled in this, they assaulted the front, but were charged and driven back with severe loss and three hundred prisoners, and several stands of colors captured. They having been repulsed with severe loss on the extreme right, they now attempted to assist the attack on French's division by assailing him on his right to turn his flank, but they were met and checked by the Fourteenth Indiana and Eighth Ohio Volunteers, and by canister from Captain Tompkin's battery First Rhode Island artillery. Having been under an almost continuous fire for nearly four hours, and the ammunition nearly expended, the division now took position immediately below the crest of the heights on which they had so gallantly fought, the enemy making no attempt to regain their lost ground.

On the left of General French, General Richardson's division was hotly engaged. They advanced in line with General Meagher's brigade on the right, General Caldwell's on the left, and Colonel Brooks' in support. They moved steadily, and soon became engaged with the enemy posted to the left and in front of Roulette's house. Pressing on under a heavy fire to the crest of the hill, they found the enemy posted in a continuation of the sunken road and cornfield before referred to. Here the brave Irish brigade opened upon the enemy a terrible musketry fire. After suffering terribly in officers and men, and strewing the ground with the enemy as they drove them back, their ammunition nearly expended, and their commander, General Meagher, disabled by the fall of his horse shot under him, the brigade was ordered to give place to General Caldwell's, which advanced to a short distance in its rear. The lines were passed by Meagher's brigade breaking by company to the rear, and General Caldwell's by company to the front as steadily as on drill.

The ground over which Generals Richardson's and French's division were fighting, was very irregular, intersected by numerous ravines, hills covered with growing corn, inclosed by stone walls, behind which the enemy could advance unobserved upon any exposed point of our lines. Taking advantage of this, the enemy attempted to gain the right of Richardson's position in a cornfield near Roulette's house, where the division had become separated from that of General French's. A change of front by the Fifty Second New York and Second Delaware Volunteers of Richardson's division, and the attack made by the Fifty-third Pennsylvania volunteers sent further to the right to close this gap in the line, and the movement of the One hundred and thirty-second Pennsylvania and Seventh Virginia Volunteers of French's division, before referred to, drove the enemy from the cornfield and restored the line.

The brigade of Caldwell, with determined gallantry, pushed the enemy back opposite the left and centre of Richardson's division, but sheltered in the sunken road, they still held our forces on the right of Caldwell in check. Colonel Barlow, commanding the Sixty-first and Sixty-fourth New York regiments, seeing a favorable opportunity, advanced the regiments on the left, taking the enemy in the sunken road in flank, and compelling them to surrender, capturing over three hundred prisoners and three stands of colors. The whole brigade, with the Fifty-seventh and Sixty-sixth New York regiments, of Colonel Brooks' brigade, who had joined Caldwell's, now advanced with gallantry, driving the enemy before them in confusion into the corn-field beyond the sunken road. The left of Richardson's division was now well advanced, when the enemy, concealed by an intervening ridge, endeavored to turn its left and rear.

Colonel Cross, Fifth New Hampshire, by a change of front to the left and rear, brought his regiment facing the advancing line. Here a spirited charge arose to gain a commanding height, the opposing forces moving parallel to each other, giving and receiving fire. The Fifth gained the advantage, faced to the right and delivered its volley. The enemy staggered, but rallied and advanced desperately at a charge. Being reinforced by the Eighty-first Pennsylvania, these regiments met the advance by a counter-charge. The enemy fled, leaving many killed, wounded, and prisoners, and the colors of the Fourth North Carolina, in our hands.

Another column of the enemy, advancing under shelter of a stone wall and corn-field, pressed down on the right of the division; but Colonel Barlow again advanced the Sixty-first and Sixty-fourth New York against them, and with the attack of Kimball's brigade, of French's division, on the right, drove them from this position.

Our troops on the left of this part of the line having driven the enemy far back, they, with reinforced numbers, made a determined attack in front. To meet this, Colonel Barlow brought his two regiments to their position in line, and drove the enemy through the corn-field into the orchard beyond, under a heavy fire of musketry, and a fire of canister from two pieces of artillery in the orchard, and a battery further to the right, throwing shell and case-shot. This advance gave us possession of Piper's house, the strong point contended for by the enemy at this part of the line, it being a defensible building several hundred yards in advance of the sunken road. The infantry fighting at this point of the line now ceased. Holding Piper's house, General Richardson withdrew the line a little way to the crest of a hill, a more advantageous position. Up to this time the division was without artillery, and in the new position suffered severely from artillery fire, which it could not reply to. A section of Captain Robertson's horse battery now arived and opened, and soon after Captain Graham's battery took position on the crest of the hill, and silenced the guns in the orchard. Graham's battery, however, being smooth-bores, was unable to reach a rifled battery of the enemy, of greater range, further to the right, and was forced to retire. General Richardson was here mortally wounded.

General Hancock was placed in command of the division after the fall of General Richardson. Meagher's brigade, now commanded by Colonel Burk, having refilled their cartridge-boxes, again advanced and took position in the centre of the line. The division now formed one line of battle in close proximity to the enemy, and Colonel Morris, with the Fourteenth Connecticut and a detachment of the One-hundred-and-eighth New York, was sent by General French to reinforce them, and were placed in an interval in the line between Caldwell's and Burk's brigades. Hancock's division, though suffering severely from the enemy's artillery, was able to hold its position, but not to attack the enemy's artillery, as it was too weak to form a second line of battle, and was, by its advanced position, enfiladed by the enemy's batteries on the right.

With the exception of some minor fighting and the repulse of a heavy line of infantry by General Pleasanton with sixteen guns, the operations on this portion of the field closed.

About noon General Franklin's Corps arrived having left Crampton's Pass at six A. M. It was at first determined to hold them in reserve, but the right under Sumner and Meade being hardly pressed it was at once sent to their relief. On nearing the field, finding that battery A, Fourth United States Artillery, was hotly engaged without support, two regiments were sent to its relief. Afterwards the remaining regiments of Hancock's brigade with Captains Frank's and Cowen's batteries were also sent there. Finding the enemy still advancing, the Third brigade of Smith's division commanded by Colonel Irwin, Forty-ninth Pennsylvania Volunteers was ordered up, and drove back the advance until abreast of the Dunker Church. As the right of the brigade came opposite the woods it received a destructive fire, which checked the advance and threw the brigade somewhat into confusion. It formed again behind a rise of ground in the open space in advance of the batteries.

General French having reported to General Franklin that his ammunition was nearly expended, General Brooks, with his brigade was ordered to reinforce him. The brigade was formed on the right of General French, where they remained during the remainder of the day and night, frequently under the fire of the enemy's artillery.

The advance of General Franklin's Corps was opportune. The attack of the enemy on this position, but for the timely arrival of his Corps, must have been disastrous, had it succeeded in piercing the line between General Sedgwick's and French's divisions.

General Porter's Corps was stationed on the east side of the Antietam upon the main turnpike leading to Sharpsburg, and opposite the centre of the enemy's lines to act in case the enemy should attempt to pierce the centre and turn our rear, as well as capture or destroy our supply trains.

Towards the middle of the afternoon, General McClellan found that Sumner's, Meade's and Mansfield's Corps had met with serious losses, that several general officers had been carried from the field severely wounded, and the aspect of affairs was anything but promising. Orders were given to reinforce this portion of the line with two brigades from Porter's Corps, and to renew the attack, but General Sumner expressed the most decided opinion against another attempt that day to assault the enemy's position in front. In view of these circumstances, the different commanders were directed to hold their positions, and the orders to Porter's brigades were countermanded.

General Slocum's division replaced a portion of Sumner's troops, and batteries were placed in positions in front of the woods. The enemy opened with several heavy fires of artillery on our troops after this, but our batteries soon silenced them.

In the morning, General Pleasanton, with his cavalry division and the horse batteries, under Captains Robertson, Tidball, Gibson, and Lieutenant Haines, was ordered to cross the bridge on the Keedysville and Sharpsburg turnpike and advance towards the latter place, and support the left of General Sumner's line. The bridge being covered by a fire of artillery and sharpshooters, cavalry skirmishers were thrown out, and Captain Tidball's battery advanced by piece and drove off the enemy with canister sufficiently to establish the other batteries, which opened on the enemy with effect. The firing was kept up for about two hours, when, the enemy's fire slackening, the batteries were relieved by Randall's and Van Reed's. About three o'clock, Tidball, Robertson and Haines returned to their positions on the west of Antietam, and did good service, concentrating their fire on the column of the enemy about to attack General Hancock's position, and compelling it to find shelter behind the hills in the rear. The batteries under Pleasanton were supported by five battalions of United States infantry who acted with great gallantry.

General Burnside's Corps held the left on the line opposite the bridge on the Rohrersville and Sharpsburg road, and as it was intended the attack on the right should be supported by an attack on the left, General McClellan ordered him at eight o'clock to carry the bridge, gain possession of the heights beyond, and to advance along their crest upon Sharpsburg and its rear. After much delay, the bridge was carried about one o'clock, by a brilliant charge of the Fifty-first Pennsylvania and Fifty-first New York Volunteers. Other troops were then thrown over and the opposite bank occupied, but for some reason a halt was ordered, and it was three o'clock before the advance resumed, when they gallantly charged driving the enemy from their guns, handsomely carrying the heights and a portion of them even reaching the outskirts of Sharpsburg. By this time it was nearly dark, and strong reinforcements just then reaching the enemy from Harper's Ferry, attacked General Burnside's troops on their left flank, and forced them to retire to a lower line of hills near the bridge.

General McClellan, in his report, blames Burnside for unnecessary delay, and says: "If this important movement had been consummated two hours earlier, a position would have been secured upon the heights, from which our batteries might have enfiladed the greater part of the enemy's line, and turned their right and rear; our victory might thus have been much more decisive."

During the afternoon the Reserves were withdrawn from the woods and put in position behind the first line in an open field, giving place to fresh troops. This was necessary, as their ammunition was entirely expended and they had been upon the field for nearly twenty-four hours, and suffered severely.

Thus terminated the long and desperately fought battle of Antietam, in which for fourteen hours nearly two hundred thousand men and five hundred pieces of artillery were engaged. The position occupied by the enemy was selected by their commander, General Lee, a most experienced engineer. They were driven from it on one flank, and a lodgement was effected within it on the other. Our soldiers slept that night conquerors on the field won by their valor.*

---

* See Appendix A.

The loss of the division was six hundred and one, officers and men, and of the army twelve thousand four hundred and sixty-nine. Almost one-third more of the enemy's dead were counted and buried upon the field by our own men than we lost. This is conclusive evidence that the enemy sustained much greater loss than we.

Thirteen guns, thirty-nine colors, upwards of fifteen thousand stand of small arms, and more than six thousand prisoners were the trophies we captured.

General Meade received a contusion from a spent grape-shot, and had two horses killed under him.

Captain Byrnes and Lieutenant Ross acted with conspicuous bravery, and the conduct of the non-commissioned officers and men is deserving of all praise. All the companies with the exception of one were left without officers. Never on any field did the men display more courage, discipline and self-reliance. Not one shirked, lagged or faltered, but all seemed determined, as they expressed it, to see what they could do on their own hook. Never for one moment during both day's fight, did their lines falter or break, or show any more irregularity than is incidental to all fields, excepting upon the occasion alluded to, when they were borne down by the weight of fire.

When we broke and were driven across the field, a chicken was scared up, which displayed equal alacrity with the men in its flight to the rear, and a most animated race for life or death took place between them, but the Sergeant-major seizing a favorable opportunity threw himself upon the ground and captured the prize, which furnished a most sumptuous repast.

On the 18th the attack on the enemy was not renewed, as the troops were much exhausted by the severe and protracted battle, together with the long day and night marches which they had been subjected to during the previous three days. They were in need of rations, which could not be supplied to them until late in the day, and many of them had suffered from hunger. A large number of the heaviest and most efficient batteries had expended all their ammunition, and it was impossible to supply them until near night. The infantry were also short of ammunition. Besides this, reinforcements to the number of fourteen thousand men, and the whole Pennsylvania militia under General Reynolds were expected during the day; therefore, the day was spent in collecting the dispersed, giving rest to the fatigued, removing the wounded, burying the dead, and preparing for a renewal of the battle.

By night almost all the wounded were collected in and around the different farm houses and buildings, where equal attention and kindness was shown to our own and the enemy's. Rude tables were put up, on which the operations were performed, and from which dripped the blood, while near by them were the amputated arms and legs. The wounded laid near these gazing at the sight, and patiently awaiting their turn to be lifted upon the tables, around which the surgeons stood with their sleeves rolled up, performing their operations with perfect coolness and seeming indifference. If a surgeon was to permit the feelings of sympathy to enter his heart, it might unnerve him and prove fatal to the poor sufferer. Where there are thousands of cases which require immediate attention, and which it will take the limited number of surgeons several days to attend to, the individual is overlooked for the good of the mass. When the probabilities are strongly against saving a man, he is not operated upon, but made as easy as circumstances will admit, and the same principle is applied to the saving or losing of a limb. This is an imperative necessity that the exigency of the occasion requires. After the operations were got through with, the patients were laid on straw or hay in the buildings or on the grass in rows, and over them were stretched blankets to protect them from the rays of the sun. Water, food, and stimulants were distributed to them by the nurses, and the stretcher-men removed and buried those that died.

Large numbers of farmers of Maryland and Pennsylvania visited the hospitals, bringing with them bread, cakes, pies, cooked poultry, milk, etc., which they distributed to the wounded, and every one of them appeared proud to get a soldier to take home with him to nurse.

Adjutant Cross and Lieutenant Wimpfheimer were buried in the village church yard, at Keedysville. The Adjutant was subsequently removed to Philadelphia, and over Wimpfheimer was placed a handsome stone.

In the latter part of the day, as the enemy were passing troops from the Virginia shore, our division was ordered into line, it being presumed they meditated some offensive movement, but during the night, they appeared to have altered their intentions, and abandoning their position retreated across the river, accomplishing the movement before daylight.

When our cavalry advance reached the river early on the morning of the 19th, it was discovered that nearly all the enemy's forces had crossed into Virginia during the night, their rear escaping under cover of eight batteries, placed in strong positions upon the elevated bluffs on the opposite bank. The whole army was moved forward to occupy a new position nearer the river, our division marching early in the morning to the front and right, about three miles, crossing the Hagerstown and Sharpsburg turnpike, and halting near the Potomac, above Sharpsburgh.

Our route took us over and along the enemy's line of battle, and we found the fields and woods literally covered with their dead. At one point, where they had crossed the fields and pike obliquely, and where they must have received a terrific fire of musketry, the formation of their lines was distinctly marked by their dead, who were stretched in long rows, showing at the time they received the fire, they were well dressed. The effect of this fire must have been crushing, none of their dead laying in front of their line, though to the rear, the ground was covered with them.

General Griffin, with a detachment from his own and Barnes's brigade, of the Fifth Corps, was ordered to cross the river at dark, and carry the enemy's batteries, which was gallantly done under a heavy fire; several guns, caisons, etc., being taken, and their support driven back half a mile.

From information obtained during the progress of this affair, it was conjectured that the mass of the enemy had retreated on the Charlestown and Martinsburg road, towards Winchester. To verify this, and to ascertain how far the enemy had retired, General Porter was authorized to send out on the morning of the 20th, a reconnoitring party in great force. This detachment crossed the river, and advanced about a mile, when it was ambushed by a large body of the enemy lying in the woods, and driven back across the river with considerable loss, which showed that the enemy was still in force on the Virginia side of the Potomac, prepared to resist our further advance. It was in this affair that the One Hundred and Eighteenth Pennsylvania volunteers, ("Corn Exchange Regiment,") was so badly cut up.

It having been reported that the enemy, under General Stuart, numbering four thousand cavalry, six guns, and ten thousand infantry, had crossed the Potomac to the Maryland side, at Williamsport, General McClellan sent Couch, with his division and a part of Pleasanton's cavalry, and with Franklin's Corps within supporting distance, to endeavor to capture them. General Couch made a prompt and rapid march to Williamsport, and attacked the enemy vigorously, but they made their escape across the river.

On the 20th General Williams' corps occupied Maryland Heights, and on the 22d General Sumner took possession of Harper's Ferry.

The main body of the enemy was at this time concentrated near Martinsburg and Bunker Hill, and occupied itself in drafting and coercing every able-bodied citizen into the ranks, forcibly taking their property, where it was not voluntarily offered, burning bridges and destroying railroads.

General McClellan not feeling it prudent to cross the river in pursuit of the enemy, stationed his army along the north bank in position to cover and guard the fords, and commenced the work of reorganizing, re-equipping and drilling.

On the 1st of October His Excellency the President visited the army and remained several days, during which he went through the different encampments, reviewed the troops, visited the hospitals, and went over the battle-fields of South Mountain and Antietam.

On the 10th, General Stuart crossed the upper Potomac at McCoy's Ferry, with two thousand cavalry and a battery of horse-artillery, on a raid into Maryland and Pennsylvania, and although immediate disposition of troops were made to intercept him, from the orders not being carried out, he was enabled to escape, recrossing the river at White's Ford below the Monocacy.

CHAPTER XX.

CROSSING THE POTOMAC. MARCH THROUGH VIRGINIA. WARRENTON. GENERAL McCLELLAN SUPERCEDED. REMOVAL OF GENERAL FITZ JOHN PORTER. OUR VIRGINIA FRIENDS. BOMBARDMENT OF FREDERICKSBURG. LAYING PONTOONS.

ON the 6th General McClellan received orders to "cross the Potomac, and give battle to the enemy, or drive him south." The order stated, that if he crossed between the enemy and Washington, he could be reinforced to the extent of thirty thousand men; but if he moved up the valley of the Shenandoah, not more than twelve or fifteen thousand could be sent to him. It was not, however, until the 26th, that the advance guard of the army crossed the Potomac. On that day, two divisions of the Ninth corps, and Pleasanton's brigade of cavalry, crossed at Berlin. The First, Sixth and Ninth corps, the cavalry, and the reserve artillery, also crossed there between the 26th of October and the 2d of November. The Second and Fifth corps crossed at Harper's Ferry, between the 29th of October and the 1st of November.

The plan of campaign adopted by General McClellan was to move the army, well in hand, parallel to the Blue Ridge, taking Warrenton as the point of direction for the main army; seizing each pass on the Blue Ridge by detachments, as we approached it, and guarding them after we had passed, as long as they would enable the enemy to trouble our connections with the Potomac.

Upon the death of Adjutant Cross, Lieutenant John J. Ross, who was the only officer with the regiment, excepting Captain Byrnes, was appointed Acting Adjutant until the return of Sergeant-Major E. M. Woodward, who had been promoted Adjutant. About the same time, Colonel McCandless, with a number of officers and men, who had recovered from their wounds, also returned.

Our regiment broke camp on the 26th, and marched, during a heavy rain-storm, to Berlin, which we reached on the 27th, the rain continuing all night. On the 29th, we crossed the river on the pontoons, and encamped near Lovettsville, Virginia, where we were inspected by General Seymour, and mustered for pay on the 31st.

On the first of November, we marched through Waterford, and encamped about a mile from Hamilton, where we laid the next day. While here, Lieutenant H. P. Kennedy, Sergeant James McCormick and Corporal A. McK. Storrie were detailed to proceed to Harrisburg to bring on drafted men, which they did not get.

The next day, at noon, the division marched, and before dark we passed through Philomont and bivouacked about a mile beyond, near Snicker's Gap, on a field where there had been an artillery skirmish in the morning, the ground being strewed with dead horses shells, etc. The next morning early, we moved about a mile to Uniontown, and halted there until three P. M., when we marched on, passing Franklin's corps and Couch's division at their bivouacs, and laid for the night on a high table land. That night, a number of the officers and men of the One-hundred and-nineteenth, Colonel Ellmaker's, and the Twenty-third, Birney's old regiment, visited us, all being from Philadelphia.

The next morning, (the 5th,) we moved at seven o'clock, in a southeasterly direction, fording the Panther-skin, a deep, broad creek, and, passing through Middleburg, halted on its confines for dinner. In the town, we found quite a large number of wounded "Greybacks" from Bull Run, with whom the boys conversed freely. At four in the afternoon, we took up our march again, moving slowly and tediously, halting continually, sometimes every few hundred yards, as there was a long wagon-train ahead of us, and the roads were exceedingly bad. At last, long after dark, we passed through White Plains, on the Manassas Gap Railroad, and moving two miles beyond, were halted, and then countermarched nearly a mile and put into a heavy woods to bivouac. Hardly had the boys built their fires, before orders came for our regiment to go on picket. It was then about midnight, and all were weary, for we had been fourteen hours marching sixteen miles, but as orders are given to be obeyed, we consoled ourselves with the thought, that "there is no rest for the wicked," and moved off about a mile to the front, and spent the balance of the night watching for the foe, who did not appear.

The next morning we marched into camp, and immediately took our position in the line, and moved off towards Warrenton, the infantry keeping on the fields to leave the road clear for the artillery. When we arrived within three miles of the town, at the gap between Water and Pig-Nut Mountains, through which the road passed, our regiment being in advance, we were deployed as skirmishers, General Reynolds supposing the enemy would make some show of resistance there. Companies A, B, and H, under the command of Captain McDonough, were deployed to the right of the road to feel the woods for the enemy; and companies D, E and G, under Major Neidé, to the left for the same purpose, the reserve, consisting of C and K, following close in the rear. The whole, under McCandless, advanced rapidly through the dense underbrush over the crest of the mountains, which being found clear of the enemy, they reunited beyond the Gap, our regiment then advancing upon the road, with the "Bucktails" on our right and the First on our left, until we came to the clear ground, when the flanking regiments filed into the road, and we entered the town of Warrenton at four P. M. Of course, our entrance was not received by the inhabitants with the joy that the entrance of their friends, the "Greybacks," would have been, the female portion of the community remaining in their houses, and those of the men who showed themselves, looking on in silence. Our eyes, however, were gladdened by the sight of sundry Confederates who were captured, and who, perhaps, remained behind for that purpose. Moving on about a mile, we encamped near the ground we occupied in August last, a few days preceding the second battle of Bull Run.

Warrenton, like all other towns we occupied, we found completely stripped of everything in the way of food, clothing, etc.: the chivalry having completely cleaned it out. The stores were all closed for want of goods, and business of all kinds was suspended. We found it impossible to obtain bread, or any other article of food, at any price, and although our occupation proved a great relief to the inhabitants, and those of the surrounding country, in obtaining supplies, we were not welcomed.

With the exception of a violent snow-storm, nothing of note occurred while we laid at this camp, until the morning of the 10th, when we were called out to bid farewell to General McClellan, the then love and idol of the Army of the Potomac, who had been relieved of his command, and superceded by General Burnside. His departure from the army was a scene never to be forgotten; the deafening shouts of the columns he had so often led to honor; the caps tossed high in the air; the tears, those true tests of affection, stealing their courses down the weather-beaten cheeks of the veterans of the Peninsula, truly told the deep hold he had upon the hearts of the men. The officers of some of the regiments sent in their resignations in a body, but their generals returned them, with a gentle admonition.

General Fitz John Porter soon after was relieved of his command and was subsequently dishonourably dismissed the service, by sentence of a court-martial, for his conduct at Bull Run, and forever prohibited from occupying any position of honor or trust under the Government, but we are not aware of there being any particular amount of "weeping and wailing and gnashing of teeth" at the event.

It is not clearly known to the author what plan of campaign General McClellan would have pursued if he had continued in command of the army, though it is certain he at one time contemplated an advance on Richmond, via Culpeper and Gordonsville. It is also known that he gave preparatory orders for the rebuilding of the wharves and the Aquia Creek Railroad, which clearly indicated an advance via Fredericksburg.

The plan of operations proposed by General Burnside was to throw a considerable body of troops across the river at Rappahannock Station, and make a feint as if to advance by way of Culpeper, and then by a rapid movement down the north bank of the Rappahannock to cross the river, seize and fortify the heights in the rear of Fredericksburg, and advance on Richmond, holding the railroad as his line of communication. This plan was approved by the authorities at Washington and carried out to a certain extent by General Burnside.

At eleven o'clock on the morning of the 11th, our

division moved in a southwesterly course to near Fayetteville, about two miles from the Rappahannock, where we arrived a little before dark and bivouacked among some scrub oaks.

The next day our regiment went on picket for twenty-four hours, and had a very pleasant time.

On the 16th, General Seymour, at his own request, was relieved of the command of our brigade, his health not permitting him to undertake a winter campaign. The general was a gallant and accomplished officer, a high strung and honorable gentleman, and as he had served with us in every battle up to Antietam, we parted from him with regret.

Colonel William Sinclair, Sixth Reserves, superceded him in command of our brigade.

At eight o'clock on the morning of the 17th, during a drizzling rain, we took up our march, pursuing a general course down the river, passing by Bealton Station, Morrisville, the Gold mines, and Grove Churches. About dark, and it soon became intensely dark, we were taken into a dense woods to bivouac, but such was the thick growth of underbrush it was found impossible for the men to advance, and we were "about faced" and marched out again, and ordered to seek a position somewhere in the neighborhood. The colonel selected a hill near the head-quarters of General Meade, where we slept soundly through the rain. It is the duty of the staff officer, who selects the bivouac ground to examine it and see if it is suitable, which was not done in this instance.

The next morning we moved at nine o'clock along the fields to Hartwood, where we took the road to Stafford Court House. About noon we were forced to halt, to repair the road, after which we moved on, crossing Potomac creek, and ascending an almost perpendicular hill, filled with deep ruts and large boulders, which required the united teams of several guns to haul one piece up it. The men toiled on manfully through the deep mud, for it had been raining all day. Towards dark we bivouacked on the banks of Occakeek creek, three miles from the court house.

That day the Fifth Reserves was detached from our brigade, and put into the Third, which gave their colonel, J. W. Fisher, the command of the brigade. Considerable cannonading was heard through the day, in the direction of the upper fords of the Rappahannock.

We remained in this camp until the 22d, during which time it rained constantly, and heavy details were made from the regiment for fatigue duty, to corduroy roads. To prevent depredations from being committed on private property, orders were issued to have hourly roll calls in each regiment.

On the morning above-mentioned we moved at eight through the fields bordering on the Telegraph road, passing through Stafford Court House to Brooks Station, on the Aquia creek and Frederickburg Railroad, where we arrived about noon and encamped on the brow of a hill overlooking an extensive meadow. Here we found the remains of the enemy's huts in which they spent the previous winter. The next day our sutler arrived with a load of goods, which were soon disposed of to the boys, who were particularly in need of tobacco.

On the 25th Major Horace Neidé resigned on account of disability from wounds received at the battle of Glendale.

On the 1st of December Major Pomeroy arrived and paid our regiment off, four months being due them.

While we laid here we received a full supply of clothing, some of the men being almost barefooted and without blankets, and many of them in need of stockings, under-clothing and great coats. Our rations were also made full and liberal, and the men appeared in most excellent spirits.

Our regiment went on picket once a week, and although in pleasant weather it is preferable to laying in camp, it is far from being so in winter, particularly during a rain or snow storm. Upon one occasion we were notified the line was to be changed, and the regiments were formed soon after daybreak and an aid-de-camp to General Meade came to conduct us. A snow of six inches had fallen through the night, which made our marching through the heavily ladened pines any thing but agreeable, but after plodding on for a couple of miles we reached the left of the new line and commenced dropping out the companies and regiments in their position. The line was about three miles long, and when we reached the right of it, where our regiment was stationed, we found ourselves about a half mile from camp. It is unnecessary to observe that the aid received many blessings upon his head of a questionable character.

A diagram of the line was given to an officer to establish the new line by,. who, after consultation with the proprietor of the property, proceeded to do so, being assured that there was but one road through the plantation. After the pickets were posted, however, he was dissatisfied with the line as its right rested on no natural obstruction. Finding no further information could be obtained at the house, he proceeded to examine the woods, and following what at first was supposed to be a ravine, in a half mile Aquia creek was found. The cause of the proprietor's deception was very apparent, as a small barn, several stacks of hay, a number of cows, calves, and chickens were found in this out-of-the-way place, and a large fishing house was located on the creek. The line was immediately changed, to the infinite disgust of our friend, who of course, aside from his own interest, would like to have had it defective. It is unnecessary to observe that no account of stock was taken upon our arrival or departure.

The field and staff of our regiment and the Eighth, made Mr. S——'s house headquarters, where, in despite of circumstances, they were soon on most sociable terms with the family. This is a matter most easily accomplished if rightly managed; all that is necessary being to show a due respect to their feelings and sentiments, and to get the right side of the old lady. Before we had been in the house long, some of the officers were busily engaged in assisting in the household affairs, cutting wood, cleaning the clock, white-washing the parlor chimney, and chasing the sheep back into the pen. In fact we made ourselves at home and generally useful, and only one incident occurred to mar our pleasure, and that was, at precisely eight o'clock, P. M., the old gentleman bid us good-night, and with his family retired. This was equally annoying to the young ladies as it was to us, and was a serious evil that required remedying. Many were the plans of operations devised during the ensuing week, but our picket turn came before any was matured. To turn the clock back was a stale trick that probably the old gentleman had had played upon him before, and something new must be devised. But "fortune favors the brave" and luckily the old gentleman was slightly indisposed. Of course he applied to our most estimable surgeon for relief, and then it was that a bright idea entered the doctor's head. After due examination a couple of opium pills were administered, with a good glass of old Cognac to rinse them down. About seven o'clock the old gentleman commenced nodding, and soon afterwards showed decided symptoms of drowsiness, and every few minutes rallying himself he would inquire the time, and fearing we reported wrongly he got up frequently and examined the clock himself. He then tried to walk the floor, but all to no purpose, and at last with eyes half closed and unable hardly to speak, he retired much to the satisfaction of all.

Mr. S—— had three daughters, the oldest possessing an excellent education and most fascinating manners, she being the lady of the family, and the others were almost her reverse, though all possessed honest and warm hearts. They told us frankly they were secessionists at heart, and that they had two brothers in the Confederate army, but situated as they were, they had no objection to entertaining Union officers whose duty placed them upon their property. They conversed freely about the war, sung "My Maryland," "The Bonny Blue Flag," "Dixie," and other Confederate songs for us. The mother showed us many times the daguerreotype of her darling "Charley," a boy of sixteen, who belonged to the Forty-seventh Virginia infantry, whom we promised, if we caught, to spank and send home to her.

We remained at Brooks' Station until December the 8th, when we struck tents and marched at six o'clock in the morning; the weather being clear and cold, and the roads so hardly frozen that the artillery and trains did not cut them up much, but the horses being smooth-shod, slipped continually, and were much worried in their march of eight miles, which the infantry accomplished by noon. Our encampment was in a meadow not far from White Oak Church. While we laid here all the detailed men were ordered into the ranks and sixty rounds of cartridges supplied to each man.

THE BOMBARDMENT OF FREDERICKSBURG, DECEMBER 11TH.—At three o'clock on the morning of the 11th, our bugles sounded the reveille, awaking the boys from their slumbers on the hard frozen ground, and soon the valleys and hills for miles around were lit up by innumerable fires, around which they gathered to prepare their coffee. In half an hour we took up our march, the bright stars in the blue vault of heaven lighting us on our way, and, as the columns defiled through the gorges and woods, the steady tramp of men alone disturbed the death-like stillness of the morning. Soon the booming of heavy guns in front announced that the ball had opened, and moving on to within a mile of the river we halted, loaded, and stacked arms in a piece of heavy pine woods, where we laid for the day and night.

In the mean time the roar of artillery had become incessant along the river bank in our front, and the men clustering on the neighboring hills had a fine view of the bombardment of Fredericksburg, which had commenced in earnest. The engineers had attempted to lay six pontoon bridges, four opposite the city and two about four miles below, but they had not got more than two-thirds of the distance laid before they were driven off by the enemy's sharpshooters posted in the houses of the town. To dislodge these, one hundred and forty-three guns were put into position, the larger portion of which opened upon the town. The sight was a magnificent but sad one, and just before dark it became grand in the extreme. The town was on fire in several places, the flames and smoke ascending high into the heavens, while shells were seen bursting in almost every quarter. During this time the enemy's sharpshooters kept up a vigorous fire upon the cannoneers and officers who lined the bank, their bullets at that long range whizzing wickedly by. Finding it impossible to drive the sharpshooters away with artillery, the pontoon boats were filled with infantry and run quickly across the river under a heavy fire, and landing, the men rushed up into the streets and houses and drove the enemy away, killing, wounding, and taking many prisoners. In fifteen minutes after the detachment landed, our men began building the bridges, and in half an hour more they were completed.

When the boats first went over, Joseph Cline, a boy of sixteen, belonging to Company C, being where they started from, could not resist the temptation and went over with them, capturing a Mississippi rifle and accoutrements from a "Grayback" he killed.

CHAPTER XXI.

BATTLE OF FREDERICKSBURG. LOSS OF OUR ARMY. INCIDENTS. CAUSES OF THE DEFEAT. RE-CROSS THE RAPPAHANNOCK.

THE BATTLE OF FREDERICKSBURG, DECEMBER 13TH.—Early on the 12th, we marched down to the lower pontoons, and at eleven A. M., crossed, halted and formed in line of battle on the bottom land beneath the elevated plain. Here the men commenced making coffee and eating dinner, as no one could tell when they would have an opportunity to build fires again. While they were thus engaged and every one was expecting in a short time to go into battle, four young boys were quietly seated, playing cards upon a blanket. For two of them it was their last game. Soon after we were moved up on the plateau, and the whole army was formed into line of battle, with the artillery and cavalry all posted. It was one of the most magnificent sights the eyes of man ever rested upon.

Some slight picket skirmishing took place in our front, and on the right, the enemy opened with artillery, but soon retired. The "Bucktails" were ordered to the extreme left for picket duty, and our regiment sent to occupy the buildings and out-houses at Smithfield, and to hold the bridge across Deep run, near where it emptied into the river The main building was Dr. Thomas Platt's large brick house, which, being unoccupied, we entered through a window, and found it very handsomely furnished. Around this building the men were posted, and it was occupied by us during the night. Upon our arrival, Colonel McCandless caused the arrest of the overseer and two other white men, and sent them to General Meade's head-quarters, who caused them to be detained until the battle was over. With the exception of the exchange of a few shots every thing passed quietly through the night.

The field upon which the battle of Fredericksburg was fought, consisted of a plateau, extending from the bluffs of the river to a range of heavily-wooded heights, commencing on the Rappahannock, above and in the rear of Fredericksburg, and extending to the valley of Massaponax, a distance of between four and five miles, its greatest breadth being two miles. On this plateau was drawn up the Union army, Major-general E. V. Sumner, commanding the right grand division, Major-general Joseph Hooker commanding the centre grand division, and Major-general William B. Franklin commanding the left grand division.

Early on the morning of the 13th, the enemy threw out foot and mounted skirmishers, on our left, and Colonel McCandless ordered Companies B, Captain McDonough, and H, Captain Mealey, to the support of the "Bucktails," and it soon after becoming evident that the enemy meditated an attack upon that point, the balance of the regiment was moved up. Soon after the remainder of the Pennsylvania Reserves, under General Meade, moved forward, and Doubleday's division passing to our left, we advanced and formed the first line of battle with Gibbons' division on our right. Crossing the Bowling Green road, we advanced to within about one thousand yards of the base of the mountain and laid down on the crest of the field, behind the batteries we were to support.

Our division formation was, the First brigade in line of battle, with the Sixth regiment deployed as skirmishers; the Second brigade in rear of the First, three hundred paces: the Third brigade by the flank, its right flank being a few yards to the rear of the First brigade, having the Ninth regiment deployed on its flanks as skirmishers and flankers; the batteries between the First and Second brigades.

This disposition had scarcely been made, when the enemy opened a brisk fire from a battery posted on the Bowling Green road, the shot from which took the division from the left and rear, As there were indications of an attack from that quarter, the Third brigade was faced to the left, thus forming, with the First, two sides of a square. Simpson's battery was advanced to the front and left of the Third brigade, and Cooper's and Ransom's batteries moved to the knoll on the left of the First brigade. These batteries immediately opened on the enemy's battery, and, in conjunction with some of Doubleday's batteries in our rear, on the other side of the Bowling Green road, after some twenty minutes' firing, silenced and compelled the withdrawal of the guns.

During this artillery duel, the enemy advanced a body of sharpshooters along the Bowling Green road, under cover of the hedges and trees at the roadside. General Jackson, commanding the Third brigade, promptly sent out two companies of marksmen from his brigade, who drove the enemy back, and no further demonstrations were made on our left and rear.

During this time a dense fog, which had hung over the field, was dispelled by the rays of the sun, and revealed to the enemy our magnificent lines drawn up in battle array. As our division had been chosen by General Reynolds, who commanded our corps, to storm the heights, Ransom's battery was moved to the right and front of the First brigade, and Amsden's battery was posted on the right of Cooper's, and the Third brigade changed front, and formed in line of battle on the left of the First brigade, its left extending so as to be nearly opposite to the end of the ridge to be attacked. The formation was barely executed before the enemy opened a sharp fire from a battery posted on the heights to our extreme left. Cooper's, Amsden's and Ransom's batteries were immediately turned on it, and, after about thirty minutes rapid firing, the enemy abandoned the guns, having had two of his limbers or caissons blown up, the explosions from which were plainly visible.

It was now twelve o'clock, M., and we had been laying under a terrific fire of round shot and shell for over three hours, which plowed up the earth in deep furrows, or went howling and bursting over our heads, filling the air with iron hail and sulphur. Though this is the most trying position soldiers can be placed in, there is little danger from it, not a man of our regiment being hurt, though the flagstaff was cut in two. But we were tired of lying still and being shot at without returning the fire, and when the order came for us to advance, it was received with joy by all. Upon the explosion of the caissons, the order to advance was given and received with loud cheers, the First brigade advancing over the field into the woods, driving the enemy before them. Having passed through a severe flanking fire from a rifle pit, which lined the base of the woods and mountains, we crossed the Richmond and Fredericksburg Railroad and drove the enemy from behind the embankments, and then making a half wheel to the left, gained the rear of the pit, and poured into its occupants a most destructive fire, by which they were slaughtered like sheep. Many of them attempted to escape by running the gauntlet in front of our regiment, they becoming perfectly wild with fright, not heeding our calls to halt, but with their arms up to shield their heads, some of them staggered to and fro up the hill, within a few yards of us, meeting certain death. The balance of our brigade being on our right, and a heavy fire being received from that direction they obliqued over to that side, and our regiment pushed on to the front.

In the mean time, about one company of scattered men were pouring into the rifle-pit, at the distance of fifty yards, a murderous fire, to which no response was given, but unfortunately the Seventh Reserve were in the field in front of the pit, and pouring into it a heavy fire, which harmed not the foe, but was received by our men, who in the excitement of the battle supposed the shots came from the pit. It was therefore almost impossible to stop the fire of our boys, until at last the adjutant cased his sword, and taking off his cap advanced between the two lines, and asked the enemy if "they wished to fight or surrender." "We will surrender, if you will let us," was the reply. This stopped the fire of our regiment. The adjutant not wishing to weaken his own regiment by sending men with them to the rear, and to prevent treachery from the enemy, took several of them with him, and advancing in front of the rifle-pit, succeeded in stopping the fire of the Seventh, upon which he got the rest of the prisoners, numbering over three hundred, out, and sent them over to the Seventh.* At least one hundred men laid dead or wounded in the pit and immediately in its rear. When the men left the pit to go into our lines, from their dirty and ragged appearance, they resembled the emptying of an almshouse more than any thing else, but under these soiled and torn jackets, there were many brave hearts, fighting for what they believed a holy and just cause. They were the Nineteenth Georgia infantry. Our regiment numbered but one hundred and ninety-five muskets.

In the meantime our brigade pressed vigorously on, and continued forcing the enemy back until the crest of the heights was crowned, we crossing the main road that runs along there, breaking down a fence and entering the open ground or plateau, across which we swept, passing rows of the enemy's muskets stacked, taking them by utter surprise and reaching their reserve and getting within sight of their ambulances. So vigorous and sudden was the attack, that the enemy in some instances had not time to get under arms before we were upon them. At this point we were assailed by a very severe fire from a large force in front, and a battery opened upon us from the right, completely enfilading us, and a few moments afterwards we received a heavy fire

---

* In the official report of General Meade of the battle, doubtlessly by mistake, the Seventh regiment is wrongfully credited with the capture of the rifle-pits, prisoners, and a standard.

on our left flank. After holding the ground here for a considerable time under these withering fires, and finding no support was coming to us, we were compelled to fall back to the railroad.

The second brigade, which advanced in our rear, after reaching the railroad, received so severe a fire on their right flank that the Fourth regiment halted, formed and faced to the right, to repel this attack. The other regiments, in passing through the woods, being assailed from the left, inclining in that direction and ascended the heights, the Third regiment going up as the One-hundred and twenty-first, then attached to our brigade, was retiring. The Third continued to advance until they met the balance of our brigade, when all retired together. The Seventh engaged the enemy on the left, and continued to advance until they encountered the enemy's reinforcements, when they were driven back.

The Third brigade had not advanced over one hundred yards when the battery on the heights on its left was remanned, and poured a destructive fire into its ranks. General Jackson attempted to outflank the battery on the right, and succeeded so far that some of the regiments advanced across the railroad, and ascended the heights in their front, but here the gallant Jackson was killed, and so severe a fire of both artillery and infantry was opened upon them, that they were compelled to withdraw.

Upon our reaching the open ground General Meade requested Colonel McCandless, who was now in command of our brigade, as Colonel Sinclair had been severely wounded, to rally the men. Our flag and that of another regiment was brought to the front, and we partially reformed and maintained our ground for some twenty minutes, but such was the severity of the artillery and infantry fire concentrated upon us, we were again forced to retire. Moving on across the field we reached our batteries, behind which we found General Birney's troops. The enemy did not follow us but a short distance from the woods, when they retired to their original position.

General Gibbons, whose division laid on our right, ordered his First brigade forward when he saw us advancing. Finding they faltered, he shortly afterwards ordered up the Second brigade, but such was the severity of the fire he could not get them to charge. He then ordered the Third brigade to form in column on the right of his line, and they went in on the bayonet and advanced as far as the railroad, the enemy's outer line, at the base of the heights, but this was not until we were being driven back by the concentrated force of the enemy on our front and flanks.

General Meade stated, prior to the assault, that he could take the heights, but could not hold them without support, which he fully expected. He sent three different times to General Birney by three staff officers, twice requesting him to advance to his support, and the third time ordering him to advance, and then he came up. To the first request he answered, he was under the orders of General Reynolds, and could not move without his orders. When he received the order to advance he sent four regiments under General Hobart Ward, who arrived just as we had retired from the woods, and they, with a portion of the Reserves and Gibbons' division, prevented the enemy from advancing beyond the edge of the woods.

General Birney, in his testimony before the "Committee on the Conduct of the War," states that he only received one message from General Meade requesting support; that the enemy charged within fifty yards of his guns; that General Ward, with his four regiments, advanced beyond where the Reserves had; that his command was *immediately* in the rear of General Meade's during the attack, and that he was requested to try and stop the *rout*, and deployed two regiment for that purpose, but the fugitives broke through his lines. These statements would not be noticed if they were not in so direct variance with those of General Meade and other officers, and with what is known to be the facts by the majority of the officers and men of our division who were present upon the field.

Birney ordered to stop the fugitive "Pennsylvania Reserves" from running!!! No one was ever ordered to do that, for when they retired no troops ever went in after them!

General Franklin, who commanded the left grand division, received orders from General Burnside "to seize, if possible the heights near Captain Hamilton's, on this side of the Massaponax, taking care to keep it well supported and its line of retreat open." "Holding these heights (on the right of our line), with the heights near Captain Hamilton's, will, I hope, compel the enemy to evacuate the whole ridge between these points." The troops under his command to accomplish this, were his own grand division numbering forty thousand men, and two divisions from Hooker's grand division under the command of General Stoneman, numbering from fifteen to twenty thousand men, making a grand total of from fifty-five to sixty thousand men. He also had twenty-three batteries, one hundred and sixteen guns, besides sixty one guns, some of them of very large calibre, stationed on the north bank of the river to protect the bridges. A portion of these guns under Captain De Russy, had obtained complete control of the Massaponax, from its mouth up to the position occupied by the enemy. With all this force at his disposal, General Franklin saw proper to order the attack to be made by two divisions, the Reserves numbering four thousand five hundred, and Gibbon's division something over five thousand men, in all at the outside ten thousand men. This was the force it was contemplated to make the attack with, though our own division was in reality the only one that crossed the railroad, and we reached a point almost three-quarters of a mile beyond. General Franklin deemed it necessary to keep between forty-five and fifty thousand infantry and a large number of guns to hold the bridges, that were two miles from the enemy, when twenty thousand men would have been amply sufficient, and if the heights had been held no infantry whatever would have been required for the purpose.

But the General in his testimony before the "Committee" states, "I never dreamed that this was considered as a strong attack at all until since the battle took place. At that time I had no idea that it was the main attack, but supposed it was an armed observation to ascertain where the enemy was." "That night," the General continues, "General Burnside sent for me, and I supposed his object in sending for me was to tell me what kind of attack was to come off the next day." It is rather surprising that General Franklin with all his known and admitted ability, should have fought through the memorable battle of Fredericksburg without "dreaming" that anything more than "an armed reconnoissance" had taken place. He was subsequently suspended from his command for not being a better dreamer.

The position held by the Confederates, and which our division attacked, was very faulty, as shown by our own maps afterwards, and the one captured from General Jackson. Jackson was thrown down on our left much too far, and if General Meade had received sufficient support to have enabled him to have held his position, it is believed that a portion of Jackson's forces and six or seven batteries could never have retired. And it is the unanimous opinion of the officers of the army, that being in the rear of the enemy's left, they would have been so shaken on the ridge, that the position in front could have been easily stormed and carried.

But the crown of victory was snatched from the brow of the Reserves.

While these operations were transpiring on the extreme left, the right was busily engaged, but with less success. General Sumner having received orders to storm the enemy's works on the extreme right immediately in the rear of Fredericksburg, selected the corps of Generals French and Hancock for that purpose. The works to be taken consisted of three tiers, the first an embanked stone wall, four or five hundred yards long, behind which infantry were posted, and with artillery enfilading it. The next tier was a more formidable row of fortifications, situated one mile in the rear on a higher position still. Between these were large masses of infantry. In the rear of this were other fortifications on still higher positions. The first line of works was repeatedly assaulted, but in spite of all the efforts of the officers our men were driven back. The enemy held their fire until our troops arrived close up to the wall when they rose up and poured into them a fearful volley, their artillery enfilading the column at the same time on both sides. No troops could stand such a fire as they received.

At two P. M., General Hooker was ordered to assault the same position and after trying to dissuade General Burnside from making the attack, he brought up all his available batteries, with a view to break away the barriers by the use of artillery. With these he continued to play with great vigor until sunset upon one point, but with no apparent effect upon the enemy or their works. About this time General Humphrey's division was ordered to form in column of assault. The men took off their knapsacks, overcoats and haversacks, as all troops do upon such occasions, and at the word "Forward," they moved up to the works with empty muskets and with great impetuosity. The head of the column arrived within fifteen or twenty yards of the wall, when they were hurled back as quickly as they advanced, leaving one thousand seven hundred and sixty of their number out of about four thousand upon the field. The whole of the advance and retiring did not occupy fifteen minutes, and they probably did not kill a man.

In addition to the musketry fire that the men were exposed to, the crest of the hills surrounding Fredericksburg form almost a semi-circle, and these were filled with artillery, and the focus was the column that moved up to this assault, and it was within good canister range. This was the favorite point of assault of General Burnside, and he persisted in butting against it all day long.

More or less artillery fighting was kept up all along the line through the day.

After remaining behind the batteries for some time our division was marched to the ground occupied the night before, where it was held in reserve.

The loss of the army during the day was:

Killed,		1,152
Wounded,		9,101
Missing,		3,234
Total,		13,487
Treated in Hospital,	1,630	
Killed,	1,152	
Total,	2,782	

There is little doubt that the aggregate of cases returned as treated in hospital and the returns of killed will very nearly cover the whole amount of disabling casualties occurring at the battle.

The return of killed may be too small, but the amount returned as treated in hospital is nearly sufficiently liberal to compensate for any such deficiency.

The loss of the First Corps was:*

FIRST DIVISION,—GENERAL A. DOUBLEDAY.

Officers,	12
Men,	199
Total,	211

* Taken from the official report of Major-general John F. Reynolds commanding First Army Corps.

SECOND DIVISION,—GENERAL JOHN GIBBON.

Officers,	76
Men,	1,180
Total,	1,256

THIRD DIVISION,—GENERAL GEORGE G. MEADE.

Killed.

Officers,	13
Men,	158
Total,	171

Wounded.

Officers,	52
Men,	1,150
Total,	1,202

Missing.

Officers,	12
Men,	457
Total,	469

Aggregate.

Officers,	77
Men,	1,765
Total,	1,842

Recapitulation.

First Division,	211
Second Division,	1,256
Third Division,	1,842
Total,	3,309

It will be observed that our division lost more than both the others added together.*

There are some incidents that occurred during the battle that are worth relating. When we laid under a terrific shelling, prior to the charge, private John A. Camp, Company A, Eleventh Reserves, was killed in the rear of our regiment, and General Meade, through some queer fancy, ordered one of our officers to have him buried. A grave was dug with bayonets and hands, and wrapping the soldier in his blanket he was laid in his honorable grave, while the shells were singing his requiem over head. Nearly eighty dollars was found upon his person, which was turned over to the officer commanding his company.

Young Charles Upjohn, Company K, captured the Nineteenth Georgia's flag, but the captain of Camp's company unjustly and ungenerously took it from him, and claimed the honor himself.

A boy of about fifteen shot a Union soldier, and dropping his rifle, ran, but was pursued by two men, who were on the point of bayonetting him, when an officer interfered and saved his life. It was some time before the boy could comprehend what the intention of the officer was, and so thoroughly convinced was he that the Yankees would kill him, that he followed the officer through the hottest portion of the battle, preferring to run his risk with him, than to trusting himself with any one else.

An amusing incident occurred during the charge. A captain of the ——— regiment received a slight wound on his knee, and down he went to the ground, but fortunately a stretcher was near, and he was lifted helplessly upon it, and started for the rear. They had not proceeded far, with their precious charge, before a shell exploded in close proximity, when the wounded officer, springing to his feet, cried out, "Hike out, boys, that's too

* See Appendix A.

hot for me," and, suiting his action to his words, ran like a deer, leaving the amazed carriers far in the rear.*

Color-sergeant William Derr, who was as brave a boy as ever wore a blue coat, was shot on the plateau as we were crossing the fence. Colonel McCandless ordered a couple of men to carry him to the rear, but he refused to permit them, telling them to "take the flag and go on."

Our flagstaff was cut in two, by a round shot, when we were lying down. The boys, jumping to their feet, gave three cheers and then laid down again.

Dr. Donnelly having been detailed to division field hospital, Dr. Coleman was left in charge of our regiment, and before night all our wounded men were collected together in one house, where they received all the kindness that could be bestowed upon them. Coffee and gruel was soon furnished them, and hardly a groan escaped their lips.

Every thing passed off quietly through the night, and the next day, although we were under arms several times, and cannonading continued off and on all day. Colonel William Sinclair, having been severely wounded, the command of our brigade devolved upon Colonel McCandless, and Captain McDonough having received an injury in his eye the day before, Captain Mealey took command of the regiment.

On Saturday night, General Burnside determined upon the insane renewal of the assault upon the works in the

* No one is more entitled to our pity than he who, having entered the army without consulting his own heart, discovers in the hour of danger, that he is deficient in courage. If he continues in the service, he will assuredly be covered with disgrace; and if the army regulations would permit him to resign, except for disability, the reason will be discovered, whatever pains he may take to conceal it; thus in either case he will find himself exposed to the derision and contempt of his comrades. A clergyman may impose upon the world by the exterior of gravity, and may feign a piety which he does not feel, but the coward cannot long maintain with success that of bravery, for the trial is too severe.

rear of Fredericksburg, on the following morning, and the column of attack was formed, but through the urgent solicitation of General Sumner, who represented that he did not know of any general officer who approved it, he countermanded the order. Through Sunday night there was considerable picket firing, and on Monday a flag of truce was agreed upon, to bring off the wounded and bury the dead, for which purpose details were made from the various regiments.

On Monday night, the 15th, soon after dark, we were got under arms, and leaving our camp fires brightly burning, moved slowly and noiseless towards the river, which we crossed on muffled pontoons, and moved back about a mile. The crossing on the right was soon afterwards commenced, and by morning the whole army was safely over, without the loss of a man or a gun. A more complete or successful evacuation of a position had not been made during the war.

The battle of Fredericksburg was lost, the bright hopes of the Nation and the army were blasted, and the victory that was within our grasp was gone forever. Let us review briefly, some of the causes of it. On the 17th of November, General Sumner arrived at Falmouth, opposite Fredericksburg, which at that time was garrisoned by about five hundred Confederate troops. The general expected to find the pontoons there when he arrived, or very soon afterwards If such had been the case, he would have seized the crest in the rear of the town, and the enemy would have been forced to have given battle at some other point nearer Richmond. The pontoons did not arrive for over three weeks afterwards, thus enabling the enemy to concentrate his forces and to fortify his extraordinarily strong position.

If General Burnside had kept himself properly posted as to the whereabouts of the pontoons, and had not advanced on Fredericksburg, thereby divulging to the enemy his plan of campaign, until the time of their arrival, and had made feint movements towards Culpeper, he might have taken the enemy by surprise at Fredericksburg, and have accomplished the same end.

It has been shown if General Franklin had properly supported Meade's charge, a victory was almost certain to have resulted to our arms.

While these faults are apparent on our side, it is equally clear that the enemy did not make proper use of his victory. If he had set fire to Fredericksburg, at any time between the close of the battle on the 13th and the night of the 15th, and have opened with all his guns and made a grand charge with his infantry, the result must have been most fearful to the Union army.

The Union force upon the south side of the river was about one hundred thousand men, not more than fifty thousand of whom were engaged in battle. The Confederate forces have been variously estimated at from one hundred to two hundred thousand men, but probably eighty-five thousand is nearer the mark. The Union army never went into battle in better spirits than they did that day, they being confident of victory and believing it would be the last great battle of the war.

CHAPTER XXII.

PICKET TRUCE AND FIGHTING. FAREWELL OF GENERAL MEADE. THE MUD EXPEDITION. GENERAL BURNSIDE RELIEVED BY GENERAL HOOKER. ORDERED TO ALEXANDRIA. TO FAIRFAX COURT HOUSE. PICKET AT BULL RUN. CAPTURE OF GENERAL STOUGHTON. PROMOTIONS.

UPON our re-crossing, our regiment and the "Bucktails" were immediately detailed to guard the river below the lower pontoon bridges, and opposite the Bernard House, and before daylight we had a number of good rifle pits dug to shelter the men in. As daylight approached, a few stragglers could be seen hurrying towards the river, and some hours afterwards the enemy's scouts appeared; but lo—the blue birds had flown. On the left of our line, the most amicable relationship was established between the pickets, they coming down to the river banks and conversing freely, expressing their mutual regrets that they had no means of visiting one another.

"How are you Yanks; I guess you found it rather unhealthy over here."

"How are you Rebs; how did you like Antietam?"

"About as well as you liked Bull Run."

"Can't you sing us 'My Maryland.'"

"D—n Maryland, can't you rig up a raft and come over and trade?"

Late in the afternoon some of the boys of Company C, got permission of one of our officers to come down and talk with them.

"Why don't you officers go home, and let us privates settle the war."

"How do you want to settle it?"

"Why, you Yanks go home and let us alone, and we won't come up north to fight you."

"Then you want your independence acknowledged?"

"Certainly; that's what we are fighting for."

And this is the universal sentiment throughout the whole South. They have been willing and anxious for peace from the beginning, but only on these inadmissible terms.

On the right of the line, these amicable relations were not maintained. A fine horse was discovered on the south side of the river, and some of Company H determined to kill it. Soon after several shots were fired, a battery posted in our rear, supposing we were engaged with the enemy, opened fire, one shell blowing a small fraction of the Southern Confederacy into atoms. Two others at the same time were wounded. Some of the shells, however, were cut short, and a piece of one struck one of our officers on the hand and buried itself between his feet, without inflicting more than a painful blow. Soon after, Captain Mealey, while standing behind a rifle-pit, received a most painful wound in the right arm from a sharpshooter behind a tree. Companies B and H immediately opened an enfilading fire upon the tree, and there is no doubt the rascal was killed. Captain Mealey's loss was severely felt, he being one of our most gallant officers. The senior officer present declining to assume the command, it devolved upon the adjutant.

About this time the extreme right, became briskly engaged with the pickets across the river, some of whom occupied a frame house. The "Bucktails" mounted a "Quaker gun," and going through all the motions of the gunners fired in volleys, skedaddling the enemy from the house, they at first being deceived by them. Towards night, the enemy called over that as we had wounded some of their men whom they wanted to get and take care of, and as it was getting cold, we had better stop fighting, build fires, cook our suppers and go to sleep. The proposition was at once agreed to, and soon bright fires lined both banks of the river, and the boys were talking and joking as if they were old friends.

Towards night Captain Connors rejoined and took command of the regiment, he having recovered from his wound at Bull Run. Late that night we were relieved by some New York troops, and proceeded to a neighboring woods, built fires and slept with the Twenty-fourth Michigan Volunteers.

The next morning we marched into camp, where Captain McDonough assumed command of the regiment. The day after at noon we struck tents and marched about five miles and bivouacked in an open field. The next morning, the 20th, we marched early, about one mile, and formed an encampment in a thick pine forest on a hill-side near White Oak Church.

Here the boys made themselves as comfortable as circumstances would permit. Some of them dug pits about two feet deep which they logged up some distance above ground and stretched their shelter tents over. Comfortable fire-places and chimneys were built, and with an abundance of dry leaves to sleep upon, they got along quite comfortably. Two or four generally bunked together, and by splicing blankets and laying "spoon fashion" they slept quite warm.

Nothing of importance occurred until the 25th, when Major-General Meade being assigned to the command of the Fifth Army Corps, bid farewell to our division in the following order:

GENERAL ORDER, NO. 101.

HEADQUARTERS, THIRD DIVISION,
December 25th, 1862.

In announcing the above order, which separates the commanding general from the division, he takes occasion to express to the officers and men, that notwithstanding his just pride at being promoted to a higher command, he experiences a deep feeling of regret at parting from those with whom he has been so long associated, and to whose services he here acknowledges his indebtedness for whatever reputation he may have acquired.

The commanding general will never cease to remember that he belonged to the Reserve Corps; he will watch with eagerness for the deeds of fame which he feels sure they will enact under the command of his successors, and, although sadly reduced in numbers from the casualties of battle, yet he knows the Reserves will always be ready and prompt to uphold the honor and glory of their State.

By command of
MAJOR-GENERAL MEADE.

(Signed.)

EDWARD C. BAIRD,
A. A. G.

The command of our division now devolved upon Colonel Horatio G. Sickel, of the Third Reserves, who was one of our most gallant officers, he having served with great credit and ability through all the battles we had fought.

While we laid here we experienced constant and heavy rain and snow storms, that turned our encampment into a vast mud puddle, and rendered the roads almost impassable. Almost daily details were made from the regiments to corduroy the roads, and we passed our time about as disagreeably as possible.

As early as the 26th, orders were received to have three days rations in haversacks and sixty rounds of cartridges per man, and to be prepared to move at a moment's notice.

On the 30th, a thousand picked cavalry with four pieces of artillery under General Averill, crossed the Rappahannock at the upper fords intending to make a complete circuit of Richmond, destroying bridges and railroads on their route, and join General Peck at Suffolk, where they were to be transferred back to Aquia creek by steamboats. It was the intention that the main army should advance at the same time, and turn the enemy's right or left flank, but through the unauthorized interference of Generals Cochrane and Newton, who had proceeded to Washington, the President was induced to suspend the movement.

The order to hold ourselves in readiness to move, was however, repeatedly renewed up to January 20th, when at twelve M., we broke camp and moved up the river ten miles, where we halted at dark and bivouacked in a thick scrub oak forest. About four o'clock it commenced raining, and continued so to do without intermission all night. By the next morning the roads and the whole face of the country was impassable. We, however, were got under way about daylight, marching some three miles, and halting near the river back of Bank's Ford. Here the army was brought to a stand still, it literally having stuck in the mud. The pontoon trains could not move at all. The supply trains were in the rear unable to come up, and twenty-eight horses stalled with a cannon. It was next to impossible to get our camp-fires lit, and the cold rain descended in torrents all day. The enemy, who for some time, had known of a contemplated movement, were more definitely posted from the fact of General Sumner having moved his wagons and artillery on the crest of the hills back of Falmouth, in full view of them, and they were in force on the opposite bank at the Ford to meet us, and tantalizingly offered to send a brigade over to help us lay our pontoons.

We remained here until the morning of the 23d, when finding the utter impracticability of carrying out the enterprize, the commands were ordered to retrace their steps back to their various old camps, and we reaching ours late in the afternoon. Our division ambulances were sent out and brought in twenty loads of prostrated men. During this movement not a particle of forage was furnished for the field and staff horses.

Thus ended "Burnsides' mud expedition."

Soon after Major-general Joseph Hooker was appointed to the command of the Army of the Potomac, General Burnside being relieved at his own request.

Nothing of interest occurred in camp until dark on the 5th of February, when a telegram was received from General Doubleday, our division commander, stating that in consideration of the arduous and gallant services of the Reserves, they were to be withdrawn to Washington "to rest and recruit," which news was received with great joy. In despite of the raw and unpleasant weather, the camp fires were soon burning brightly, around which the men were gathered, talking of the good times coming. The next morning early, the men were all up and soon every thing was packed to move. At three, P. M., the order to march came, and soon after the bugles rang out the joyful "assembly," and bidding farewell to our old camp, and the gallant One-hundred-and twenty-first Pennsylvania Volunteers, who had been temporarily attached to us before the battle of Fredericksburg, we took up our march for Belle Plains, which though but four miles distance, on account of the bad state of the roads, was not reached until after dark. Here, in the freezing cold and deep mud, we had to stand until two o'clock the next morning before we could embark, soon after which we were on our way up the Potomac, and landed at Alexandria at nine, A. M., the same day. After some delay, we marched through the city to near the Cemetery, where we laid last April, and there on a bleak hill bivouacked.

Captain McDonough being taken sick was sent home, and the command of the regiment devolved upon Captain P. I. Smith. Our stay here was very unpleasant, we having little or no wood to cook with; and on the morning of the 12th, at eight o'clock, we marched to the depot of the Orange and Alexandria Railroad and embarked upon the platform cars, and proceeded to Fairfax Station, where we alighted, and marching to Fairfax Court House proceeded about one mile beyond and encamped in a heavy woods.

On the 20th Lieutenant-colonel Woodward arrived in camp and superceded Captain Smith, and the next day, at daylight, our regiment started for Bull Run to go on picket. On arriving at Union Mills, our colonel reported to General Hays, who sent a dashing young aid, all covered with gold to receive us. Upon his arrival he inquired for Captain Reitzel, who was temporarily in charge of the regiment. It should be mentioned here, that the officers of the Reserves were never particularly noted for their fine uniforms and gold lacings, and especially after going through the memorable campaign of 1862. In fact, Captain Reitzel wore nothing to indicate he was an officer but his sword, and that was concealed under his overcoat. Besides, the captain, like many other old campaigners, went out provided with the implements of comfort, an axe and frying-pan. The aid was duly saluted by the captain, who informed him he was the individual sought for, but his indignation at the impudence of the "pioneer," as he called him, waxed exceedingly warm, and he was on the point of running him down when he discovered his mistake, which created a hearty laugh all round, in which the little German aid joined. In the mean time, a fine brass band, sent by the general, arrived and escorted us to our encampment. As this was the first time we had ever been escorted any where, except to the battle-field, the boys stepped off quite lively to the soul-inspiring strains.

The nice little aid, before parting, made us generous promises of plenty of tents, clothes and food, with fresh beef and bread to boot, and we really began to think we had got into good quarters, when along came an abominable orderly, with orders for us to fall in to relieve the pickets. It was now night. We had just got our fires started and were preparing our coffee, but strike tents and fall in was the order, so off we started through the forests and over the hills of Bull Run to the fords. Soon a blinding snow-storm set in, bewildering and almost benumbing us. It was daybreak the next morning before our left companies reached their posts, our line extending over seven miles. The snow continued falling all the next day, giving us but little opportunity to erect comfortable shelter. Our posts at the fords were almost nightly visited by the guerrillas, who exchanged a few shots with the pickets and disappeared. When a shot was fired, not knowing the strength or object of the enemy, the reserve at the post was turned out, and as this occurred several times through the night, the men's sleep was constantly liable to be disturbed. This tour of duty lasted sixteen days, and we were all glad when it was over.

At the camp near Fairfax Court House there were left over forty men under the charge of the adjutant, composed of the guard, the sick, and those in arrest for going home on "French." At midnight on the 1st of March we were all aroused by heavy firing in the front, and the men being got under arms were started for a swamp in the rear of the camp, when an order came from Colonel Woodward, commanding our brigade, for us to report to Captain Taylor, commanding the "Bucktails," where we stayed until morning.

The next night, about twelve o'clock, orders were received to send two officers and twenty-five men on picket, on the Aldie road. Not having that many men to detail, those in arrest were offered their release if they would go, which they gladly accepted. All, however, passed quietly through the night. These alarms occurred almost nightly.

Near midnight on the 8th, a body of the enemy's cavalry quietly came into Fairfax Court House, and seized Acting Brigadier-General Stoughton, a number of his staff and guard, at the house of Miss Ford, and carried them off. The affair was a bold, dashing act, and the officer in command deserves great credit for the adroitness with which he managed it. No one was to blame for the mishap but the colonel himself, whose nomination to a brigadier-generalship was consequently withdrawn by the President.

The regiment was relieved at dark on the 8th, and marching down to Union Mills, we laid there through the night, and returned to camp the next day under Captain Smith, he again being the senior officer.

During the absence of the regiment, Captain John M. Clark's caisson company (F) reported in camp. They were a fine set of Pennsylvanians, numbering sixty muskets, and were welcomed by all. Before our return wedge tents had been drawn for the regiment, and put up by F, in a fine heavy woods were the boys found every thing comfortably prepared for them.

On the 16th, Colonel Sinclair returned and took command of the brigade, and at noon the same day, we broke camp, and moved to the outskirts of the town, and commenced throwing up rifle pits which commanded the Centreville road. The cause of these precautions were that the enemy's cavalry having crossed the Rappahannock, were operating on General Hooker's right, and as far north as this neighborhood.

With the exception of the usual night alarms, and heavy rain and snow storms, nothing of note transpired until the morning of the 28th, when we broke camp and marched across the fields and through the woods to Fairfax Station. The distance was but four miles, but as it had been raining hard all night and day, it took us as many hours to march it. It was amusing to see the men laugh and joke and swear by turns, trying to keep up their good spirits as they toiled, under their heavy knapsacks, and plunged through the mud up to their knees, and wet to the skin. It was late before our wagons arrived, and temporarily pitching our tents for the night, we managed to get along pretty comfortably. The next day our camp was regularly laid out in a heavy pine woods, and all things put to rights.

About this time Lieutenant Justus was appointed acting quartermaster, *vice* A. Q. M. Ross, who was detailed on recruiting service.

On the 23d of April, Captain McDonough arrived in camp and assumed command of the regiment.

Considerable labor was expended in arranging our camp, in felling the trees not required for shade, cutting the stumps off close to the ground, burning the brush and rubbish, and thoroughly policing the whole neighborhood. The avenues and streets were planted with rows of heavy cedar trees, which afforded a cool and pleasant shade, and buried our camp in a grove.

About the 1st of May, the commissions of the following named offices, promoted for gallant conduct were received:

Lieutenant-colonel William McCandless to be Colonel from November 1st, 1861, *vice* Wm. B. Mann, resigned. Major G. A. Woodward to be lieutenant-colonel from June 30th, 1862, *vice* William McCandless promoted. Sergeant-major E. M. Woodward to be adjutant, from September 18, 1862, *vice* Aug. T. Cross, killed. Quartermaster Charles F. Hoyt to be captain and commissary-sergeant from July 1st, 1862. Commissary-sergeant W. A. Hoyt to be quarter-master from January 6th, 1863, *vice* Charles F. Hoyt, promoted.

Company A.—First Lieutenant Daniel H. Connors to be captain from June 30th, 1862, *vice* Horace Neidé, promoted. Second Lieutenant John J. Ross to be first lieutenant from June 30th, 1862, *vice* Daniel H. Connors, promoted. First Sergeant Daniel Craig to be second lieutenant from June 30th, 1862, *vice* John J. Ross, promoted.

Company C.—First Sergeant Andrew Casey to be second lieutenant from June 30th, 1862, *vice* James R. Nightingale, killed.

Company D.—First Sergeant Thomas Canavan to be first Lieutenant from November 25th, 1862, *vice* John M. Curley, honorably discharged. Second Sergeant Robert R. Smith to be second lieutenant from December 3d, 1862, *vice* George H. Young, honorably discharged.

Company E.—First Sergeant John Taylor, to be first lieutenant from July 12, 1862, *vice* J. Baxter Fletcher, killed. Second Sergeant Andrew McLean, to be second lieutenant from October 25th, 1862, *vice* Alexander Black, honorably discharged.

Company F.—First Lieutenant John M. Clark to be captain from August 1st, 1862, *vice* John E. Barnacle, honorably discharged. Second Lieutenant Robert J. Clark to be first lieutenant from November 23d, 1862, *vice* John M. Clark, promoted.

Company G.—First Sergeant Elisha P. Woodward to be Second Lieutenant from September 17th, 1862, *vice* Max Wimpfheimer, killed.

Company H.—First Sergeant William McGlenn to be Second Lieutenant from December 25th, 1862, *vice* Richard Clendenning, honorably discharged.

At the same time Sergeant Joseph Benison, Company H, was appointed sergeant-major, from January 1st, 1863, and George W. Fernon, Company C, commissary-sergeant, from January 6th, 1863.

The guerrillas about this time became exceedingly troublesome, frequently attacking the picket posts and railroad trains. In one of these attacks a private of the Seventh Michigan Cavalry named Andrew McClain, was wounded and brought to our hospital, where he lingered for nine days. Upon a post-mortem examination being made it was found that a pistol ball had entered his backbone and passed up through the spinal marrow eight inches, which should have produced almost instant death. From his shoulders down he was completely paralyzed, and mortification had commenced in his nether limbs.

Towards the latter part of May, Colonel William Sinclair commanding our brigade, resigned as colonel of the Sixth Reserves, to take command of a battery of horse artillery in the west, and Colonel McCandless succeeded him in the command.

Lieutenant-colonel Woodward being relieved from duty at Washington, took command of our regiment, Captain McDonough was appointed Major, Sergeant-major Joseph Benison, second lieutenant of Company H, and Sergeant D. H. Pidgeon of Company K, sergeant-major.

On the 2d of June we were paid off by Major Gideon Ball, six months being due us.

About this time, Brigadier-general S. W. Crawford was appointed to the command of our division, and established his headquarters near our brigade. As the enemy were concentrating on Hooker's right flank, considerable skirmishing took place below in the neighborhood of the Rappahannock, and the trains were constantly conveying forage and provisions there, and bringing up wounded soldiers and prisoners.

CHAPTER XXIII.

OUR PETITION. MARCH TO PENNSYLVANIA. HAPPY DAY. BATTLE OF GETTYSBURG. LOSSES OF THE ARMIES.

SHORTLY after the defeat of our army at Chancellorville, Governor Curtin became thoroughly convinced that the enemy contemplated an invasion of Maryland and Pennsylvania, and although he made strenuous efforts to induce the General Government to adopt measures for defence, he could not prevail upon them to act, until the enemy had crossed the Potomac. His representations and advice were unheeded and many of the newspapers treated with levity his "unnecessary alarm." But at last, after much valuable time had been lost, the authorities awakened to the realization of the fact, and commenced vigorous preparations to repel the invaders.

On the 15th, long trains of ambulances, wagons and the reserve artillery from the army on the Rappahannock passed by our camp moving northward. The same day General Hooker and staff passed by, and towards night the Twelfth Army Corps arrived. All were in most excellent spirits and were confident of victory in the coming battle. On the 17th, the main body and the rear guard of the army arrived and resting a night and part of a day moved on.

To see the whole army moving to meet the enemy whom we knew were in Pennsylvania threatening our homes and loved ones, and for us to remain behind was rather mortifying, and although we had sent officers to Washington to intercede for marching orders for us, we met with no encouragement. On the 17th, we therefore, addressed the following communication to Colonel McCandless, who forwarded it through the proper channel to Washington, where it materially assisted in producing the desired effect:

HEADQUARTERS SECOND REGIMENT INFANTRY, P. R. V. C.
FAIRFAX STATION, VA., *June 17th*, 1863.

To Colonel WILLIAM MCCANDLESS,
Commanding First Brigade,
Pennsylvania Reserve Volunteer Corps.

COLONEL:—We, the undersigned, officers of the Second Regiment Infantry, Pennsylvania Reserve Volunteer Corps, having learned that our mother State has been invaded by a Confederate force, respectfully ask, that you will, if it be in your power, have us ordered within the borders of our State, for her defence.

Under McCall, Reynolds, Meade, Seymour, Sinclair and yourself, we have more than once met and fought the enemy, when he was at home. We now wish to meet him again where he threatens our homes, our families and our firesides.

Could our wish in this behalf be realized, we feel confident that we could do some service to the State that sent us to the field, and not diminish, if we could not increase, the lustre that already attaches to our name.

We are, Colonel,

Very respectfully, your obedient servants,

GEO. A WOODWARD, Lieutenant-colonel Second regiment P. R. V. C, commanding the regiment,
P. MCDONOUGH, Major Second regiment,
E. M. WOODWARD, Adjutant Second regiment,
JAMES C. JUSTUS, Acting Quartermaster Second regiment,
E. A. JACKSON, Assistant Surgeon Second regiment,
DANIEL H. CONNORS, Captain Company A,
JAMES C. MANTON, Lieutenant-com'ng Company B,
JAMES N. BYRNES, Captain Company C,
THO'S CANAVAN, First Lieutenant Company D,
JOHN TAYLOR, First Lieutenant Co. E,
ANDREW MCLEAN, Second Lieutenant Company E,
JOHN M. CLARK, Captain Company F,
ROBERT J. CLARK, First Lieutenant Company F,

W. D. REITZEL, Captain Company G,
J. L. RHOADS, First Lieutenant Company G,
E. P. WOODWARD, Second Lieutenant Company G,
WILLIAM MCGLENN First Lietenant-com'g Company H,
JOSEPH BENISON, Second Lieutenant Company H.

In the mean time Generals Reynolds and Meade had both applied to the War Department to have the Reserves attached to their corps. General Reynolds was offered in lieu a full division, which he declined. General Meade, however, succeeded in having us assigned to his corps, but the day we joined him, he left us to assume the important post of commander of the Army of the Potomac, the proudest position any general in America could aspire to.

At last, on the 25th, orders were received to move immediately, and at five that afternoon we left Fairfax Station, and marched in a northwesterly direction through Vienna, near which we bivouacked at eleven o'clock that night. Just as we started it commenced raining and continued so to do all night. The next morning at four o'clock we resumed our march, continuing in the same direction passing between Drainesville and Leesburg and making Goose creek that night. Through the day the rain was most violent and constant, rendering the roads almost knee-deep in mud, and as we were making forced marches many of the wearied boys fell out, and did not get up with us until daylight the next morning. Rain, however, is preferable to dust.

The Third brigade, Colonel J. W. Fisher, joined us in the morning from Alexandria; the Second brigade, Colonel H. G. Sickel, being retained for the defence of Washington. The next morning, at daylight, we resumed our march, passing near a portion of the field of the "Ball's Bluff massacre," and crossing the Potomac at Edwards' Ferry on pontoons. That night we made the mouth of the Monocacy in spite of the heavy roads.

Sunday the 28th was a clear and pleasant day, and at

daylight we moved off and soon crossed the aqueduct of the Chesapeake and Ohio Canal over the Monocacy, and passing through Buckeystown we bivouacked about two miles from Frederick. Here we came up with the main army, and reported to General Sykes, commanding the Fifth Army Corps, to which we were assigned. This corps, until then, had been commanded by General Meade, who had made application to have us sent to him, but the day of our arrival General Hooker was relieved of the command of the army, and he assigned to it.

We started the next day at noon, and moving a few miles halted in a lane nearly all the afternoon, and at seven crossed the Monocacy bridge on the Baltimore pike, and turned up the banks of the stream heading north. Soon after we waded the stream and struck across the fields, and about ten o'clock bivouacked in a wood, having made a tiresome day's march of but ten miles. This slow marching was occasioned by our being the rear guard of the Reserve artillery, which consisted of two hundred and forty-eight guns, supplied with two hundred and fifty rounds of ammunition each, making in all six-two thousand rounds. Before night that day the enemy's cavalry entered Frederick. That night heavy details were made from our regiment for a wagon guard.

The next morning we marched early, passing through Liberty, Union Bridge and Union Town, where a pontoon train that accompanied us that day created much wonderment among the rustics, who did not believe we could do much with our "gun boats" up in the mountains. We marched twenty miles and bivouacked near dark two miles beyond Union Town and mustered for pay.

The next morning, July 1st, we moved at five o'clock, and ascertaining that the enemy's scouts had been in the neighborhood the day before, each regiment threw out flankers to the right and left, in which way we advanced for several miles, when the country became of such a nature that cavalry could not operate against us, and they were called in. About two we halted within a few hundred yards of the Pennsylvania State line, and rested ourselves. That day was one of the happiest of our lives, and every heart beat warm with the thought, we would soon press the soil of our mother State, in whose defence we were marching. The brigade bands and regimental drum corps poured forth their soul-inspiring airs from morning till night, and light was the tread of our feet to their notes. About three o'clock we were drawn up to hear a patriotic address from General Crawford, after which we marched on, and as we crossed the line, cheer after cheer rang out from the regiments, which rolled over the hills and through the valleys until lost in the far distance. Soon we came to a fine open woods where we halted until night, rolling on the good old soil of Pennsylvania and listening to the sweet airs of the bands. Abundance of rations and sixty rounds of cartridges per man were distributed, the former for ourselves and the latter for our friends the "Graybacks."

While lying here, through the branches above, amidst the bright sunshine, a large star was discerned shining over us with all the brilliancy of a heavenly visitant, which was gazed upon by all with great interest, and received as an omen of victory, which, happily, it proved to be.

While here all our wagons were sent to Westminster, some twenty-five miles from the battle-field, and the ammunition wagons and ambulances were pushed forward. At dark we again took up our march, and a long weary one it proved. We did not rest until two the next morning, when we laid down in an open woods having made twenty miles during the day and being awake twenty-two hours. But in one hour's time the drums beat the reveille, and soon after we were again in motion, moving slowly and cautiously along the roads and across the fields, and about noon we struck the pike and soon filed off to the left into a field in the rear of the line of battle.

THE BATTLE OF GETTYSBURG, JULY 1ST, 2D, AND 3D.—The enemy, who, as early as the 13th ult. gave battle to General Milroy, at Winchester, Virginia, and the next day precipitated him to a disastrous and disgraceful flight, with their advance guard, one thousand five hundred strong, under General Jenkins, entered Chambersburg, Pennsylvania, at eight and a half P. M., on the 15th, but being without infantry support, evacuated the same on the 17th and withdrew to Hagerstown, Maryland with the horses and cattle they had plundered the defenceless farmers of. The enemy continued to cross the Potomac in force, and on the night of the 30th had concentrated within a short distance of Gettysburg, seventy-six thousand infantry and a large number of cavalry. Confronting this was the First Corps, General Reynolds, eight thousand strong; the Eleventh Corps General Howard, fifteen thousand; and six thousand cavalry under General Buford, making a total of twenty-nine thousand men.

For this little band of Union troops to give battle to such an overwhelming force of the enemy, seemed the extreme of rashness, but the eagle eye of Reynolds saw at a glance, that to secure and hold, until the main body of our army arrived, the ridges and positions upon which the great battle was subsequently fought was of vital importance to the success of our arms. He was too true a soldier to shrink from the responsibility of defeat, when the good of the cause demanded battle, and he hesitated not to engage the enemy.

On the morning of the 1st of July, at half past nine o'clock, General Buford dismounted a portion of his cavalry and commenced skirmishing with the enemy, who had debouched his infantry through the mountains on Cashtown, and about ten o'clock several pieces of light artillery were brought into play. Soon after General Reynolds moved around the town of Gettysburg and advanced on the Cashtown road, and immediately deploying his advance division, attacked the enemy, and at the same time sent orders for the Eleventh Corps, General Howard, to advance as promptly as possible.

Soon after making his disposition for attack, General Reynolds fell mortally wounded; the command of the First Corps devolving on Major-general Doubleday, and of the field, on Major-general Howard, who arrived about half past eleven, A. M., with the Eleventh Corps, then commanded by Major-general Schurz. General Howard pushed forward two divisions of the Eleventh Corps to support the First Corps, now warmly engaged with the enemy on the north of the town, and posted his third division, with three batteries, on the Cemetery ridge, on the south side of the town. Prior to the arrival of the Eleventh Corps the First had fought with determined bravery, double their number, for two hours, and not only held their own, but drove the enemy back in their furious charges, and about one P. M. Wadsworth's division captured General Archer and his whole brigade, numbering about one thousand five hundred men, who had attempted to flank them.

Between one and two o'clock the enemy received reinforcements on the Cashtown road, and Ewell's Corps came in on the York and Harrisburg roads and formed a junction, which enabled them to bring vastly superior forces against both the First and the Eleventh Corps, outflanking our line of battle and pressing it so severely that, about four o'clock General Howard deemed it prudent to withdraw these two corps to the Cemetery ridge, on the south side of the town, which operation was successfully accomplished, but not, however, without the loss of about two thousand five hundred prisoners, who being much crowded in passing through the streets, and somewhat confused, were unable to repel the enemy who pressed hard upon them. At this time the combined forces of Heath, Pender, Rhoads, and Early, amounted to forty thousand men, while those opposed to them did not exceed twenty thousand. At one time, during the alternate advance and backward movements, we lost one thousand nine hundred prisoners, all of whom were retaken, and a Mississippi regiment, numbering eight hundred men made prisoners.

About the time of the withdrawal, Major-general Hancock arrived upon the field and took command, and in conjunction with General Howard proceed to post the troops on Cemetery ridge, and to repel the attack that the enemy made on our right flank. This attack was not, however, very vigorous; the enemy, seeing the strength of the position occupied, seemed to be satisfied with the success he had accomplished, desisting from any further attack that day.

About seven o'clock, P. M., Major-generals Slocum and Sickles, with the Twelfth Corps and part of the Third, reached the ground, and took position on the right and left of the troops previously posted. At one o'clock the next morning, General Meade arrived and assumed command.

Early on the morning of the 2d, the Second and part of the Fifth Corps, with the rest of the Third arrived, and were posted as follows: the Eleventh Corps retaining its position on Cemetery ridge, just opposite to the town; the First Corps was posted on the right, the Eleventh on an elevated knoll, connecting with the ridge and extending to the south and east, on which the Twelfth Corps was placed, the right of the Twelfth Corps resting on Rock creek, a small stream at a point where it crossed the Baltimore pike, and which formed on the right flank of the Twelfth something of an obstacle.

Cemetery ridge extended in a westerly and southerly direction, gradually diminishing in elevation, till it came to a very prominent ridge, called "Round Top," running east and west. The Second and Third Corps occupied the continuation of Cemetery ridge, on the left of the Eleventh Corps und Fifth Corps; and pending their arrival the Sixth Corps was held in reserve. While these dispositions were being made, the enemy was massing his troops on an extreme ridge, about one mile and a half distant from the line occupied by us.

At two o'clock, the Sixth Corps arrived, after a march of thirty-two miles, which was accomplished from nine P. M., of the day previous. The Fifth Corps was immediately moved to the extreme left, and the Sixth taking its place as a reserve for the right.

About three, General Sickles, not fully apprehending his instructions in regard to the position to be occupied, advanced his corps a half or three-quarters of a mile in the front of the line of the Second Corps on a prolongation which it was designed his corps should rest. General Meade, perceiving the movement, hastened to the spot, and was about arranging for the withdrawal of the corps, from its too far advanced position, when the enemy opened upon them with several batteries in front and flank, and immediately brought forward columns of infantry, and made a vigorous assault. The Third Corps sustained the shock most heroically, and troops from the Second Corps were immediately sent to cover their right flank, and soon after the assault commenced.

The Fifth Corps most fortunately arrived, and the First and Second divisions were immediately posted on the left of the Third by Major-general Sykes. Soon the cannonading became general along our left and centre, answered by the guns of the enemy, of which more than one hundred were placed in circuit on the Seminary Ridge and on the hill east of the town. Our troops went forward in gallant style and engaged the enemy in a most terrific struggle at Sherby's peach orchard and the adjoining grounds near the Emmetsburg road. Both parties fought with desperation, but at last our men overpowered began to give way. Rallied by their officers, they arrested and hurled back the advancing column for a short time; but finding themselves hard pressed by an overwhelming mass of the enemy, they gave way a second time. This was the most critical moment of the day. The point aimed at by the enemy was to break our left and flank us, and this they would have accomplished, if succor had not speedily arrived.

At this movement, about half-past five o'clock, the Pennsylvania Reserves, which until then had been held in reserve, were brought forward and formed by brigades in columns of regiments, on the brow of "Little Round Top," upon which was posted one of their batteries. Before them, from the base of the rugged height, stretched a broad meadow, skirted on its outer edge by heavy timber, from which emerged the victorious enemy, driving before them the scattered regiments of the First and Second divisions of the Fifth Corps and the Third. Most gallantly did the brave fellows dispute the ground, but the overpowering masses of the enemy swept victoriously on, and their wild shout of triumph rang through the valley. Our battery to the right belched forth its sheets of flame and smoke, hurling its missiles of death over the heads of the flying mass into the enemy. Immovable and firm stood the Reserves, resting on their arms, silently gazing on the magnificent and grand sight, until our broken masses had passed to the right, and the enemy had advanced within fifty paces, when the gallant Crawford, seizing the standard of the First, whose bearer had been shot down, waved it aloft and cried out, "Forward, Reserves." With a simultaneous shriek from every throat, that sounded as if coming from a thousand demons, who had burst their lungs in uttering it, on swept the Reserves, delivering, as they started, a solid volley, and careering victoriously over the field, halted not a moment until they reached the stone wall, bordering on the skirting of woods, where the surprised enemy made their last desperate rally to retrieve the day. Not a moment was lost. On went the glorious flags to the wall, standard bearer after bearer was shot down, but with empty muskets the column pressed on, and leaping over, bayonetted and scattered in flight the proud foe, from whose brows they wrenched the laurels of victory.

One loud shout of triumph rang through the valley and over the hills, and it was with the utmost difficulty the men could be restrained from following the enemy further. But prudence forbade it, and our regiment was ordered to halt and fall back to the wall by Captain Smith.

After the excitement and heat of battle is over, every one is suddenly taken with thirst, and to get water is the first care of the soldier. Down the centre of the meadow we crossed, run a small creek—Plum run—and to it the thirsty ones repaired, to fill their canteens. It was found almost choked with the dead and wounded, who had fallen in, while attempting to cross. It was the only place from which we could get water. After this we set to work gathering our wounded and those of other regiments who had been driven from the field, and who lay thick in every direction. This work occupied many of us the most of the night, but it was light labor to relieve the sufferings of our comrades. Nor were the enemy's wounded neglected, they being treated with the same kindness and care that our own received, as every old soldier holds that after the battle is over there are no enemies upon the field.

The Third brigade of the Reserves being posted to our left on "Round Top," and that position and flank being threatened by the enemy, they had not the opportunity of participating in the charge, with the exception of the Eleventh regiment Colonel Jackson, who being next to us, could not resist the temptation and went in. We won the Eleventh fairly that day, and soon after at the solicitation of its officers it was wedded to our brigade.

That night a heavy line of pickets were thrown out in front, under Lieutenant McLean, ammunition was distributed, and the boys stretched their weary limbs to rest, and slept, regardless of the skirmishing of the pickets which was kept up off and on all night. But the balls whizzed harmlessly over head, and the noise disturbed not their slumbers.

During the assault on the left, the Sixth Corps and part of the First, together with detachments from the Second and Twelfth Corps, were all brought up at different periods to assist in the repulse, and about eight P. M., an assault was made on the Eleventh Corps from the left of the town, which was repulsed by the assistance of troops from the Second and First Corps.

During the absence of a portion of the Twelfth, the line on the extreme right was held by a very much reduced force. This was taken advantage of by the enemy, who, during the absence of General Geary's division of that corps, advanced, and occupied part of the line. The musketry fighting here continued from seven until half-past nine o'clock.

General Geary having returned during the night, and being reinforced by a portion of the Sixth Corps, at dawn of day on the third, opened upon the enemy with artillery at the point where they had penetrated our lines the evening previous. This was followed by a general infantry attack, and soon the battle raged furiously, and was maintained with desperate obstinacy on both sides from half-past four to half-past ten, A. M., when the enemy were driven back with great slaughter and our former position re-occupied.

At daybreak on the 3d, the enemy's line of skirmishers in our brigade front being reinforced, they opened with great spirit, the noise of the musketry almost resembling that of a regular battle. Our own line was promptly reinforced by volunteers who freely responded to them, but soon after the fire on both sides slackened and settled down to the common-place picket fighting. This work was kept up until about five P. M., during which time we were much annoyed by the sharpshooters posted in the trees, and a number of men of the other regiments were killed and wounded by them. This kind of fighting gave excellent opportunities for the display of individual bravery and address, and the manœuvring of the boys to get good shots at times created considerable amusement. When some enterprising "Confed." was well posted and annoyed us much two or three would arrange their plans to knock him over, and creeping up cautiously from different directions, one of the men would draw his fire, while another on his flank would shoot him. One scamp got up a tree and succeeded in killing several men, when his locality was discovered; two of the boys started after him, and got under the tree before he saw them. He immediately cried out he would come down, to which they replied, they knew that very well, and they rattled him through the branches a few moments afterward. Another individual whom they afterwards discovered doing an extensive business in the same style, they left hanging in the crotches of a tree with his head and feet towards the ground. The boys never showed any mercy to these "tree frogs."

Thus the day wore on until one P. M., when the enemy opened upon our lines with over one hundred and thirty guns, playing principally upon our left and centre. This fire was immediately responded to on our side, and for over two hours the most terrific cannonading probably ever witnessed on this continent was kept up. The guns poured forth their missiles of death that went whizzing, screaming and bursting through the air, until the earth fairly trembled, and it seemed as if the very vault of heaven had been rent asunder.

About half-past three o'clock, the enemy in two long and massive lines was seen emerging from the woods of Seminary ridge to the south of McMillan's orchard, and moving over the plains towards the left centre. When they had reached one-third of the distance between the two opposing lines, our artillery opened upon them with shell and grape, staggering them for a few moments, when, with a terrific yell, they rushed to the charge. Our men quietly awaited until they had approached within short range when they opened upon them a deadly fire of musketry that mowed them down like grass. After a desperate struggle, the enemy were driven back with great slaughter, losing three thousand five hundred prisoners, and fifteen stands of colors. During this assault Major-general Hancock commanding the left centre, and Brigadier-general Gibbon commanding the Second Corps, were severely wounded, and of the enemy Generals Kemper was severely wounded, Armistead mortally, and Garnett was killed.

During the afternoon, the enemy had been annoying the Third brigade of Reserves, who held "Round Top," and attempted to turn the left flank, and heavy skirmishing was kept up between them. Our own front had been greatly annoyed by the enemy's sharpshooters and a battery posted about one thousand yards distant on the crest of a gentle elevation. To get rid of these, General Crawford ordered Colonel McCandless to "capture the battery and clean the enemy out," with his brigade, for which purpose the "Bucktails," the First, the Second, and the Eleventh were advanced in line of battle over the stone wall, and through the skirting of woods to a wheat field, where they drew the fire of the battery, upon which they were laid down until it ceased, when they were again put in motion to the left and then to the right, thus displaying themselves and drawing the fire, until the Sixth, under Colonel Ent, had crept up close to the battery, which they stormed with great gallantry, and through a shower of grape and canister captured one gun and two caissons.

When the Sixth had become fairly engaged, Colonel McCandless marched the balance of his brigade by the right flank, and filing left formed in line of battle in a woods at right angles with the stone wall, and deploying skirmishers to the front, right and left, charged on double quick over the field for half a mile, receiving the enemy's fire from the woods on three sides. Half wheeling to the right and pouring a few volleys into the woods, they charged through them up to the crest, driving every thing before them. Here, halting for a few moments, they about faced, wheeled the line a little to the right, and charged through the woods in their rear, running like hounds, and yelping like devils down through the meadow and up over the steep acclivity on the opposite side, surprising the enemy and taking them on the flank, and doubling them up and driving regiments and brigades pell-mell before them in utter confusion. The gallant efforts of their officers to rally them were useless, we had them fairly on the run, and did not cease following them until we had penetrated far into their lines.

The trophies of this brilliant raid into their line of battle, besides those captured by the Sixth, were six thousand stand of arms, the flag of the Fifteenth Georgia, and three hundred prisoners, including a colonel and many line officers. The ground was strewn with their dead and wounded, and the remainder of their division was scattered in flight. Night was now fast approaching, we were nearly two miles from our starting point, and we had entered the open ground, where the smallness of our force could be discovered. Prudence demanded we should withdraw, and therefore McCandless with his brigade retraced his steps for some distance; when halting, we encircled ourselves with pickets, and slept upon our arms.

Such was the surprise of the enemy at our last charge, that their prisoners told us, that at the time we attacked them, they supposed we were nearly a mile off. Even their butchers were killed while engaged in skinning beeves, and a fatigue party who were burying their dead was captured. A prisoner was asked what regiment he belonged to, and replied, the Nineteenth Georgia. "Why, we captured you at Fredericksburg." "Are you the Second Pennsylvania Reserves? d—n you, you always give us h—ll when you meet us."

With this may be said to have ended the battle of Gettysburg, and it was looked upon as one of the most brilliant exploits of the field. Colonel McCandless displayed cool courage and military genius of the highest order, handling his brigade in most splendid style, and withdrawing it at the right time. The conception of the idea of making a raid directly into the enemy's line of battle, of throwing out skirmishers in the front and on both flanks, of charging the enemy on the right and left front and rear by turns, in fact being outflanked and having our rear turned at the same time, was bold and dashing, and showed the full confidence of the leader in himself and men.

Generals Meade, Sykes, and Crawford and many other officers from "Round Top," saw the brigade start, and watched it as long as in sight. With the din and lull of battle their hopes arose and fell, and when they found it receded far from them, though knowing we were driving the enemy, they feared the ultimate result, and sent support, which met us on our way back, and received us with hearty cheers. When an aid announced to them the complete success of the raid, they shook hands and congratulated each other, manifesting the liveliest satisfaction.

As soon as we halted for the night, stretchers and ambulances were sent to gather up our wounded who had laid upon the field from the day before, and who had suffered the pangs of many deaths. All night long and until noon the next day, were we thus engaged in the willing but painful work. The poor fellows had suffered terribly for water, and had been robbed of all their money and valuables, and some of them of their clothing. Large details were also made to collect the arms and before morning over six thousand rifles and muskets were gathered and taken to the rear.

Ammunition was procured and distributed to the men during the night, and at two o'clock on the morning of the "glorious Fourth," our regiment and the Sixth were moved to a more advanced post as pickets, and soon after daylight the enemy discovering us, their pickets opened upon us, which we returned with much spirit. About nine o'clock the Regulars, who composed the second division of our corps, advanced a splendid line of skirmishers, supported by two lines of battle, driving in the enemy's pickets and fully drawing their fire, when the object for which they advanced, viz.: to ascertain the position, strength and composition of the enemy, being obtained they withdrew to the rear again. When they advanced, our boys opened briskly upon the enemy, to draw their fire from the skirmishers, and some of them joined in the advance. Upon their retiring, the enemy fired a few shells, and then quietly advanced their picket line again, and settled down to exchanging an occasional shot in the usual quiet manner. While here, three thousand rounds of ammunition were distributed to the men. About one P. M., we were relieved, and during a heavy rain moved to our old position at the stone wall, having been under an almost constant fire for forty-three hours.

Never in any battle did the Reserve show more reckless and determined bravery than they did upon this field, for all felt that they were defending their own homes. One whole company of the First regiment were raised in Gettysburg, and some of the men fought on their own farms. All the field and staff officers determined to go in mounted, and did so as far as their horses could go. General Crawford and his staff, Colonel McCandless and his Assistant Inspector-general, Captain Coates, all displayed intrepid bravery. Lieutenant colonel Woodward, who from his wounds walked with difficulty in the early part of the action, received a contusion of the ankle, and was unable to accompany us in our charges, but remained upon the field.

The loss of our regiment, and in fact, of the brigade, was remarkably small which is attributed to the impetuosity of our charges, which gave the enemy but little chance to inflict damage upon us. The proportion of killed was very small, though among the wounded the mortality was subsequently very heavy.*

---

* See Appendix A.

Our regiment went into battle with one hundred and forty-seven men and its loss was heavier than any other regiment in the brigade.

The enemy numbered ninety thousand men and two hundred pieces of cannon, we had sixty thousand men and about an equal number of guns. Our total loss was four thousand killed, twelve thousand wounded, and four thousand prisoners, in all about twenty thousand; whilst the enemy's loss was five thousand five hundred killed, twenty-one thousand wounded, nine thousand prisoners, and four thousand stragglers and deserters, making a total of about forty thousand.

About one o'clock in the afternoon the Regulars relieved us at the stone-wall and we were moved back to "Little Round Top," where we received rations and remained until the afternoon of the next day, during which time it rained severely.

CHAPTER XXIV.

FALL OF REYNOLDS. THE BOY'S SWORD. MARCH. UNDYING LOVE. FALLING WATERS. LEE CROSSES THE POTOMAC. WAPPING HEIGHTS. MANASSAS GAP. ANECDOTE. MARCHING IN A CIRCLE.

BEFORE leaving the field of Gettysburg let us refer to Major-general John F. Reynolds, in the death of whom, a most skillful officer, brave soldier, high-minded and honorable man, and courteous gentleman, the army and country sustained a great loss, but nowhere was it more sincerely felt than in the First brigade of the Reserves whom he had moulded in their infancy and led to honor and glory on many fields. It will be remembered, at Harrison's Landing the men of this brigade determined to present the General with a handsome testimonial of their regard, which on account of the active service in which they were soon after engaged, was not procured until a short time before we left Fairfax Station, and no opportunity being afforded to present it, it was taken into Pennsylvania with the intention of presenting it to him on the battle-field, but, alas! when they arrived within hearing of his guns, he had passed to immortality.

In this gift the men felt great pride, as it was known that the general had refused to receive similar ones when tendered by officers, but he could not refuse this, prompted as it was by the pure and disinterested feelings of the men's hearts. And it was such a one as any general would have been proud of. It consisted of a costly sword of most exquisite workmanship, and was accompanied by a sash, and belt embroidered with heavy bullion. The blade of the sword was of the finest Damascus steel, and the scabbard of pure gold, having inscribed upon it on a scroll:

"Presented to Major-general John F. Reynolds, by the enlisted men of the First, Second, Fifth and Eighth regiments of the First brigade of Pennsylvania Reserves, in testimony of their *love and admiration.* Mechanicsville, June 26th, 1862."

Upon the grip was a black onyx, in the centre of which was set in diamonds the initials J. F. R., surrounded by a wreath of precious brilliants. On the reverse, in a handsome scroll was inscribed—"*Vincit Amor Patriæ.*" Crowning the grip was a solid globe of gold, chased with the map of the world, around which was the belt of the Union in blue enamel, with thirteen diamond stars, while entwined around the guard was an exquisitely-shaped serpent, with its venomous tongue protruding as if to steal one of the stars from the galaxy. The shield of the hilt was formed of the coat of arms of the State of Pennsylvania, cut from a solid plate of gold. Beneath this, on the scabbard, was a fine figure of the Goddess of Liberty modeled from the statue surmounting the Federal Capitol. In style and workmanship it was exquisitely gotten up, every touch upon it being given by hand, it resembling a fine piece of jewelry.*

Subsequently, W. H. Grier, a brave and gallant sergeant of the Fifth was chosen to proceed to Philadelphia and presented it to the general's sister, Mrs. Henry Landis.

On the morning of the 5th, it being ascertained that the enemy was in full retreat by the Fairfield and Cashtown roads, the Sixth corps was sent in pursuit on the Fairfield road, and the cavalry on the Cashtown road, by Emmetsburg and Monterey passes. As these passes were reported by Major-general Sedgwick as being very strong, General Meade determined to follow the enemy by a flank movement, and accordingly leaving a brigade of cavalry and infantry to harass the enemy, he put the army in motion for Middletown, Maryland.

Major-general French, in anticipation of orders, moved from Frederick and reoccupied Harper's Ferry and seized Turner's Pass, in the South Mountains. He also pushed his cavalry to Williamsport and Falling Waters, where he destroyed the enemy's pontoon bridge and captured its guard.

At five o'clock in the afternoon of the 5th, we moved off in a southwesterly direction over exceedingly bad roads, and at twelve o'clock at night bivouacked in an open field and threw out pickets. The next morning, about eleven o'clock, we marched to the State line, where a congratulatory address from General Meade was read to us and we bivouacked for the remainder of the day and night.

At four the next morning we moved off, passing near Emmetsburg and continuing along the base of the South Mountains, marching on the fields skirting the pike and passing through Graceham and Creegarstown, and bivouacked about dark, six miles from Frederick, having marched tweuty-one miles over very heavy roads.

---

* The designs in many respects were entirely new and original, and the sword has been pronounced one of the most chaste and beautiful ever made in this country. It was manufactured by Mr. E. Kretzmar.

The Catholic Convent at Emmetsburg since we passed there, has received a bright gem into its cloisters, the melancholy story of which is peculiarly interesting to the Reserves. A young lady, possessed of all the charms and attributes of womanly graces, won the heart of one of the Reserves' ablest generals. Her love was too pure and holy to look to this world alone for bliss, and although their hearts and hands were plighted, she postponed the happy hour that was to make them one, while she plead with him with all her earnestness to come into the folds of her church. The general, though one of the most upright and moral of men, could not be induced to leave the faith he had been reared in, and thus while their hearts were trembling between love and piety, and love and manly virtue, the hero sealed his devotion to his country by pouring out his heart's blood to hold the ground until the Army of the Potomac could concentrate at Gettysburg. And how fitting the sequel! Bowed down with the loss of her brave and gallant hero, she consecrated her fortune to charity and her life to her God.

At six o'clock on the morning of the 8th we marched, heading nearly west, and passing over fields soon struck the Catoctin Mountains, up the rugged sides of which we clambered through a heavy rain that had been falling all night. Arriving at the summit we commenced the descent along a narrow and rough road, and soon had a fine view of the magnificent valley, in which Middletown is situated, and a large number of troops were laying. Passing through Middletown, which was filled with moving columns of troops and wagons, we turned to the left and bivouacked about a mile to the south. During the night rations were served out to the companies.

The next morning we marched at six, and crossed the South Mountains at a point where the left wing of our army had gained a glorious victory on the 14th of September last. Descending the western slope we bivouacked about two miles from Keedysville, within sight of Antietam's glorious field. Through the day we heard heavy firing in the direction of Williamsport. A full supply of shoes and stockings, which were much needed were received and distributed during the night.

The next morning we commenced our march at six o'clock, and soon afterwards heard heavy cannonading. Passing near Keedysville and La Roy, we struck Antietam creek, passing by Delamont Mills, where the enemy had been in the morning, and some of their officers had ordered dinner, which they did not remain to eat. Just beyond here we halted and threw out cavalry and infantry skirmishers, who occasionally exchanged shots with the enemy for over two hours.

On the morning of the 11th we moved forward cautiously to near the Sharpsburg and Hagerstown turnpike, where we deployed in line of battle, and rested until four in the afternoon, at which time the division moved forward in columns of companies with the regiments at deploying distance, with a heavy body of skirmishers in front, and the pioneers to tear down the fences. Having advanced about two miles, the division halted, and our regiment and five companies of the Fifth, under Colonel Woodward, were sent out on picket. We found the Second Corps pickets engaged with the enemy on the pike for the possession of a piece of woods, and did not succeed in making our connection with their line until after dark, when we occupied the inner edge of the woods in dispute. The Second Corps fell back and changed their line twice through the night, and we had to alter ours to correspond with theirs.

The next morning, Sunday, we advanced our line, occupying the woods in dispute without opposition, crossed the pike and posted our line on the elevated ground beyond, sending Companies C and H, Captains Byrnes and Mealey, to occupy a piece of heavy timber further in advance and to the left within close proximity to the enemy's picket pits. Soon after, heavy artillery and musketry firing was heard on our right, and about four o'clock orders were received to withdraw our line about half a mile to the left. Here we formed the division, and soon afterwards were ordered to throw out our line as skirmishers, beyond the pike fronting the woods. Some sharp firing took place but without occasioning any loss on our side.

The division moved back about dark to their former position, and at nine o'clock that night we were relieved and joined them.

July the 13th was a rainy and disagreeable day, and we did not move until nearly three o'clock in the afternoon, when we were formed and marched to a long line of rifle-pits that the division had thrown up, and soon after to a field in front, where we laid all night.

That night orders were received to march early with the greatest secrecy, but when the morning came there was no occasion for this as the enemy had evacuated their position through the night. As we advanced we found three long lines of most formidable rifle-pits advantageously posted which the enemy had abandoned leaving many of their tools behind them. We also found a number of arms, and many prisoners were brought in, who proved to be the dirtiest set of mortals we had yet seen. During the march the "Bucktails" were posted on the right, and we on the left as flankers, and at ten A. M., we arrived within sight of Williamsport on the upper Potomac. At noon we re-commenced our march and proceeded to Falling Waters, where we arrived too late to participate in the brush with the enemy. Here our cavalry overtook the rear guard and captured two guns, three flags and a number of prisoners, and killed General Pettigrew. Lee's army crossed the night before on a trestle and boat bridge. We remained in position until about four o'clock, when we moved to a clover field and bivouacked.

The question has frequently been asked why did Meade permit Lee to escape? It must be remembered that our army was much fatigued by their late hard fighting and marching, and was seriously reduced in number. That upon the arrival of Lee upon the banks of the Potomac, he immediately commenced the erection of breastworks, and that the greatest difficulty General Meade experienced, was the impossibility of reconnoitring the enemy's position on account of the character of the country. A council of war was called and the five corps commanders present, decided against an attack, and it showed a proper prudence on the part of General Meade not to order a blind attack when ignorant of all essential matters, having therefore, no clear view that success was probable against a splendidly posted, desperate and powerful enemy. Had an attack been made on the 13th, Lee's whole army would have been found behind their works, as not a man left his lines until after dark that night. A defeat would have lost all the benefit of the past victory, and placed the North and Washington again at the command of Lee and his army.

The next morning, the 15th, at four o'clock we commenced our march, nearly retracing our steps, passing near Delamont and down the Hagerstown and Sharpsburg pike to the Keedysville road, and halted to make coffee about noon on the site of the "Smoketown Hospital." Near by was the burial ground with a handsome wooden monument about twelve feet high erected in the centre, by the convalescents. We were now on the battle-field of Antietam, whose rolling fields were covered with luxuriant grain ready for the harvest, and the deep forest was clothed with new foliage that sighed above the graves alike of friend and foe, peacefully slumbering together awaiting the last reveille. Moving on, we crossed the Antietam. passing through Keedysville, and over South Mountains by the same road we came, and encamped near its eastern base. The day was very warm, and the march was over a rough and hilly country, in many places with the roads very muddy, and the distance made being twenty-three miles, the men were much worn out.

We moved the next morning about five, skirting along the eastern base of South Mountains through Berkettsville and Petersville, and halted about two miles from Berlin and encamped in a fine woods about eleven A. M. The next day our wagons came up and the officers got a change of clothing, the first they had since we left Fairfax Station.

It rained heavily all night and through the day of the 17th, until four in the afternoon, when we moved off towards the Potomac, which we crossed on a pontoon bridge at Berlin and trod once more the soil of our adopted State. Moving on to Lovettsville, three miles beyond, we bivouacked in the rear of it, being the first infantry that had crossed. The inhabitants of this section are almost all loyal to the Union.

The next day our regiment was detailed as guard to the corps' wagon train, and starting at eleven, reached Wheatland at three P. M.

On the 19th, we marched at six o'clock in the morning and passing through Purcellville, bivouacked in a woods at ten A. M. We passed on the route a number of prisoners belonging to White's cavalry, captured by Kilpatrick's. Our movements were now rather cautious, as we had a large train, and the enemy's cavalry were in the neighborhood.

The next morning we sounded reveille at two, and moved at four o'clock, almost over the same ground we did last year under McClellan, passing by Philomont and our old camps, near Uniontown, and encamped about noon on Goose creek, in a woods on a hill side. Our route laid through a finely watered and picturesque country with fine farms and houses; one of the handsomest of which was that of Mr. Delaney's, a wealthy Englishman, who owned two thousand acres of land in detached parcels, but so thoroughly had been the destruction of the roads and landmarks, that he stated he could not trace the lines of any of his property, excepting the tract upon which his house is situated. Surveyors will reap a rich harvest in Virginia when the war is over.

The next day was spent in camp, the boys occupying their time in writing home, bathing, and washing clothes. In a long stone wall in the meadow in front of us, some copperheads were discovered, and soon nearly half of the division was at work with sticks and clubs hunting them, and in an incredibly short time the wall was leveled with the ground.

At two o'clock on the afternoon of the 22d, we marched off over the fields and along by roads to Rectortown and encamped near the Manassas Gap Railroad in a heavy woods. The next morning we formed a field hospital in a fine woods, and left all our wounded and sick in charge of a suitable number of surgeons and a guard, with provisions, medicines, etc. Among those left was Acting Sergeant-major H. C. Hostetter, who died and was buried there. He was a good soldier, an exemplary young man, and his death was regretted by all.

The next day we marched early keeping along the general course of the railroad, passing through Markham, Petersville, and Linden. Last fall the enemy tore up the rails of this road and heating them on piles of burning ties, bent and destroyed them. About three o'clock we reached the eastern base of the Gap, and soon after skirmishing commenced on Wapping Heights, which lasted until near dark, when the enemy were driven back with loss. Soon after we moved on past Wapping, which consisted of a defunct tavern, an empty store, and several shanties, and encamped about half a mile beyond. That day we marched twenty-five miles.

Being in the presence of the enemy, no "calls" were sounded. The next morning at seven o'clock we marched up the railroad, and moving to the right formed in columns of division and moved in by the right flank, and advanced up the sides of a steep mountain, covered with a heavy growth of timber and underbrush. So steep was it that the field officers found it impossible to descend the western slope on horseback. Having reached its base, the ascent of a still steeper and higher mountain was commenced, which required great exertion to accomplish, and by the time the command had crossed, the men were completely fagged out. The day was excessively hot, several men were sun struck, one broke his neck, and another was accidentally shot through the head by a comrade. A small force of the enemy could have held us at bay, and probably repulsed our brigade, as by the nature of the obstacle, the companies and regiments became mixed up together. A line of skirmishers properly supported would have been more effective. Upon arriving at the western base, the men were collected and reformed in a little valley, and after a half hour's rest, we marched back to our old bivouac. Soon after we moved two miles back and encamped, where we had fresh beef served out to us.

The Third brigade, which moved on the left of the railroad, captured several prisoners.

Through the day we learned that General French had captured eleven hundred head of cattle, a number of wagons, and about three hundred and fifty prisoners. From a high mountain back of where we laid, we had a magnificent view of the valley of the Shenandoah, the scenery of which equalled any we have ever seen. A large column of the enemy's cavalry or wagons were seen in rapid motion up the valley, as the sudden appearance of our army at the Gap made them fearful lest a portion of their army should be cut off. They effected their withdrawal by way of Strasburg, and retired to the Rapidan.

On the 25th, we sounded reveille at three, and moved at six o'clock, retracing our steps for some miles and then turning to the right, followed along the foot hills of the Blue Mountains, and halting about three in the afternoon, on an open field, where we bivouacked. We had been short of provisions for several days, the men living mostly on blackberries, which grew in luxuriance in this section, care being taken to halt us wherever a large patch was found. On our route we passed the house of Mr. James Marshall, which had been ransacked by stragglers. Mr. Marshall was a violent secessionist, and upon the approach of our troops fled with his family to Richmond. Occupied houses are seldom if ever touched by the men, but when one is found deserted, they generally take what they want.

The next morning we marched at five o'clock, passing a large number of prisoners near Orleans, who appeared in an exceedingly good humor. At noon we halted in a clover field about two miles from Warrenton, having made thirteen miles with a halt of but fifteen minutes.

While we laid here General Crawford was saluted with the cry of "crackers" from his hungry boys, which annoyed him so much that he went to General Meade and demanded rations. "Why, my dear General," replied the commander, "you should not let that annoy you." "One night at White Plains where I marched the boys a couple of miles out of the road they actually called me a 'four-eyed son of a b—h,' and upon my soul I could not get mad at them."*

On the march, Dr. E. O. Jackson one of our Assistant Surgeons was taken sick and sent from Warrenton to Washington where he died. He was a young gentleman of high professional talents and fine social qualities, and his death caused much regret.

Here Captain John M. Clark, Lieutenant Andrew McLean, Sergeant John McDonough, Sergeant Dennis O'Brien, Corporal Jeremiah Dooling, Corporal Thomas M. Fisher, were detailed to go to Pennsylvania after drafted men to fill our regiment, none of which they got.

At four in the afternoon we got into motion and marched six miles, passing to the west of Warrenton, and encamping in a low open field, where we were annoyed for the first time during the war by mosquitoes.

The next morning we sounded no reveille, but woke

---

* The General wore spectacles.

the men up early and marched at five o'clock towards Fayetteville, near which we halted at eight in the morning, for the night and day.

On the 28th, on account of the scarcity of water, we moved about a mile to a new position, where we laid until the 1st of August, spending one day of our time on picket. While here Lieutenant John Taylor commanding Company E, was appointed an aid on Colonel McCandless' staff.

On the 1st, we marched at five in the afternoon two miles towards Warrenton and bivouacked. There was through the afternoon, considerable cannonading heard towards the Warrenton Sulphur Springs, occasioned by our cavalry and light artillery skirmishing.

On the 3d, we moved at eight A. M., about three miles to our old bivouac of the 26th ult. The weather was so oppressively hot that in this short distance many men gave out and several were sunstruck. We remained there until dark, when we marched to our old bivouac of the 28th, where we laid two hours, when we again got under way and marched by a circuitous route eight miles and bivouacked at two the next morning within two miles of our last starting point, on our old camp ground of November last, under Burnside.

On the 4th, we moved camp about one mile. In the afternoon, during a heavy thunder storm, our own and the enemy's cavalry, supported with light artillery, met accidentally south of the Rappahannock, and had a heavy skirmish in which our men drove them and took a number of prisoners. The day before they had an encounter at Kelly's Ford with the same result.

On the 6th, General Gibbon took temporary command of our corps, Colonel McCandless of our division and Colonel William Cooper Talley of our brigade. Major Wiley paid the regiment off, and Lieutenant Craig, Company A, rejoined us, having recovered from his wounds received at Fredericksburg.

On the 8th, we marched early, and at noon arrived at

Rappahannock Station where we formed a regular encampment.

During our late marching and countermarching a large portion of our troops were sent to the City of New York (the left wing of Lee's army), to enforce the draft, with which a powerful mob had been permitted by the City and State authorities to interfere, and we being in the presence of a superior and vigilant foe it was necessary to deceive him as to our numbers, for which purpose we moved continually in a circle of some fifteen miles diameter, and the tramp of troops and the moving of artillery and wagons was heard night and day. At every stopping place orders were issued to lay out our camp regularly, dig sinks, and erect bough arbors over our tents, but no sooner were they finished than orders to march were received. In this manner, the enemy's spies and the inhabitants were utterly deceived, and when our army was reduced to probably twenty-five thousand men, the Richmond papers reported us as receiving large reinforcements and numbering over eighty thousand. The men soon understood and appreciated the strategy of General Meade.

This depletion of our army to maintain the authority of the Government and to enforce the laws at home, paralyzed the movements of General Meade, and virtually brought to a close the campaign at a season most favorable to its prosecution, and at a time auspicious of its success.

CHAPTER XXV.

RAPPAHANNOCK STATION. THE SWORD BANQUET. MILITARY EXECUTION. MARCH TO CULPEPPER COURT HOUSE.

IN our camp at the Station, wells and sinks were dug, bough arbors erected, clothing and an abundance of rations issued, our sutler's tent kept well supplied, mail facilities afforded, and the "Philadelphia Inquirer," the soldier's paper, received the day it was published. The usual routine of camp, guard mounting, drills and dress parades, were established, and the discipline which is so apt to become relaxed during an active campaign was re-established.

While here the boys who were always fond of bathing had ample opportunity of enjoying that luxury, but unfortunately one day Samuel Black of Company F was drowned.

Nothing of moment occurred until the middle of the month, when late one afternoon, notice was received that the enemy was advancing upon us, and orders were issued to be in readiness to fall in prepared for action at a moment's notice. A signal gun was fired from corps' head-quarters, upon which a large number of troops crossed the Rappahannock, but the night passed over without any sound of battle. The next morning it was ascertained the alarm had been occasioned by an aid having "a rush of rats to the head," which caused him to mistake our returning scouts for the enemy.

The officers of the Reserves having determined some time previous to present to General Meade a testimonial of their esteem and admiration for him, as an officer and leader, had procured through their chairman, Colonel McCandless, a costly sword of most exquisite workmanship, a sash, belt and a pair of gold spurs to offer for his acceptance. On the 28th the presentation took place.

Invitations were extended to Governor Curtin and a number of gentlemen prominent in civil and military life, who were present. The banquet was one of the most magnificent affairs of the kind ever gotten up in the Army of the Potomac. For ten days one hundred men had been engaged in decorating the grounds, building green arbors, arches and towers of the most exquisite taste and artistic style. The day was a most beautiful one, and about five in the evening, there gathered upon the ground a large assemblage of officers, of our division and the army, and among them some of the most distinguished heroes of the war, all dressed in full uniform, with sash and belt, but without swords. General Meade, surrounded by a staff of distinguished *personnel* mounted the stand, and General Crawford, taking the sword from the case, in a neat and appropriate speech, handed it to the general, who stepped forward, amid the most vociferous cheering, and responded as follows:

"GENERAL CRAWFORD AND OFFICERS OF THE DIVISION OF THE PENNSYLVANIA RESERVE CORPS:—I accept this sword with feelings of profound gratitude. I should be insensible to all the promptings of nature if I were not grateful and proud at receiving a testimonial of approbation from a band of officers and men so distinguished as has been the division of the Pennsyvania Reserve Corps, during the whole period of this war. I have a right, therefore, to be proud that they should think my conduct and my course have been of such a character as to justify them in collecting together here so many distinguished gentlemen, as I see around me, from different parts of the country, and our own State, to present to me this handsome testimonial. It in effect says to me, that in their judgment I have done my duty towards them and towards the country. I began my career in this army, by commanding the Second Brigade of your division. I faithfully endeavored, during all the time I held that command, and also the command of your division, to treat the officers and men in a manner that would express to them my high appreciation of their conduct as soldiers and brave men.

"I am very glad, sir, that you have mentioned your distinguished guest, the Governor of Pennsylvania. I have a personal knowledge of his patriotic efforts in behalf of the soldiers. To him the country is indebted for putting into the field in its hour of sorest need this splendid corps, and I have watched with pleasure and satisfaction the solicitude he has always shown, to see that all its interests and wants are attended to. I have been with him on the occasions when he has visited the officers and men from our State, and I know that they are indebted to him for many comforts, and that the country is indebted to him for words of eloquence which he addressed to them to inspire them with increased patriotism and courage. I am gratified that he is here to witness this presentation, and I heartily join you, sir, in the hope that his fellow-citizens will remember, on election day, his services in promoting the interests of the country and the suppression of the rebellion.

"In speaking of the pride which I experience in receiving this sword, I feel myself justified, even at the risk of being charged with egotism, in saying a few words about the services rendered by this division. I say unhesitatingly here before this assembly, and I am quite sure that when the history of the war is written, that the facts will vindicate me, that no division in this glorious army of the Potomac—glorious as I conceive it to be—is entitled to claim more credit for its uniform gallant conduct, and for the amount of hard fighting it has gone through, than the division of the Pennsylvania Reserve Corps. I do not wish to take any credit to myself in this. It is not of my own personal service that I would speak, but of the services of the soldiers—of the privates of the Pennsylvania Reserve Corps, and I have only to appeal to Drainesville, where the first success that crowned the arms of the Army of the Potomac was gained, unaided and alone, by a single brigade of the Pennsylvania Reserves. I have only to refer to Mechanicsville, where the whole of Longstreet's Corps was held in check for hours, and victory really won, by only two brigades of the Reserves. I refer you to New Market Cross roads, sometimes called Glendale, and refer emphatically to that battle, because certain officers of the army, not knowing the true facts of the case, and misled at the time by the statement of others equally ignorant with themselves, and whose statements have since been proved incorrect, brought charges against this division on that occasion. I was with the division during the whole fight, and until dark, when it pleased God that I should be shot down and carried off the field.

"I have been told that the division ran off, but I know that I stayed with it until it was dark, and my men were engaged in a hand-to-hand contest over the batteries with the enemy. I do not say that there were nôt some who ran away, but that is nothing singular. There are cowards in every division; there are bad men in every corps. I do say, however, that the large body of the gallant men of the Pennsylvania Reserves remained on the field until dark, and did not leave it until the enemy had retired. Those guns were never captured from them. They remained on the field, and were not taken until ten o'clock the next day. I refer to South Mountain, and it is not necessary for me to say much of their conduct there, for their gallant ascent of the height in the face of the enemy, and turning their left flank, was witnessed by the commanding general, and they received full credit for it. I speak of Antietam, where, on the 16th of September, the Pennsylvania Reserve Corps, always in the advance, boldly attacked that portion of the Confederate army in its front, without knowing its strength, and continued to drive it until dark, and then held the position it had gained until morning, when the battle was renewed. I speak again of Fredericksburg, where the Pennsylvania Reserve Corps crossed the railroad, and led the advance, unaided and alone, up the heights, and held their position for half an hour. Had they been followed and supported by other troops, their courage that day would have won a victory. I repeat, therefore, that I have a right to be proud and grateful when the officers and men of such a command, who can with truth point to a hard-earned and dearly-bought record of bright deeds, present me, who have had the honor of commanding them, with such a testimonial.

"While, however, I give expression to these feelings, they are not unmingled with others of a sad and mournful nature, as I look around you and reflect that so many of the brave officers and soldiers who originally composed this division sleep their last sleep, and that others have been obliged to return home crippled and maimed for life. It is terrible to think that there should be any necessity for so much misfortune and misery! Sad, that in this country, a land flowing with milk and honey, and in which we are all brothers, we should raise our arms against each other, and such scenes should be enacted as I have been a participant in. It is sad that there should be an occasion like the present, for the presentation of a testimonial such as this. These are sad, sad thoughts to me, but at the same time I am sustained in my present position by a consciousness that I am acting from a high and proper sense of my duty to my country. It is impossible that this great country should be divided; that there should be two governments or two flags on this continent. Such a thing is entirely out of the question. I trust that every loyal man would be willing to sacrifice his life before he would consent to have more than one government and one flag wave over the whole territory of the United States. This re-union, gentlemen, awakens in my heart new sorrow for an officer which it vividly recalls to my mind, for he commanded the division when I commanded one of the brigades. He was the noblest as well as the bravest gentleman in the army. I refer to John F. Reynolds. I cannot receive this sword without thinking of that officer. When he fell at Gettysburg, leading the advance, I lost not only a lieutenant of the utmost importance to me, but I may say that I lost a friend, aye, even a brother. I miss other faces which were familiar to me in your midst—Bayard, of the cavalry; Jackson, of the Third brigade; Simmons, of the Fifth; McNeil and Taylor, of the Rifles; young Kuhn, who came from Philadelphia to assist me in the field; Dehone, and a host of others whose memories you all cherish.

"It is oppressive, gentlemen, to me to go over the list of these officers who have been sacrificed; but if I could remember and name every soldier of your division that has fallen, what a long list, and what a trying recital it would be to us all! How many men who once belonged to the Pennsylvania Reserve Corps now sleep in the grave, or are lingering on earth, joyfully expecting death to end their sufferings.

"I thank you, General Crawford, for the kind manner in which you have conveyed to me this elegant testimonial, and I also thank these gentlemen who have come so far to be present. I trust, sir, this sword will be required but a short time longer. Affairs and events now look as if this unhappy war might be brought to a happy termination. I have to request of you, gentlemen, who are in civil life, that, when you return home, you will spare no efforts to make the people understand that all we want are men to fill up our ranks. Send these to us. Give us the numbers, and the war will soon be concluded. I think the Confederates are now satisfied that their struggle is only a matter of time, as we have the force on our side, and that as soon as they see that we are bringing out that force in earnest they will yield. Permit me, before I close, to mention what I intended to refer to before this, but it escaped my memory. I intended to express my delight, sir, on hearing that at Gettysburg, under your command, the Reserve Corps enacted deeds worthy of their former reputation, showing that they had lost none of their daring, and could always be relied on in the hour and post of danger. I expected that this would be the case, it was particularly gratifying to me to hear it from your immediate commander on that occasion. Thanking you for your gallantry there, and again thanking you for your kindness, I will conclude."

The general was followed by Governor Andrew G. Curtin, in a patriotic and soul-stirring speech, in which he paid a touching tribute to our dead, and spoke with the highest admiration and deepest regret of the lamented Reynolds. After his Excellency followed Colonel R. Biddle Roberts, late of the First Reserves, the Honorable Morton McMichael and Colonel John W. Forney after which all retired to the banquet hall, where was spread all the delicacies that a refined taste and epicurian palate could suggest. After passing a most happy evening, about ten o'clock the mirthful party broke up, the civilians taking the cars at Bealton Station, and the officers dispersing to their various camps.

The day following the banquet, the execution of five substitute deserters took place in the presence of the Fifth Corps, to which they belonged. The spot chosen was well fitted for the occasion, the troops being drawn up on the slope of a hill from which all could witness it. A death procession, composed of the culprits, a priest, a rabbi, the guard, the firing party, and the band, to the most beautiful and solemn dirges, passed down the line and halted in front of the graves. The prisoners seated themselves upon their coffins, were blindfolded, a short prayer was said, the orders, "ready"—"aim"—"fire"—given, and the culprits fell back dead. Their graves were filled up, and the troops marched back to their camps with their bands playing merry tunes. Men who sell their blood for money and then desert, deserve no sympathy.

On the first of September Lieutenant-colonel G. A. Woodward left us, he having been transferred to the Invalid Corps, on account of wounds received at Glendale, which incapacitated him for field service, although in his crippled condition he served through the Pennsylvania campaign.

The command of the regiment devolved upon Major McDonough.

On the 15th orders were received to march, and the next morning at eight we moved, crossing the Rappahannock at Beverly's Ford, and halted for the night near Mountain run. Early the next morning we moved on, passing through Culpepper, which is a fine town and encamped about four miles beyond. Beyond the town the country was more hilly and wooded, and on an elevated range we found the marks of the artillery fight of the preceding Sunday. The trees were torn and shivered, and the carcasses of numerous horses emitted a most intolerable stench. Some of the rascally rebs took the trouble, and that under fire, of driving some of their wounded horses to the neighboring wells and tumbling them in, to spoil the water for us. On the outskirts of the town is a soldiers' burial ground, containing about a regiment, formed in column of companies, with the graves neatly sodded and marked with head-boards.

About this time Adjutant Woodward was honorably discharged the service on account of disability, and Lieutenant John L. Rhoads, commanding Company G, appointed his successor.

CHAPTER XXVI.

LEE'S ATTEMPT TO FLANK. BACK TO THE RAPPAHANNOCK. TO BRANDY STATION. THE BATTLE OF BRISTOE. TO CENTREVILLE AND FAIRFAX COURT HOUSE. VICTORIES AT RAPPAHANNOCK STATION AND KELLEY'S FORD. REBEL CABINS. CROSSING THE RAPIDAN. BATTLE OF MINE RUN. WINTER QUARTERS AT BRISTOE. FLAG PRESENTATION. REORGANIZATION OF THE ARMY.

NOTHING of importance occurred while we laid here until early in October, at which time the contending forces occupied opposite banks of the Rapidan river, our line extending from near Falmouth on the left to Robertson's and Hazel rivers, beyond Thoroughfare Mountain on the right, the centre being in front of Culpepper Court House. On the 9th it was discovered that the enemy had commenced advancing northward, evidently with the intention of interrupting our line of communication with Washington. A corresponding movement was necessary on our part, and orders were issued that night to the army to be prepared to move at short notice. At two o'clock the next morning, our division moved towards Culpepper, and then turning to the left marched around Poney Mountain and bivouacked at Racoon Ford, where we remained until two the next morning, when we marched back to our old camp. Early in the morning we were again in motion, acting as the rear guard of the army and passing through Culpepper moved in the direction of Rappahannock Station, where, upon our arrival, we were drawn up in line of battle, in which position we remained until night, when we crossed the river and bivouacked in our old camp of August and September last. The enemy followed us up closely through the day, and at Brandy Station a smart fight took place between our and their cavalry, in which the latter was handsomely repulsed.

On the 12th, General Meade, for the purpose of ascertaining the true extent of the enemy's demonstration, sent several corps back across the river. Early in the morning we crossed the river at Beverly's Ford, and formed in line of battle and laid there until near sundown, when we advanced to Brandy Station. Our cavalry commenced skirmishing about ten, A. M., and by night drove the enemy back to Culpepper. At midnight we marched for the river again, but in the darkness getting separated from our corps, we did not arrive at our old camp until three o'clock on the morning of the 13th.

In this movement General Meade was successful, and on the same night Lee crossed the river further up. At seven o'clock on the morning of the 13th we moved towards Warrenton some distance, and then inclining to the right, marched for Catlett's Station, near where we bivouacked.

The two armies were now pushing forward on parallel lines, the intention of General Lee being to seize the heights of Centreville with a portion of his army, and with the remainder to fall upon our flank and rear, hoping by a sudden and determined attack to rout our army.

THE BATTLE OF BRISTOE STATION, OCTOBER 14TH, 1863.—At four o'clock on the morning of the 14th we took up our march, moving nearly abreast of the Second Corps, and halting for rest after crossing Broad run. On the Second Corps reaching Bristoe Station, they found Hill's corps drawn up in line of battle. The troops which had advanced on the left of the railroad were double quicked to the right, and the cut and embankment, which Hill had neglected to occupy, were taken possession of. General Warren hastily formed his troops under cover of the cut and embankment, and the enemy making an impetuous charge upon his left flank, the men rose from their cover, and at close range, poured volley after volley into them. During the short but severe engagement that followed, the enemy were repulsed, they flying from the field, leaving their dead and wounded, several hundred prisoners and seven guns, two of which they subsequently recovered.

Our division had hardly crossed Broad run before the enemy opened upon us with a battery, when we were double quicked out of range, and formed behind a wood, while a battery was got into position, which soon silenced theirs. The division was then ordered forward to support the Second Corps, and re-wading Broad run, advanced, but by the time we arrived upon the field it was dark, and the fighting had mostly ceased. We then continued our march, fording Bull run about three o'clock the next morning, and laid down for a few hours rest.*

And at nine the same morning we were again on the move, passing through Centreville to Fairfax Court House, where we bivouacked in a woods, near the town, and remained until the morning of the 17th, when we advanced to Centreville and remained there all night, the next morning returning to Fairfax Court House.

On the 19th, at four, A. M., we again moved, retracing our steps towards Centreville, fording Bull run, and that night sleeping on the battle-field. Here we found our dead mostly as they had fallen, and we laid down and slept among the bones of our comrades.

The next morning, the 20th, reveille was sounded at one o'clock, but we did not move until six, we passing Gainesville and halting near New Baltimore, where we remained until the 26th, when we marched as wagon guard to New Auburn. While we laid here, Major McDonough was mustered in as lieutenant-colonel, and Captain R. Ellis as major. The first mentioned appointment gave satisfaction to all.

On the 30th at six A. M., we marched to Warrenton Junction, and remained there until the 7th of November

---

* See Appendix A.

THE VICTORIES OF RAPPAHANNOCK STATION AND KELLEY'S FORD, NOVEMBER 7TH.—The enemy had in the mean time entrenched themselves on the north and south banks of the Rappahannock, near Rappahannock Station, and deeming themselves secure from interference, had commenced the construction of huts on the south side, with the expectation of remaining there during the winter. To their surprise, however, early in the afternoon of the 7th, General Sedgwick with the Fifth and Sixth Corps, arrived before their works, and driving their skirmishers before him, occupied a crest less than a mile distant, and posted his guns. Our corps was held in reserve, under cover of favorable ground, near our old camp. An artillery duel commenced, and during its progress a storming party, consisting of four regiments, of Russell's brigade, and two of Colonel Upton's, was organized, and with a cheer made a desperate assault upon the forts and rifle-pits. To reach the works half a mile of open plain had to be traversed, but regardless of the heavy fire that was opened upon them, they moved steadily forward at double-quick without firing a single shot until they reached the works. Here a desperate hand-to-hand struggle commenced and continued for about twenty minutes, resulting in a complete victory to our troops, and the surrender of the enemy. Four guns and two thousand stand of arms were captured, and about one thousand six hundred officers and men taken prisoners.

In the meantime General French had been sent with the First, Second, and Third Corps to Kelley's Ford, where, after a brief but warm engagement, he succeeded in capturing the rifle-pits and a large number of prisoners and their arms.

Late in the afternoon, our regiment was advanced towards the river, and a detail of seventy men under Captain Byrnes sent out as pickets to hold Fordmand's Ford, on the south side of which the enemy were in considerable force, and had a long line of rifle-pits erected. During the night the enemy withdrew.

The next morning, the 8th, we reached Kelley's Ford, and about one P. M. crossed the Rappahannock, and massed in column of division, halted awhile, and then advanced about two miles and took possession of the fine winter quarters built by A. P. Hill's Corps, which we found much more comfortable than our own shelter tents. They were composed of log cabins with shingled roofs, ample chimney-places, and furnished with bunks, tables, and stools. Here were captured three thousand pair of drawers, a large lot of harness, muskets, horse-shoes, blacksmith's coal, etc.

On the 10th we marched to Mountain run, where we also found comfortable quarters, which the enemy had erected in expectation of enjoying a pleasant winter's rest. We remained here until the 24th, during which time we were paid off by Major Smith, had several inspections, and drilled continually.

On the 24th we broke camp, and marched in the direction of the Rapidan, but on account of the violence of a rain storm that set in, we countermarched and returned to our quarters where we remained until the 26th.

On the 26th, we again marched from our quarters towards the Rapidan, which we crossed at Culpepper Mine Ford, and advanced on the Culpepper Plank road, and halted near its junction with the Orange Plank road, and bivouacked for the night within three miles of Chancellorsville.

On the 27th was fought the battle of Locust Grove, which resulted in the success of our arms and the retreat of the enemy, with heavy loss. That morning we marched to New Hope Church, where we found Gregg's cavalry division, which we relieved, and then throwing out skirmishers, formed in line of battle, and laid down all day under a heavy shelling without pulling a trigger.*

* See Appendix A.

On the 28th, the enemy were pursued towards their defences on the west bank of Mine run, a small tributary of the Rapidan. Their position was a very strong one, the line being formed on a series of ridges with enfilading positions for batteries, while in front stretched an extensive marsh. That morning we moved to the right and halted at Robinson's tavern.

On the 29th, we advanced to Mine run, and formed a line of battle, and bivouacked there for the night. On the 30th, we were advanced to the right and deployed as skirmishers, and then moved into a woods where we laid until the 2d of December. The shelling on both sides was for a time very heavy, but little damage, however was done.* The men suffered severely from the cold, some being frozen to death, and others carried to the rear, totally benumbed. General Warren reported that the enemy's right could be carried, but after a careful examination of the position, General Meade concluded it could not be done without a fearful sacrifice of life. Accordingly a retrograde movement was decided upon, and on the 2d it was commenced, a large portion of the army returning to their old quarters at Brandy Station, while a portion was stretched along the Orange and Alexandria Railroad for its protection.

On the evening of the 2d, we commenced falling back, and crossed the Rapidan at five o'clock the next morning, when we took a couple of hours rest, marching again at eight o'clock for Brandy Station, where we bivouacked for the night. On the 4th, we moved across the Rappahannock, and arrived at Bristoe Station on the 5th.

During this movement, the army suffered much from cold, many times being in positions that forebade the building of fires. Yet they stood the fatigues and hardships with great fortitude, and were as rugged and hearty as ever.

Our encampment laid on the south side of Broad run,

See Appendix A.

on a hill overlooking the surrounding country. We had the good fortune to occupy the log cabins built by the One-hundred-and-forty-ninth regiment Pennsylvania volunteers, which we found quite comfortable, and regularly laid out in company streets. Surrounding all was a rifle-pit.

About two miles to the southeast laid the almost deserted village of Brentsville, the county town of Prince William. This village, like most others in Virginia, being deprived of all the active portion of its population and trade, was soon deserted by those that remained, who had no other alternative but starvation. Daily the soldiers entered the deserted village and carried off doors, windows, weather-boards, bricks, etc., to their camps, and soon but little was left of the village, except a few occupied houses, the chimneys and innumerable cats and dogs. Many of the latter were brought to camp, each mess having its pet, which, though very agreeable companions by day, sometimes made night hideous with their noise.

During the winter, the guerrillas became exceedingly bold and annoying, sometimes approaching quite near our picket lines, and several skirmishes took place with them. On the 28th of January, 1864, John Hoover, Company F, was ambuscaded by them, and wounded in the arm, which it was necessary to amputate.

About this time Lieutenant James C. Manton, of Company B, while being conveyed home, died at Alexandria. He was a brave young officer of much promise, and had been in command of his company for a long while. He was buried in Philadelphia.

On the 17th of February, First Lieutenant Robert R. Smith, Company D, joined us, he having recovered from his wound received at Antietam.

Nothing of interest occurred until the 14th of March, when a Committee of the Cooper Shop Volunteer Refreshment Saloon, consisting of Messrs. Joseph Megary, Philip Fitzpatrick, E. S. Cooper, William Cooper, Jr.,

Samuel W. Nichols, Charles McDonough, William Dougherty and Joseph T. Packer, visited camp, charged with the presentation of a beautiful silk flag and markers to the regiment. The day was a beautiful one, and the presentation ceremony took place in the presence of the brigade, which was formed on three sides of a square, with the Second as the base.

About two o'clock, the Committee, accompanied by Colonel McCandless, commanding the division, and Colonel Talley, commanding the brigade, their respective staffs, and a number of ladies, rode to the centre of the square and dismounted, when Mr. Megary stepped to the front with the flag, which he presented in a neat and patriotic speech, which was responded to on behalf of the regiment by Colonel McCandless. The color-guard then advanced, and the Color-sergeant, Joseph F. Sweeton, received it, amid the loud cheers of the boys and patriotic strains of the band. The colonel and the committee then took position and the brigade passed in review, after which they repaired to the camp of the Second, where a handsome collation had been prepared in a large tent, beautifully decorated with evergreens. After the removal of the cloth, toasts were drunk, and patriotic speeches, abounding in wit and humor, were made, and at taps all retired to their quarters.

About this time the reorganization of the Army of the Potomac was commenced, some of the army corps, divisions, and brigades, being broken up and consolidated with others. The three brigades of the First division of the Fifth Corps were consolidated into two brigades, and the Second Division was consolidated into one brigade, all designated as the First Division, Fifth Corps, commanded by Brigadier-general Charles Griffin.

The Second brigade of the Third Division, First Corps, was transferred to the Second division, First Corps, and this division was designated the Second Division, Fifth Corps, commanded by Brigadier-general J. C. Robinson.

The old Third Division (Pennsylvania Reserves) Fifth

Corps, was retained as the Third Division, Fifth Corps, commanded by Brigadier-general S. W. Crawford.

The First brigade of the Third Division, First Corps, was transferred to the First Division, First Corps, and this division was designated as the Fourth Division, Fifth Corps, commanded by Brigadier-general J. S. Wadsworth.

The command of the Fifth Corps was assigned to General Warren, General Sykes being relieved.

From this time every thing passed off comparatively quiet until the 29th of April, when we were relieved by Burnside's Corps. At ten A. M., on that day we broke camp, and marched one mile beyond Warrenton Junction, where we bivouacked. The next morning we marched at five o'clock, crossed the Rappahannock and encamped about a mile to the east of the Culpepper Court House, where we remained until the 4th of May.

CHAPTER XXVII.

POSITION OF THE ARMIES. OPENING OF GRANT'S CAMPAIGN. THE BATTLE OF THE WILDERNESS. THE BATTLE OF SPOTTSYLVANIA COURT HOUSE. ENGAGEMENT AT GUINNEY'S STATION. ENGAGEMENT AT NORTH ANNA. TERM OF SERVICE EXPIRES. THE REGIMENT RESOLVES TO REMAIN. THE BATTLE OF BETHESDA CHURCH. THE PARTING. MARCHING HOME. RECEPTION IN HARRISBURG AND PHILADELPHIA. PRESENTATION OF MEDALS.

AT this time our army was consolidated near Culpepper Court House, about ten miles north of the Rapidan, the Confederate army was mainly at Orange Court House, about ten miles south of the river: the outposts and pickets of both armies reaching that stream, on either side. On the morning of the 3d of May, orders for the advance of our army were issued. The crossing of the Rapidan was effected during that day and the following night, mainly at Germanna and Ely's Fords, twelve and eighteen miles east of Culpepper. Instead of marching directly south upon Lee's strong position at Orange, and the entrenchments on Mine river, a few miles distant, which Meade had found in November too strong to be assailed, and which were now doubtless still stronger, General Grant's plan was to turn them upon the right, that is, to the east, and thus throw himself between these positions and Richmond. The effect of this movement would be that Lee must either come out of his entrenchments, and defeat this advance upon open ground, or fall back towards Richmond. This line of advance would compel Grant to traverse the region locally known as the Wilderness.

The Wilderness is a broken, sterile tract of country, in Spottsylvania County, commencing not far from the south bank of the Rapidan, and stretching ten or fifteen miles in each direction. The region is intersected in every direction by gullies and ravines of no great depth, but with steep sides, interspersed here and there with swamps. The low hills and swells are covered with a thick growth of stunted pines, dwarf oaks, and underbrush, hardly reaching the height of a man, but so dense as to be almost impenetrable. The roads which straggle here and there, crossing and recrossing, are, with one or two exceptions, mere paths, impassable for the rudest vehicle, even in good weather, and converted into quagmires by a few hours' rain. Here and there, at the intersection of these roads, is a tavern or store, with half a dozen rude dwellings grouped around it. Besides these, and here and there a solitary dwelling, the whole tract is almost bare of inhabitants. Across this desolate region Grant's army must pass in order to carry out the design of turning the works at Mine run. That it would be attacked by the Confederates, whose intimate knowledge of the region would give them a decided advantage, was a probability which had to be taken into consideration in venturing upon the movement.

The army, under the immediate lead of General Meade—Lieutenant-general Grant, who accompanied it, taking the general direction of the whole series of combined movements—crossed the Rapidan in the course of Wednesday, May 4th. The passage was made mainly on pontoon bridges, which had been thrown across during the previous night. It was effected without opposition, apparently before the enemy, some miles distant, were aware of the intention. The Fifth Corps, under Warren, and the Sixth, under Sedgwick, crossed at Germanna Ford; The Second, under Hancock, crossed at Ely's Ford; the Ninth, under Burnside, being held in reserve, on the north bank. The army moved in light marching order, carrying six days' rations, leaving its train to follow after. That night the army encamped beyond the south bank of the Rapidan.

On the 4th we broke camp and crossed the river about eleven A. M., and bivouacked on the Lacy farm. The next morning Companies A, D, E and H, under Captain Mealey, were detailed with a like number of the Sixth regiment, as train and ambulance guard, and did not rejoin us until the 11th.

The Battle of the Wilderness, May 5th, 6th and 7th, 1864.—At three A. M., the line of march was taken up through the Wilderness. The enemy being within striking distance, it was necessary to assume and maintain a line of battle fronting towards him—to the west—while we at the same time moved slowly southward. Our line stretched from the northwest to the southwest and moved left in front, Hancock holding the advance and left, Sedgwick the rear and right, with our corps—Warren's—in the centre. The movement had hardly begun, and before Warren's corps had got into position, before the enemy were discovered approaching in force, Lee evidently intending to repeat his favorite movement of hurling his troops in masses upon the weakest point of our lines. The attack was made by Ewell's and Hill's corps, first upon one point, and then in succession upon others. Some of these assaults were successful at the outset; in one, nearly a thousand prisoners and two guns were captured; but the enemy in the end was foiled in each, and utterly failed in his purpose to break our lines or force us to recross the Rapidan.

The battle extended far into the night, and the loss, which was heavy, was probably about equal on both sides; though they took some seven hundred more prisoners than we did. The battle was indecisive, and both armies rested upon their arms in their respective positions upon the field.

When the enemy was first discovered advancing, our division was moving to its position, on the right of Hancock, and was immediately double-quicked and deployed into line of battle, our regiment being thrown out as skirmishers. In this formation we advanced to a clear piece of ground, bordering on the Wilderness, where the enemy's skirmishers were discovered on our left and front, with their main force to our right. Here General Crawford detached the Second, Seventh and Eleventh regiments of our brigade, and ordered McCandless to move in upon the enemy. The colonel filed the men to the right, until he had obtained his front, when he ordered them to advance. A most spirited and exciting fight now took place, we driving the enemy for about a half mile on to Wadsworth's division, who were before hardly pressed. Here a stubborn resistance was attempted by them, and McCandless seeing the critical position of Wadsworth, ordered a charge, heading it in person, and followed by Dr. Donnelly, Lieutenant Taylor, and other members of his staff and his orderlies. Animated by the heroic conduct of their commander, the brigade followed on the run with loud cheers. The enemy were soon broken, and driven from their position, but such was the impetuosity of the charge that most of the brigade staff, Captain Byrnes, and many others were captured; McCandless himself escaped by running the gauntlet of their fire, and passed out unscathed.

General Crawford having changed the position of the balance of the division, our battalions were in imminent danger of being captured, the enemy attempting to turn our left flank. This movement, however, was foiled by making a left half wheel to the rear, and then by doubling around a hill and woods for four miles, under an infantry and artillery fire, we were brought off, and rejoined the division near the Lacy farm. Here rifle-pits were improvised, and we laid down for the night in line of battle.

The scene during the battle was of the most exciting nature, the underbrush taking fire and wrapping the Wilderness far and near in dense clouds of flame and smoke, through which the brave boys went, and in which many of their wounded comrades perished.*

On the 6th, both Generals Grant and Lee resolved to take the offensive, but Lee, who had been joined by Longstreet during the night, however, got the start, and repeated his tactics of the preceding day, with even more determination. Grant also tried the offensive, and the two lines of battle, irregularly formed among the dense thickets, swayed back and forth during the whole day, first at one point, and now at another. Upon several instances, the enemy succeeded in breaking through our lines, but in every case they were signally repulsed.

The last and most desperate of these attempts was made just at nightfall, when a furious dash was made upon the extreme right of Sedgwick's corps, which had remained for hours almost unassailed. Seymour's and Shalers's brigades were swept away, and both generals captured. The whole right wing was in great peril, and if it had been crushed the entire army would have been severed from its supplies across the Rapidan, and unless the enemy had been checked a ruinous defeat would have been almost inevitable. Sedgwick, however, rallied his forces and checked the enemy. In the gathering dark-

* See Appendix A.

ness they were probably unaware of the extent of their success, and moreover, they were exhausted by the terrible struggle of the day, and withdrew under cover of the darkness.

At eight o'clock that morning, our brigade, in support of the Third, advanced about one mile, and met the enemy, who, with their skirmishers, we drove back some distance, when they took post in a ravine, which offered them protection equal to a breastwork. General Crawford, deeming the advantage to be gained by carrying it, would not warrant the heavy sacrifice it would require contented himself in holding them in their position, which he did until four o'clock, by laying the men down in front of it. About this time General Warren rode up, and after reconnoitring the position, ordered us to fall back to our old place, near the Lacy house.

About dark an aid came dashing down and ordered us to fall in, and in a moment we were double-quicking down the Plank road to Sedgwick's relief. Upon arriving we were put into position, but soon after moved to the left, where we succeeded in re-establishing his lines. About ten o'clock we were relieved by his troops, and marched back to our old position, where we arrived about two the next morning.

The whole battle, like that of the day before, was a series of desperate assaults, successful at first, but finally signally repelled. The battle was a drawn one, yet we were edging a little out of the Wilderness on to ground where we could use artillery, the fighting heretofore being confined to musketry, resembling Indian bush-fighting on a large scale.

At daybreak on the 7th, our artillery on the right opened fire, but could not elicit any response. Skirmishers were thrown out, and the whole line advanced, but as no regular opposition was met with, it was evident that the Confederates were falling back. Our army was immediately put in motion, marching southward by a road nearly parallel with the enemy's, the aim of both being Spottsylvania Court House. Lee arrived there first, and took up a strong position, that had been previously fortified.

THE BATTLE OF SPOTTSYLVANIA COURT HOUSE, MAY 8TH, 9TH, 10TH, 11TH, 12TH, 18TH AND 19TH.—Our regiment, after considerable countermarching, was sent on picket, and did not move with the main body. In the afternoon a sprinkling fire took place between the lines, in which Captain Smith was slightly wounded. That night we were withdrawn, and on the 8th marched to Spottsylvania Court House, a distance of fifteen miles, passing over the ground cleared by Sheridan's cavalry, and acting as rear guard. Upon our arrival, we found our division engaged, and we went under fire about two P. M. The battle soon after became furious, but in spite of the burning woods, and the fire of the enemy, we broke, and then drove them nearly two miles, when finding we were going too far, we halted, and soon after returned to our original position and slept upon the field. Our loss was heavy, including Colonel McCandless, who received a painful wound in the arm.*

We believe that "The Blue Coats," are a good hearted, glorious set of boys, and that heaven was made for Blue Coats and pretty ladies, but it is with deep humiliation and sorrow that we are compelled to acknowledge that we cannot vouch for their honesty. Will you believe it, reader?—just think how cruel it was—after the innocent Second had marched fifteen miles, and fought a hard battle, some rascally Blue Coats stole all their meat and left them to go supperless to bed. We said our prayers a little, and then forgave them as they were Blue Coats—but if we had found out what regiment it was, and had once have laid eyes on their commissary stores, they would have had nothing to eat for a week. But fortunately for us, the trains arrived through the night, and rations were distributed to the whole army.

---

* See Appendix A.

Colenel McCandless being wounded, and Colonel Talley having been taken prisoner, the command of our brigade devolved upon Colonel Jackson of the Eleventh.

The 9th opened comparatively quiet, but early in the afternoon, the enemy made an unsuccessful assault on Wilcox's division; and there was sharp skirmishing at various points of the line, in one of which the gallant General Sedgwick was killed. His loss was severely felt by the army. Towards dusk General Grant threw several divisions across one of the branches of the Mattapony. Through the day there were the usual charges and repulses, without any definite result, the Confederates holding a semi-circular line around the Court House, and we closely confronting them.

Early in the day, we were ordered to the right, where we took a position, and threw up breastworks. Hardly had they been completed before our line was slightly changed, which rendered it necessary to throw up new ones. Soon after we moved to the right, and crossing a deep ravine, advanced to a road through a growth of scrub oaks, in which we received a heavy fire, but so high that the minnies only tipped our bayonets. Crossing the road, we charged, driving the enemy before us, until within forty yards of a heavy woods, when we in turn were driven back by a new line that suddenly emerged from it. When we reached the road, the boys rallied and handsomely repulsed the enemy, who contented themselves with annoying us with a desultory and long-ranged musket fire. Here we again threw up temporary entrenchments.

The morning of the 10th was opened by a sharp cannonade, preparatory to a general attack, which was to be made along the whole line. The contest through the day, though most furious was indecisive in its results, though upon the whole strongly in our favor. In the morning we were engaged in building rifle-pits, and afterwards our regiment was sent on picket. The enemy in our front became restive about noon, and soon we became engaged in a spirited skirmish, which was continued until dark, when it ceased by mutual consent.*

Before daybreak on the 11th, Hancock's corps was massed, and our division deployed to occupy the ground left vacant by them. It rained heavily throughout the day, and all remained quiet until the afternoon, when some slight skirmishing took place.

General Grant in an official report to the Secretary of War, dated this day, says: "We have now ended the sixth day of very heavy fighting. The result to this time is very much in our favor. Our losses have been heavy, as well as those of the enemy. I think the loss of the enemy must be greater. We have taken over five thousand prisoners in battle, while he has taken from us but few, except stragglers." * * * *

During the night, the position of the corps were changed, Hancock, finding himself in front of the Confederate division, under General E. Johnson, who were strongly entrenched. At daylight on the 12th, these works were charged and carried with a rush, the whole division, with its commander, being made prisoners. During the day, there was hard fighting along the lines, we taking between three and four thousand prisoners, including two general officers, and over thirty pieces of artillery. The fighting was of the most obstinate nature, lasting until after dark, and being renewed about nine o'clock continued off and on with more or less vigor all night.

At one A. M., we moved into rifle-pits, and at daybreak the enemy opened upon us a heavy fire of artillery, to which our guns promptly responded. Between us and the works occupied by the enemy, there was a valley, covered by a heavy pine and scrub underbrush, the pits of each party crowning the opposite crests. Through the morning our guns having silenced the fire of the enemy's, we leaped over the pits, and charging down through the valley, we went up to the breastworks,

---

* See Appendix A.

and planted our banners upon them, but such was the terrible fire of the enemy and the stubborn resistance that we were driven back to our own works. The boys were then laid down behind the pits and told to rest themselves and make coffee, after which we opened the fight again, charging twice over the valley and being driven back each time with heavy loss, Lieutenants Robinson, Company C, being severely, and Clark, Company F, mortally wounded. In the last charge, we maintained our position for a long while, and did not retire until relieved by Colter's brigade.*

The 13th passed in comparative quietness, the rain that had been falling for two days past still continuing. On the 14th, we advanced southward crossing the Po, and passing the 15th and 16th without any fighting. On the 17th, we marched some distance, and threw up intrenchments within sight of the Court House.

On the 18th, the battle that had lulled for several days past, was renewed, Hancock attacking the enemy's right, carrying two lines of his intrenchments and capturing six guns. General Burnside at the same time attacked and drove the enemy's left some distance, but subsequently withdrew.

The 19th was passed in unusual quietness, until about six o'clock, when a sharp fire of musketry was heard to our right, and well to the rear. It was evident that the enemy had attempted to turn our right, for the purpose of cutting off our supplies on the Fredericksburg pike. Troops were immediately put in motion to meet them. A portion of General Tyler's division, consisting for the most part of raw recruits, being nearest, were the first to encounter them, and succeeded in recapturing the ambulances and wagons and driving the enemy back into the woods, but were in turn repulsed themselves and compelled to retire. The balance of the division, however, coming up, the prize was again wrenched from their hands and the enemy signally repulsed. Our loss

---

* See Appendix A.

was only nine hundred killed and wounded, while that of Ewell's was one thousand two hundred and fifty, besides five hundred taken prisoners.

When the firing was first heard, our division was put in motion and double-quicked up the plank road to the field, but, as by the time we arrived, the battle was over, we returned to our position and rested for the night.

Everything was quiet on the 20th, and the enemy in our front showing a disposition of friendliness it was reciprocated on our part, the boys exchanging newspapers, etc. That night, General Grant began to manœuvre to draw General Lee out of his intrenchments, for which purpose Hancock moved to the left, and in the evening advanced southward. He continued his march the next day, and in the evening occupied Bowling Green. Hancock's movement was discovered by the enemy and Longstreet an hour afterwards moved south also.

ENGAGEMENT AT GUINNEY'S STATION, MAY 21ST.—The next day, the 21st, at noon, our division marched to the crossing of the Fredericksburg and Richmond Railroad, at a stream three miles south of Guinney's Station, where we arrived about three o'clock in the afternoon. We crossed the stream and advanced some five hundred yards, when a terrific fire from some twenty pieces of artillery was opened us, but quickly advancing a short distance we laid down behind a gentle rise of ground, and let the missiles pass harmlessly over our heads. As we had not the slightest idea under these circumstances, of interfering with the enemy's arrangements, and as they did not in the least disturb us, we had a comfortable rest of nearly two hours, during which time there was a great deal of harmless wrath vented upon us. The enemy afterwards withdrew and we occupied the heights.

ENGAGEMENT AT NORTH ANNA, May 23d.—On the 22d we went on picket, and the next afternoon, at two o'clock, we marched down the Telegraph road, past

Mount Carmel Church, to Jericho Ford, where we crossed the North Anna river about five o'clock. There we found the enemy in force, and after the usual preliminary shelling, he advanced his infantry to a charge, but they were signally repulsed. The battle lasted with considerable spirit until night, our division taking over four hundred prisoners, mostly South Carolinians.

On the 24th, we moved to the left and intrenched ourselves, and remained inactive and quiet until the 26th. By this time Grant's entire army was between the North and South Anna rivers, and within twenty-five miles of Richmond. On the north bank of the latter river was General Lee's new line of defence.

On the 25th, the three years term of service of our regiment expired, and General Crawford put the question to the boys, whether they would go home alone, or remain until the 31st, when the other regiments of the division would be relieved. They unanimously decided to remain with their comrades and see the old division through. This decision was highly gratifying to the General and all the officers.

On the same day, Lieutenant Justus, Acting Quartermaster, while out procuring forage for division headquarters, was captured by the enemy.

To all appearances, it was Grant's intention to assault Lee in his new line, as he did the former one along the Po. But, on the 26th, he commenced re-crossing the North Anna, and on the 31st he had his whole army south of the Pamunky and within ten miles of Richmond, with a new base of supplies established at White House.

On the 26th, our corps, bringing up the rear of Hancock and Wright's, crossed the North Anna and marched for the Pamunky, which we crossed on the 28th, at Hanovertown Ford, Gregg's cavalry division skirmishing and driving the enemy's before them. On the 29th, we advanced to Hawes' shop, meeting with no opposition.

THE BATTLE OF BETHESDA CHURCH, MAY 30TH.—On

the 30th, General Warren pushed forward our division, the left of his corps, from Hawes' shop towards Mechanicsville, we passing Bethesda Church about noon, and reaching the neighborhood of Shady Grove church about two o'clock, where we met the enemy's skirmishers. It was about this hour of the day, and at this place, that we met the enemy under similar circumstances just before the battle of Mechanicsville, our first fight. Skirmishing soon commenced, and we fell back, making but little resistance until we reached the road running from Mechanicsville to Hanover Court House. Here we commenced throwing up breastworks, but had not worked more than half an hour before we were attacked on both flanks with great fury. From some of the prisoners taken, we ascertained that the attacking force consisted of Rhode's division and one brigade of Early's division of Ewell's corps, and orders were given to fall back. We retired slowly for three-quarters of a mile, delivering so steady and heavy a skirmish fire that the enemy did not follow us up vigorously.

Reaching a favorable position, the division was halted, and the line of battle formed across the road and through some fields into the woods. The Third brigade, Colonel J. W. Fisher, held the right of the line, the First brigade, Colonel M. D. Harden, the centre, and Kitchen's brigade of heavy artillery, armed as infantry, the left, with two sections of a Michigan battery posted near the centre. Our whole force did not number over five thousand five hundred men. After the line was formed, the Second regiment was moved to the rear and left, and posted to hold a piece of woods. The men immediately went to work throwing up breastworks, which were so formed as to enable us to deliver a cross fire. The artillery commenced shelling the woods in front at different points, feeling the enemy's guns, from which they soon received a response. Soon after, near sundown, the whole of Ewell's corps emerged from the woods, formed in three lines, and advanced to the charge. Scarcely had they moved, before the Third brigade opened upon their flank a severe cross-fire, which turned them over upon the First and Kitchen's brigades.

About twenty-five yards in front of the First brigade's rifle-pits was a fence and some bushes that concealed our pits and men from view. The enemy advanced to the fence in most excellent order, and as they reached it, our whole line, which had not fired a shot, opened upon them a crushing fire of musketry, while the artillery poured in canister and one-second fuse shells. Their repulse was instantaneous and complete. What were not killed or wounded of the first line threw themselves upon the ground, and the balance precipitately fled. Our men then slackened their fire, but whenever those who had laid down got up to run, they were shot. Finally, an officer called out to them, that if they would throw down their arms and come in, they would be spared, and about four hundred of them surrendered, including two colonels, three lieutenant-colonels, one major, and twenty line officers.

The enemy's loss was calculated to be very little short of one thousand men. General Ransom, of North Carolina, was left dead upon the field, and his sword was presented by one of the boys to General Crawford. Colonel Terrill, of the Twenty-seventh Virginia, a brother of the Union General Terrill who was killed at Shiloh, was also killed. The Confederate Colonel Hoffman was cut in two by a shell. The color-bearer of the Fifty-second Virginia came to the fence, when he was struck by a shell and literally torn to pieces. Some of his comrades, however, saved their flag. Our loss was not heavy, except in the first engagement on the Mechanicsville road, where we were compelled to leave our wounded in the hands of the enemy. It amounted to fifteen killed, fifty-four wounded, and eighty-five missing, in all one hundred and fifty-four.

This signal repulse of Ewell's corps, with such slaughter, by a force of less than one-third of their number, and within a short distance of the victorious field of Mechanicsville, where we opened the "Seven days battle," was a fitting close of the glorious career of the Pennsylvania Reserves. That night we slept victors upon our last field of victory.

The next morning we buried our fallen comrades, and those of the enemy, on the field of honor, and left them to "sleep their last sleep," peacefully, side by side, until the last trump "shall wake them to glory again."

In the course of the morning, the following orders were received and read to the division:

HEADQUARTERS, FIFTH ARMY CORPS,
MAY 3D, 1864.

Soldiers:—With this is the order for the return of the Pennsylvania Reserves, whose term of service expires to-day. The General commanding begs leave to express to them his great satisfaction at their heroic conduct in this arduous campaign. As their commander, he thanks them for their willing and effective efforts, and congratulates them that their successful engagement of yesterday, closing their term of service, and being the last of many battles bravely fought, is one they can ever remember with satisfaction and pride.

By command of
MAJOR-GENERAL WARREN.

(Signed,)
A. G. MANN, A. A. G.

HEADQUARTERS THIRD DIVISION,
PENNSYLVANIA RESERVE VOL. CORPS, FIFTH ARMY CORPS,
JUNE 1, 1864.

Soldiers of the Pennsylvania Reserves:—To-day the connection which has so long existed between us is to be severed forever. I have no power to express to you the feeling of gratitude and affection that I bear to you, nor the deep regret with which I now part from you.

As a division you have ever been faithful and devoted soldiers, and you have nobly sustained me in the many trying scenes through which we have passed with an unwavering fidelity.

The record of your service terminates gloriously, and the Wilderness, Spottsylvania Court House and Bethesda Church, have been added to the long list of battles and triumphs that have marked your career.

Go home to the great State that sent you forth three years ago to battle for her honor and to strike for her in the great cause of the country.

Take back your soiled and war-worn banners, your thinned and shattered ranks, and let them tell how you performed your trust.

Take back those banners sacred from the glorious associations that surround them, sacred with the memory of our fallen comrades who gave their lives to defend them, and give them again into the keeping of the State forever.

The duties of the hour prevent me from accompanying you, but my heart will follow you long after your return, and it shall ever be my pride that I was once your commander, and that side by side we fought and suffered through campaigns which will stand unexampled in history. Farewell.

S. W. CRAWFORD.
Brigadier-general Commanding Division.

(Signed,)

R. A. McCoy,
Lieutenant-colonel and A. A. G.

After the reading of these orders, an order was issued for all those whose term of service had not expired, and those who had re-enlisted to report to Colonel Carroll at headquarters. From our regiment there were Companies B, Lieutenant Cullin; F, Captain Clark, and G, Captain Woodward, with some fifty veterans and recruits. They were got together and marched over, where they stacked arms and returned to spend the day with us.

The next morning, June 1st, we were up and in line

early, and those who were to remain came over to bid us good-bye. It was one of the saddest and most trying hours of our lives We had read of comrades parting, and we had parted with friends of childhood's days, but we could not realize the strong attachment that had grown up between us, until the hour of separation came. It was the parting of those who had shared their last cracker, who had slept under the same blanket, who had picketed together through many weary hours of the night, and who had stood side by side when the storm of death was sweeping by—it was the parting of brothers. Not an eye was dry. From our general down, the tears gushed out in spite of strife to conceal them. But the hour came. From "Home sweet Home," the bands changed to patriotic strains, and the air was rent with the loud cheers of the boys as they shouted their last good-bye.

But there were other sad memories that clustered around our hearts as we marched along. We were near the fields of "The Seven Days' Battles," upon which the bones of many of our comrades lay bleaching. How vividly those scenes of strife, of glory and disappointment, arose in our vision! How we recounted the names of our dead! But their spirits still cluster around the old flag, and they are happy, at least with the consciousness that they met death gloriously and had fallen in a sacred cause.

We took up our march for White House, following closely the general course of the Pamunky, and arrived there on the afternoon of the next day.

On the morning of the 3d, we embarked, and passing down the Pamunky and York rivers, entered the Chesapeake Bay and steamed up the Potomac to Washington, where we arrived on the evening of the 4th, and disembarking marched to the Soldier's Rest, where we slept for the night.

At noon the next day, we took passage by rail to Baltimore, and at the depot formed and marched through the city to the depot of the Northern Central road. On our passage through we were received with cheers and other demonstrations of joy by the citizens who thronged the thoroughfares. We arrived at Harrisburg about ten o'clock on the morning of the 6th, and marching to the Volunteer Refreshment Saloon, partook of an excellent collation that had been generously prepared for us.

The church bells of the city were now merrily ringing out a welcome to us, and the citizens were closing their stores and gathering to receive us. The State guns were thundering forth a salute from Capitol Hill; and the different furnace and factory signals sent up one continual din and roar. The procession to receive us arrived, and we wheeled into line, they marching in the following order:

Chief Marshal William H. Kepner and Aids. Band of Music. Military escort, Captain Bate's battery, First New York Artillery. Pennsylvania Reserve Corps. Assistant Marshal. Governor and Cabinet Officers in carriages. Mayor and President of Common Council in carriage. Clergy. State Officers. County Officers. Judges and Members of the Bar. Common Council of the City of Harrisburg. Assistant Marshal. Band of Music. Officers of the Army and Navy sojourning in Harrisburg. Strangers sojourning in Harrisburg. Civic Societies. Assistant Marshal. Citizens of Harrisburg. Assistant Marshal. Band of Music. Fire Department. Assistant Marshal.

As we passed along, cheer after cheer was given and bouquets and flowers thrown, until the boys were literally covered with the richest floral offerings of June. About noon we reached Capitol Hill, where was collected a vast concourse of citizens, who made the welkin ring with loud huzzas. Reaching the main edifice, the Corps was massed in front of the Capitol portico, and Mayor Roumfort mounting the stand improvised for the occasion, delivered the following address:

"Hail, brave soldiers of Pennsylvania! In the name

of the citizens of Harrisburg, I greet you with hearty, most hearty welcome to the Capital of your State. During the last three years, by flood and by field, in the valleys and upon the mountain-tops, you have, like gallant and noble soldiers, bravely fought, bled and died for our common country, carrying the old flag from victory to victory. You have been on every battle-field, and in the extreme front of every battle and grand contest east of the Allegheny Mountains, and immortalized yourselves, winning laurels of renown unsurpassed.

"Of twenty thousand men who marched into the field an unbroken front three years ago, you now return the broken, battle-stained, shattered remnants of two thousand men. May your departed companions, whom you have left behind you in Southern graves, who have fallen in defence of our country's liberties, receive that crown of immortality which has become their heritage, as bequeathed to glory and to fame. And not only the fallen of the brave ones, whose untimely end we so deeply deplore, but at your feet, brave soldiers-in-arms, cast we our garlands of flowers. Never shall your deeds be forgotten.

"It was the intention of the citizens of Harrisburg to give you upon this very ground a reception dinner, but you are as sudden with your friends as with your enemies; you took us unawares and by surprise. You *outflanked* us. But, my gallant soldiers, the citizens of Harrisburg do not despair of entertaining you. They have all agreed to invite you into the sanctity of their homes. They will receive you there as part of their own loved families, around their tables and hearth-stones. They will remind you of the old times when you used to sit at home by the smoking hot dinner; and you can relate to them your gallant charges, your narrow escapes, and the circumstances of your glorious victories through which you have passed since you marched from your homes to the battle-fields of Rebellion. We will be glad to hear your voices in our homes, as we will be most happy and proud to entertain you. And after you have partaken of this foretaste of our gratitude, you will be permitted to go home to the dear ones there, in whose hearts your memory has become enshrined as holy in the history of our Commonwealth. My good friends, my gallant friends, I welcome you again! and when the alarums of war have ceased may you enjoy that peace you so well deserve under your own vine and fig-tree, with your household gods around you. In that day it will be merely necessary for you to say, 'I was a member of the Pennsylvania Reserve Corps,' and the answer will come from bystanders, 'Bless the brave man!'

"My friends, I expect that next Wednesday, at two o'clock in the afternoon, you and we will participate of the dinner which will be provided for you."

The Mayor was most heartily cheered, and after something like silence could be produced, Governor Curtin stepped upon the platform.

The Governor spoke substantially as follows:—

"I thank you, Mr. Mayor of Harrisburg, and you the people of this city, for this your hearty welcome to these brave men. It has been through you, brave soldiers, that the hearts of the people have been stirred. Your presence here again, my fellow-citizens (the Reserves), has stirred up emotions in our hearts, deep and glorious as our feelings are to-day, that we will never forget. I cannot find language to adequately express to you the sentiments and feelings of Pennsylvania, and when I say, as we all say, 'You have done your whole duty,' I but faintly convey to you the universal verdict of the whole people of this commonwealth. It is now nearly three years since you left this city a mighty army. Nearly that period of time has elapsed since I had the honor of handing to you these standards which you are about to return to the State, unstained with dishonor and covered with laurels of brightest martial renown. You have never set foot upon the soil of your homes since then, save *once*. Once you came back to Pennsylvania, and then we all heard of your deeds, that spoke in thunder tones with your cheers. 'Round Top' at Gettysburg will ever live as a watch-word of glory and victory. When nearly all the rest gave way before the bayonets of the enemy we heard your shouts around the hills of that devoted country, in the face of the enemy, and to you belongs the honor of driving him from our soil.

"I would speak of your gallant deeds, but they have passed into history. I have not time to enumerate the battles you have been in. History will record all you have done for your country. The record of the Pennsylvania Reserve Corps is without blemish and spotless. I am not qualified to speak of the heroic dead you have left upon nearly every battle-field of the Republic. Upon their graves centres the gratitude of this great people. But I can welcome you, who have returned with sunburnt faces and tattered flags to your homes. From the North and the South, and the East and the West, the voice of welcome is wafted towards you from the old Keystone State.

"We did not know three years ago that you would remain so long in the public service. But I can say that I refer with pride and pleasure to the part the great State has borne in this contest, from the battle of Drainesville, where you were the first to strike, until last Monday, where you struck your heaviest blow at Bethesda Church. May you all find a happy welcome at your homes! May you be all marked as brave men who served their country in times of greatest peril. May you never regret that you belonged to the Pennsylvania Reserve Corps and were in every battle of the Republic! With this welcome I bid you farewell."

At the close of the Governor's speech loud cheers were given for his Excellency, Grant, Meade and the Army of the Potomac.

Colonel Fisher, in behalf of the Corps, responded briefly, as follows:—

"Mr. Mayor, Governor and citizens of Harrisburg. In the name of the remnants of what was once a mighty division, I thank you for the reception you have given us here to-day. The people of Harrisburg, represented by their Mayor, have overwhelmed us with their kindness. In reply to these kind expressions, the only response I have to make is the speech familiar to the Pennsylvania Reserves. So, my gallant boys, let us have three cheers, and let them be such thundering cheers as you gave at Bethesda Church before we left the army."

And in response the whole Corps joined in three cheers, that made the old State House tremble from dome to foundation.

Colonel McCandless, who was severely wounded, being called for, made a brief speech in thanks for the Keystone's welcome. "He had only to say, and he did himself honor in saying, that they (the Reserves), in their consciences felt that they had done their whole duty. And we are willing for as many years as our lives shall last and our blood flow in our veins to continue to sustain the old flag which we have carried in triumph in many an engagement.

"We stand upon a sure record. We fought the first battle at Drainesville; at Malvern we were there, and whenever and wherever the Reserves were called, they were there. It shall always be my pleasure to stand by you and lead you where you wish to be led."

Colonel R. Biddle Roberts being called for, addressed the Corps in a few eloquent remarks, which were vociferously applauded by the Corps. He remarked that a hot dinner had been promised them; but he remembered the time when they had a hot dinner, a very hot dinner, with no ladies around to grace it with their smiles.

The Corps then marched to Camp Curtin, where we spent the night.

Although the citizens of Harrisburg had generously offered us a reception dinner, and pressed us to stay and partake of it, we were constrained to decline, as all were anxious to get home to receive that welcome that comes from the heart alone, without any pomp or ceremony. Therefore, the next morning our regiment accompanied by the First and Seventh, under the command of Colonel Talley, proceeded to Philadelphia, where we arrived early in the afternoon of the same day. The First and Seventh did not belong to the city but were ordered there to be mustered out.

Upon arriving at West Philadelphia a salute was fired and a Committee of Councils and other organizations were in attendance. As the battalions alighted from the cars and formed into line, loud cheers arose from the crowd and bouquets of flowers were presented to the men. The line of escort was formed on Market street, east of the bridge, and took up the march in the following order:—

Band. Committee of Councils. Committee of Citizens. Committee of Refreshment Saloons. Liberty Band. Veteran Reserve Corps. The Provost Guard. Douglas' Band. Discharged Officers and Men of the Division. The First, Second and Seventh Regiments of Pennsylvania Reserves. The wounded and convalescent soldiers of the Reserves. Mechanics' Band. The Fire Department. Ambulances.

The procession proceeded to the National Guard's Hall where the Reserves were welcomed by Colonel Small on behalf of the City, which was responded to by Colonel Talley. The line of march was again taken up from the Hall to the Cooper Shop Volunteer Refreshment Saloon, the streets through which it passed being densely packed with citizens, who at various points gave hearty cheers. The public buildings and many private houses were decorated with flags and patriotic devices, and a handsomely decorated archway was erected across Third street, at Evelina street by the Hibernia Engine Company, bearing the inscription, "Welcome, Brave Reserves." The bells of the Fire Companies were rung as the procession passed, and St. Peter's bells chimed forth a merry welcome. At the Refreshment Saloon a handsome entertainment was spread, after partaking of which the boys were dismissed to their homes.

Companies C, "Hibernia Target Company," and D of the Northern Liberty, were taken in charge by the members of their respective companies and marched to their halls where a warm reception awaited them.

As the boys marched along they were not only greeted by strangers but by friends and relatives who rushed to grasp their hands. But all was not joy and happiness that day, for there was the fond mother, the affectionate father, the devoted wife, the gentle sister and the true-hearted brother, who gazed with sadness upon the shattered ranks and thought of those—their own dear ones —whom we had left to sleep upon the battle-field. Sad indeed where their thoughts when they remembered the bright eye and flushed cheek, so full of hope, of love, of glory, that bid them farewell as they marched off to battle for the Union and Liberty, and that now are dimmed and faded away. But peacefully sleep their dead, for their blood arises like sweet incense from the altar of their country.

A few days afterwards the members were called together at the hall of the Hibernia Engine Company, to receive the medals that had been prepared for them by a Committee of Citizens. The medals which are one inch and an eighth in diameter, have on one side the Pennsylvania coat of arms inside of a wreath of laurel, with the words "Second Regiment P. R. V. C., June, 1864. On the other side are the words "Honor to the Brave," "Presented by the Citizens of Philadelphia." Colonel James Page made the presentation in behalf of the citizens, and Colonels McCandless and McDonough of the regiment responded.

Shortly afterwards the regiment was mustered out of service, and now the name and the glory of the Second Reserves is all that remains.

APPENDIX A.

KILLED, WOUNDED AND PRISONERS.

MECHANICSVILLE.

Killed.

Corp'l Isaiah McCauley, Co. A
" Jacob Kreis, D
Private Samuel Drain, A
" William Rowbotham, A
" John Williams, A
" Ignatius Gillette, B
" Joseph Nightingale,* C
" Thomas Ward,* C
" Joseph L. Fisher, D
" Thomas Hackett, D
" William Haughly, D
" John J. Reilly, D
" Joseph Simpson, E
" Calhoun White, E
" James Graham, E

Wounded.

1st Lt. Daniel H. Connors, A
" John B. Robinson, C
Sergt. George W. Fowler,† A
" Dennis Maguire, B
" James Toomey, D
Corp'l Jacob Tugent,† A
" William Drain,† A
Private William Hoff,† A
" Frederick Hibberd,† A
" John Kernan,† A
" Robert Kirkwood, A
" James McGran,† A
" Wm. Schoenewald, A
" John Shaw, B
" William F. Graff, C
" William Derr, C
" Chas. W. Nickert,† C
" Jacob L. Blight, D
Private George W. Atkins, Co. D
" Anthony W. Laws, D
" Julius C. Aitken, E
" William McFarland,† E
" Edward Barnes, K

Prisoners.

Corp'l Lambert Longshore, A
Private James Murphy, B
" Augustus Rickards, B
" James Nicholson, E

GAINES' MILL.

Killed.

Corp'l Charles Day, A
C. " Andrew Beckett,* E
Private Thomas Lyttle, B
" George Whiteman, D
" Patrick Dunn, H
" Thomas Edmonson, K
" William Shaw,* K

Wounded.

Capt. J. Orr Finnie,† E
1st Lt. Hugh P. Kennedy,† H
Sergt. Isaac E. Sharp,† E
" Henry Moore, C
" James Stewart,† E
Corp'l James Thompson. C
" John S. McBride, D
Private John Carr, B
" George Harris, C
" Charles Stump, C
" William McLain, C
" John Murphy, C
" James O'Kane, D
" Cassius P. Harvey,† E

* Died subsequently. † Taken prisoner.

Private Wm. McDonald,† Co. E
" James Kincade,† H
" Abraham Fulton,† H
" Alexander Murdock,† H
" Bernard Finnigan, H

Prisoners.

Private John Haney, A
" John Walls, B

GLENDALE.

Killed.

1st Lt. J. Baxter Fletcher,* E
2d Lt. James R. Nightingale, C
Sergt. Thos. H. Humphries, E
" William B. Jones, E
" Thomas Smith, E
" William Prentice,* E
Private Robert Smith, A
" Robert Brown, B
" Daniel Harton, B
" William McHugh, B
" Job West, B
" James McCall, C
" Edward McDowell, C
" Augustus G. Goodwin, C
" Major Whiteside, D
" William Burns, E
" Thomas Collier, E
" William Macklin, E
" James Potts, E
" Samuel Shannon, E
" Frank P. McNeill, K

Wounded.

Major G. A. Woodward.†
Capt. P. I. Smith.† K
" Horace Neide,† A
Sergt. Daniel Craig, A
" Thomas Crilly, H
" David H. Pidgeon, K
Corp. Joseph Lathrop, C
" John Collins, H
" John Phillips,† H
Private George Larkins, B
" George C. Barton, C
" Henry O'Neill, C

Private Hugh Gillen, Co. C
" William McLane, D
" Charles W. Schoeber, D
" Edward Peplow, D
" Christopher Grim, E
" James McKinney, E
" Thomas Shaw, K

Prisoners.

Corp. Asher S McCully, C
" John Conroy, C
Private Edward V. McKee, C
" Balthasar Steese, E
" Thomas G. Burns, H
Mus'n Thomas Hartman, K

SECOND BULL RUN, OR THE PLAINS OF MANASSAS.

Killed.

Private Luke Carney, B
" Wilberforce Poulson, K

Wounded.

Colonel William McCandless.
Capt. Daniel H. Connors, A
1st Lt. John H. Jack, B
" John B. Robinson, C
O. Sgt. G. Harry Zeigler, B
Sergt. Henry Moore, C
Corp. Samuel H. Garvin, B
" Edward Concannon, C
" Thomas J. Wood, C
Private George W. Kendel, D
" George W. McMullan, E
" Robert Patterson, E
" Francis Colligan, H
" Charles Weaver, H
" James Baskerville, H
" Joshua R. Cox, K

Prisoners.

Corp. Lambert Longshore, A
Private William Caleley, A
" John C. Harrison, A
" Richard Jeffries, A
" William W. Nelson, E
" George W. Swancott, K

* Died subsequently.

† Taken prisoner.

SOUTH MOUNTAIN.

Killed.

Corp'l	Wm. McClintock,	Co. B
"	Edward Booth,	E
Private	Charles Stump,	C
"	Lawrence Keefe,*	C
"	Gilbert McKeller,	E
"	Augustus Sucker,	G
"	William H. Simpson,	K

Wounded.

2d Lt.	Richard Clendinning,	H
O. Sgt.	Staughton George,	K
Sergt.	Richard P. Dillon,	B
Corp'l	Robert Ferguson,	E
Private	Alexander H. Brown,	B
"	George Molloy,	B
"	Thomas Donnelly,	B
"	Francis Higgins,	D
"	Henry Brown,	E
"	Albert R. Reel,	K

ANTIETAM.

Killed.

Adju't	Augustus T. Cross.	
2d Lt.	Max Wimpfheimer,	G
Corp'l	William McKecknie,	E
"	Jeremiah Fritz,*	G
Private	Thomas McMullin,	B
"	Andrew J. Toy,	K

Wounded.

Capt.	Timothy Mealey,	H
C. Sgt.	William J. Fulton,	H
O. "	Thomas Canavan,	D
Sergt.	Albert G. Barton,	A
"	Robert R. Smith,	D
Corp'l	Smith Barker,	D
"	William H. K. Bush,	G
Private	John Armstrong,	A
"	Patrick Fadden,	B
"	Thomas Rogerson,	B
"	Thomas J. Brines,	D
"	James Patton,	E
"	John C Young,	E
"	Lyman Price,	G
Private	Charles Reagan,	Co. G
"	John A. Hull,	G
"	Isaac Myers,	H
"	Hiram F. Chew,	K
"	George Gougler,	K
"	William J. Manning,	K

FREDERICKSBURG.

Killed.

C. Sgt.	William Derr,	C
Private	Michael Brough,	A
"	Hugh Reilly,	B
"	William Moore,	B
"	Charles Devlin,	C
"	A. P. Kennedy,	G
"	Joseph Harter,	G

Wounded.

O. Sgt.	Daniel Craig,	A
"	Michael A. Crowley,	C
Sergt.	Robert Ferguson,	C
"	James McCormick,	E
C. Cor.	James F. Morrison,†	K
"	Joseph F. Sweeton,†	K
Corp'l	Asher S. McCully,	C
"	John S. Lytle,	G
Private	William Schoenewald,	A
"	Peter Cullin,	B
"	John Hagan,	B
"	Patrick Keely,	B
"	Robert W. Davis,	B
"	William Nickert,	C
"	Hugh Gillen,	C
"	John Devlin,	C
"	Lou s Davis,	D
"	William Chandler,	E
"	L. Detwiler,	E
"	Christopher Grim,	E
"	A. Blankhorn,	G
"	J. Shoemaker,	G
"	Jno. Shalck,	G
"	F. Bitterman,	G
"	William Robb,	H
"	James Baskerville,	H
"	George Seddall,†	H
"	Charles Hanf,	K

* Died subsequently.

† Taken prisoner.

Prisoners.

Sergt. Hiram C. Hostetter, Co. G
Corp'l William Brighton, G
Private William McDowell, B
" George Blackwell, H

PICKET ON THE RAPPAHANNOCK.

Wounded.

Capt. Timothy Mealey, H

GETTYSBURG.

Killed.

Sergt. Thomas M. Savage, H
C. Cor. R. W. Linsenmeyers,* E
Corp'l George Stewart,* E
Private Thomas Burns, B
" John R. Querey,* E
" Alexander Hoffer,* F
" George Moyer,* F
" Martin H. Riggle,* F
" Samuel B. Steward, F
" Andrew Ryan, H

Wounded.

Capt. Wm. D. Reitzel, G
1st Lt. James C. Manton, B
Sgt. mj. D. Harris Pidgeon, N. C. Staff.
C. Sgt. James Toomey, D
Sergt. G. W. Cassiday, F
C. Cor. William H. Nolan, C
Corp'l S. W. Ryan, B
" Samuel A. Souder, F
Private Adam Erford, C
" William Keefe, C
" Edward Louge, C
" Henry Guy, D
" Charles F. Miller, D
" Samuel Dunlap, E
" John Wilson, E
" John Hoover, F
" William Brown, F
" Peter Bowman, F
" M. Bowman. F
" John B. Webb, F
" Robinson T. Sherman, F

Private Jacob Carter, Co. G
" Adam Erline, G
" Park J. Stackhouse, G
" John Hart, G
" Thomas G. Burns, H
" Henry McGarvey, H
" John Seadinger, H
" Oliver Wilson, H

BRISTOE STATION, OCT. 14, 1863.

Wounded.

Corp'l Samuel A. Louder,† F
Private George Graham, A

Prisoner.

Private Robert Patterson,* E

NEW HOPE CHURCH.

Killed.

Private Thomas G. Burns, H

MINE RUN.

Wounded.

Capt. Daniel H. Connors, A

Prisoner.

Private John Labold, F

BRISTOE STATION, JAN. 24, 1864.

Wounded.

Private John Hoover, F

BRISTOE STATION, MAR. 27, 1864.

Killed.

Private William Lindsay, F

THE WILDERNESS, MAY 5, 1864.

Killed.

Sergt. John A. Hull, G

Wounded.

Sergt. James B. Read, F
Corp'l W. H. K. Bush,† G

* Died subsequently.

† Taken prisoner.

Prisoners.

Surg'n E. Donnelly, Staff
Capt. James N. Byrnes, Co. C
1st Lt. John Taylor, E
O. Sgt. Michael Crowley, C
Private William A. Nickert, C
" John P. Schalck, G

THE WILDERNESS, MAY 7, 1864.

Wounded.

Capt. P. I. Smith, K

SPOTTSYLVANIA COURT HOUSE, MAY 8, 1864.

Killed.

O. Sgt. Martin Divine, G
Sergt. Rudolph M. Graff, G
Private Adam Erline, G

Wounded.

Colonel Wm. McCandless, Com'g brigade.

SPOTTSYLVANIA COURT HOUSE, MAY 10, 1864.

Killed.

Private Adam Gehrett,* F
" Abraham L. Smith, F

Wounded.

Corp'l John Smith, F
Private Joseph C. Curfman, F
" Marshal Houck, F

Prisoner.

Private George J. Halsel, F

SPOTTSYLVANIA COURT HOUSE, MAY 12, 1864.

Killed.

1st Lt. Robert J. Clark,* F
Private William Henry, E
" Alfred Cherry, F
" Robinson T. Sherman,* F

Wounded.

1st Lt. John B. Robinson, C
Sergt. Charles C. Upjohn, K
Corp'l David Cassiday, F
Private Austin Thompson, F
" William S. Wall, F

MAY 24, 1864.

Prisoner.

Lieut. James C. Justus, K

REAM'S STATION.†

Wounded.

Sergt. John Donnelly, H
Dru'r George W. Leeti, H

Prisoners.

Lieut. A. McK. Storrie, B
Sergt. John McDonough, B
" William Brighton, G
" Thomas Fitzsimmons, B
Corp'l Edward Leatherberry, A
Private Elmer E. Large, A
" Steward Graham, A
" John Elliott, B
" Charles Eckhart, G
" Michael Ernswiler, G
" Benjamin Hartman, G
" Joseph Grab, G
" Jacob Harnish, G
" John Lytle, G

* Died subsequently.
† This battle was fought after the time of the regiment was out, and the men had been transferred to the 191st Regt. P. R. V. V. C.

APPENDIX B.

ROSTER of the Second Regiment Infantry, Pennsylvania Reserve Volunteer Corps, Thirty-first of the line, with date of commission.

FIELD OFFICERS.

Colonels.

William B. Mann, April 24, 1861. Resigned October 30, 1861.
William McCandless, November 1, 1861. Wounded at Second Bull Run and Wilderness.

Lieutenant-Colonels.

Albert L. Magilton, June 21, 1861. Resigned October 3, 1861.
William McCandless, October 24, 1861. To Colonel.
George A. Woodward, June 30, 1862. To Invalid Corps, August 24, 1863. To Colonel, Twenty-second Regiment, V. R. C.
Patrick McDonough, August 25, 1863.

Majors.

William McCandless, June 21, 1861. To Lieutenant-Colonel.
George A. Woodward, April 2, 1862. To Lieutenant-Colonel. Wounded and taken prisoner at Glendale, June 30, 1862.
Horace Neide, June 30, 1862. Honorably discharged on account of disability, November 25, 1862.
Patrick McDonough, November 26, 1862. To Lieutenant-Colonel.
R. Ellis, October 28, 1863.

STAFF OFFICERS.

Adjutants.

Horace Neide, October 1861. To major.
Augustus T. Cross, April 5, 1862. Killed at Antietam, September 16, 1862.
E. M. Woodward, September 18, 1862. Honorably discharged on account of disability, September 22, 1863.
John L. Rhodes, September 23, 1863.

Quartermasters.

Charles F. Hoyt, June 22. 1861. To captain and commissary subsistence, July 1, 1862.
William A. Hoyt, January 6, 1863.

MEDICAL DEPARTMENT

Surgeons.

Thomas B. Reed, June 6, 1861. To brigade surgeon volunteers, April 20, 1862.
Edward Donnelly, April 28, 1862.

Assistant Surgeons.

John W. Lodge, June 6, 1861. Resigned December 5, 1861.
John Malone, January 7, 1862. To surgeon, 71st regiment, P. V., November 4, 1862.
A. G. Coleman, July 31, 1862.
D. W. Bashore, September 13, 1862. Discharged November 22, 1862.
E. Owen Jackson, December 17, 1862. Died August, 1863.

Sergeant Majors.

Augustus T. Cross, June 21, 1861. To adjutant.
E. M. Woodward, May 1, 1862. To adjutant.
Joseph Benison, January 1, 1863. To second lieutenant Company H.
David H. Pidgeon, June 8, 1863. Wounded at Gettysburg, July 2, 1863.
Hiram C. Hostetter, July 10, 1863. Died near Rectors Town, Va., July 24, 1863.
Andrew McK. Storrie, January 1, 1864. To second lieutenant, 191st regiment, P. V. V.

Quartermaster's Sergeants.

Wesley Mann, June —, 1861. Honorably discharged on account of disability, July, 1861.
John L. Benson, August 1, 1861. To second lieutenant, 191st regiment, P. V. V.

Commissary Sergeant.

William A. Hoyt, August, 1861. To quartermaster.
George W. Fernon, February 1, 1863.

COMPANY A.

Captains.

George A. Woodward, April 24, 1861. To major.
Horace Neide, April 2, 1862. To major. Wounded and taken prisoner at Glendale.
Daniel H. Connors, June 30, 1862. Wounded at Mechanicsville and Second Bull Run.

Robert H. Lowden, April 24, 1861. Resigned December 6, 1861.
Horace Neide, December 7, 1861. To captain.
Daniel H. Conners, April 3, 1862. To captain.
John J. Ross, June 30, 1862.

Second Lieutenants.

Horace Neide, April 24, 1861. To first lieutenant.
John J. Ross, December 16, 1861. To first lieutenant
Daniel Craig, May 3, 1863.

Orderly Sergeants.

John J. Ross. To second lieutenant.
Daniel H. Conners. To first lieutenant.
Daniel Craig. To second lieutenant. Wounded at Glendale and Fredericksburg.
George F. Buehler.

Sergeants.

Joseph Vanosten.
James Lynch.
George Drew.
William F. Huplet.
Albert G. S. Barton. Wounded at Antietam. Honorably discharged.
Isaac C. Sharp. Honorably discharged on account of disability. Wounded and prisoner at Gaines' Mills.
George Fowler. Honorably discharged on account of disability. Wounded and prisoner Mechanicsville.
William Aiken. Reënlisted.
*William Wood.

Corporals.

Michael Brough. Wounded and prisoner at Fredericksburg, Dec. 13, 1862. Reënlisted.
James Lewis. Reënlisted.
George Rossiter. Color corporal.
Lambert Longshore.
Jacob Lugend. Wounded and prisoner at Mechanicsville, honorably discharged.
Charles Day. Killed at Gaines Mills, June 27, 1862.
Isaiah McCauley. Killed at Mechanicsville, June 26, 1862.
William J. Drain. Wounded and prisoner at Mechanicsville, June 26, 1862.

Musicians.

John Clingman.
John Burns. Reënlisted.

Privates.

Armstrong, John. Wounded at Antietam. Discharged to enter the Regular Army.
Bright, Andrew J. Detailed at Division hospital.
Callelly, William.
Cockrell, James.
Craig, David. Honorably discharged for disability, August 19, 1861.
Devine, Charles. Reënlisted.
Drain, Samuel. Killed at Mechanicsville, June 26, 1862.
Ettinger, William J.
Goeteil, Daniel. Died in hospital, 1862.
Goldey, Joseph. Detached in Signal Corps, August, 1861.
Graham, George. Reënlisted.
Graham, Joseph. Died, August 28, 1862.
Graham, Stuart. Reënlisted. Taken prisoner at Ream's Station.
Gray, Joseph. Honorably discharged on account of disability, March, 1862.
Gray, Leander. Honorably discharged on account of disability, March, 1862.
Haney, John. Taken prisoner. Honorably discharged on account of disability, September, 1862.
Harrison, John.
Hay, John. Reënlisted.
Hess, William. Died, September, 1861.
Hoff, William. Wounded and prisoner at Mechanicsville. Honorably discharged, September, 1862.
Holmes, William. Died at Bristoe Station, April, 1862.
Hubbard, Frederick. Honorably discharged, September, 1862.
Jamison, William. Transferred to serve out time.
Jefferies, Richard, Jr. Reënlisted.
Jefferies, Richard, Sr. Honorably discharged, August, 1861.
*Kenny. Raphael.
Kernan, John. Wounded and prisoner at Mechanicsville. Honorably discharged, March, 1863.
Kirkwood, Robert. Wounded and prisoner at Mechanicsville. Honorably discharged, January, 1864.
Large, Elmer E. Reënlisted. Taken prisoner at Ream's Station.
Leatherberry, Edward. Reënlisted. Prisoner at Ream's Station.
Lukens, John. Drowned. February, 1863.
Mann, Wesley. Honorably discharged, August, 1861.
McCallins, John. Died, September, 1862.
McGrans, James. Wounded and prisoner at Mechanicsville, June 26, 1862.
Miller, John.
Neidé, Carroll. Transferred to Signal Corps to serve out time.
Price, James. Honorably discharged, 1862.
Quigley. Albert.
Rowbotham, William. Killed at Mechanicsville, June 26, 1862.
Sayers, Matthew.

22

Schoenewald, William. Wounded at Mechanicsville and Fredericksburg.
Schultz, William.
Scott, Charles C. Reënlisted.
Searins, Theodore.
Smith, Robert. Killed at Glendale, June 30, 1862.
Stuart, Henry. Sunstruck blind. Honorably discharged, July 20, 1861.
Sweeney, John. Honorably discharged, August 4, 1861.
*Townsend, Edward.
Trexler, David.
Wade, John. Honorably discharged, 1862.
West, James. Discharged to enter the Regular Army.
Williams, Benjamin F. Transferred to serve out time.
Williams, John. Killed at Mechanicsville, June 26, 1862.
Wolfe, Charles. Honorably discharged, 1862.

Company B.

Captains.

Patrick McDonough, April 20, 1861. To major.
John H. Jack, November 26. 1862. To captain 186th Pennsylvania volunteers.

First Lieutenants.

John D. Schock, April 20, 1861. Honorably discharged, August 27, 1861.
John H. Jack, September 2, 1861. To captain.
James C. Manton, November 26, 1862. Died, January 13, 1864.
John Cullin, January 14, 1864 Transferred to the 191st regiment, Pennsylvania volunteers.

Second Lieutenants.

John Gill, April 20, 1861. Honorably discharged, August 27, 1861.
James C. Manton, September 2, 1861. To first lieutenant.

First Sergeant.

Henry G. Ziegler. Wounded at Bull Run. To lieutenant 22d regiment Veteran Reserves.

Sergeants.

Richard Dillon. Wounded at Antietam, September 17, 1862.
Thomas Stanton. Discharged for disability, December 26, 1862.
James McHale.
Alexander H. Brown.
Dennis Maguire. Wounded at Mechanicsville. Discharged, March, 1864.

Adolph Louis Schultz. Reënlisted.
John McDonough. Reënlisted. Prisoner at Ream's Station.

Corporals.

John Wilson, Jr.
John McClintock. Killed at South Mountain.
Andrew McK. Storrie. To sergeant-major. Reënlisted. Prisoner at Ream's Station.
Samuel W. Ryan. Reënlisted.
Thomas McFall. Color corporal.

Musicians.

James Loftus.
Edwin A. Snyder. Reënlisted.

Privates.

Brown, James.
Brown, Robert. Killed at Charles City Cross-roads.
Burk, John.
Burnes, Thomas.
Carnly, Luke.
Carr, John. Discharged for disability, September 29, 1862.
Coy, Michael. Discharged for disability, February 17, 1862.
Crawford, William. Reënlisted.
Cullen, Peter.
Curry, Owen. Discharged for disability, February 17, 1862.
Darragh, William.
Davis, Garret B. Reënlisted.
Dillon, John P. Discharged for disability, January 15, 1863.
Dugan, James. Discharged for disability, July 9, 1862.
Elliott, John. Taken prisoner at Ream's Station.
Fitzsimmons, James.
Fitzsimmons, Thomas. To sergeant 191st Pennsylvania Volunteers. Taken prisoner at Ream's Station.
Freil, James. Discharged for disability, February 17, 1862.
Garvin, Samuel H. Discharged for disability, October 26, 1862.
Gillespie, James. Killed at Mechanicsville, June 26, 1862.
Gilloly, John.
Gillette, Ignatz.
Harding, Charles.
Hart, John. Discharged for disability, January 30, 1862.
Harton, Daniel.
Keener, Jacob. Reënlisted.
Keeny, William.
Kettler, John.
Larkins, George.
Laughlin, George. Reënlisted.
Lyttle, Thomas. Killed at Gaines' Mill, June 27, 1862.
May, John P.

Melville, Cornelius.
Molloy, George.
Monahan, Cornelius.
Moore, John B. Reënlisted.
Moor, William.
Murphy, James. Discharged for disability, December 31, 1862.
McConaghy, John.
McDermott, Patrick.
*McFadden, Timothy.
McGinley, Charles. Discharged for disability, February 22, 1862.
McHugh, William.
McMullin, Thompson.
Reed, Thomas.
*Richard, Augustus.
Shaw, John. Wounded at Mechanicsville, June 26, 1862.
Sipple, Joseph. Reënlisted.
Toomey, William.
Walls, John.
West, Job.
White, Richard.
Wilson, John, Sr. Reënlisted.
Rizenhart, Jonas. Discharged for physical disability, February 17, 1862.

Company C.

Captain.

James N. Byrnes, April 29, 1861. Taken prisoner at Wilderness, May 5, 1854.

First Lieutenant.

John B. Robinson, April 29, 1861. Wounded at Second Bull Run, and Wilderness, May 12, 1864.

Second Lieutenants.

Francis Fox, April 29, 1861. Resigned August 8, 1861.
James R. Nightingale, November 4, 1861. Killed at Glendale, June 30, 1862.
Andrew Casey, June 30, 1862.

Orderly Sergeants.

James R. Nightingale. To second lieutenant.
Andrew Casey. To second lieutenant.
Michael Crowley. Wounded at Fredericksburg. Taken prisoner at Wilderness.

Sergeants.

Henry Moore. Wounded at Gaines' Mills and Bull Run.
Robert Ferguson. Wounded at Fredericksburg, December 13, 1862.

George C. Barton Wounded at Glendale, June 30, 1862. To first lieutenant 192d regiment Pennsylvania volunteers.
Charles Nickert. Wounded and prisoner at Mechanicsville.

Corporals.

Edward E. McKee.
E. C. Concannon. Wounded at Bull Run. To Invalid Corps, November 10, 1863.
William H. Nolan Color corporal. Wounded at Gettysburg. To Invalid Corps.
Asher S. McCully. Wounded at Fredericksburg, December 13, 1862.
John Morris. Honorably discharged, December 6, 1862.
Thomas Wood. Wounded at Bull Run. Discharged December 21, 1862.
Joseph G. Cline. Reënlisted.
James A. Thompson. Wounded at Gaines' Mill. Discharged.
Archibald McCann. Reënlisted.
William Derr. Color bearer. Killed at Fredericksburg.
Joseph Lathrop. Wounded at Glendale, June 30, 1862. Discharged

Musician.

Josiah Wagoner. Appointed chief musician, February 1, 1863.

Privates.

Axe, Frederick. Discharged to enter battery M, Second United States Artillery.
Caldwell, Matthew. Discharged to enter battery M, Second United States Artillery.
*Carrigan, John.
Conroy, John. Discharged to enter battery M, Second United States Artillery.
Davis, Thomas. Honorably discharged, August 8th, 1861.
Devlin, Charles. Killed at Fredericksburg, December 13, 1862.
Devlin, John. Wounded at Fredericksburg. To Invalid Corps, December 10, 1863.
Dolan, John.
Duval, George. Honorably discharged, August 8, 1861.
Erford, Adam. Wounded at Gettysburg. To captain, One hundred and Ninety-second Regiment, P. V.
Fernon, George W. To commissary sergeant, February 1, 1863.
Fredericks, Reuben. Honorably discharged, May 10, 1862.
Furgeson, John.
Gaff, William F. Wounded at Mechanicsville. Discharged, April 21, 1863.
Gaffigan, John.
Gillon, Hugh. Wounded at Glendale and Fredericksburg.
Goodwin, Augustus G. Killed at Glendale, June 30, 1862.

Harris, George. Wounded at Gaines' Mill. Discharged to enter battery M, Second United States Artillery.
Hess, William. Reënlisted.
Kane, Michael.
Keefe, Lawrence. Killed at South Mountain.
Keefe, William. Wounded at Gettysburg, July 3, 1863.
Kelly, Michael.
Lawson, James. Honorably discharged, May 24, 1863.
Logue, Edward. Wounded at Gettysburg. To Invalid Corps, October 29, 1863.
Mack, John. Honorably discharged, August 8, 1861.
McCall, James. Killed at Glendale, June 30, 1862.
McDowell, Edward. Killed at Glendale, June 30, 1862.
McKeegan, William. Honorably discharged.
McLain, William. Wounded at Gaines' Mill, June 27, 1862.
Miller, William.
Moore, Edward J. Reënlisted.
Murphy, John. Wounded at Gaines' Mill. Discharged December 29, 1862.
Nightingale, Joseph. Died in Richmond, July 12, 1862, of wounds received at Mechanicsville.
Nickert, William A. Wounded at Fredericksburg. Missing at Wilderness.
O'Donaghue, Timothy. Died, 1863.
O'Neil, Henry. Wounded at Glendale, June 30, 1862.
Picket, Michael. Honorably discharged, March 31, 1862.
Scanlan, Charles. Discharged to enter battery M, Second United States Artillery.
Scarlett, Howard.
Schreaves, Francis. Honorably discharged.
Sigenthall, George. Discharged to enter battery M, Second United States Artillery.
Simpkins, Lewis.
Smith, Aaron. Honorably discharged.
Stump, Charles. Wounded at Gaines' Mill. Killed at South Mountain.
Toomey, James.
Vanhook, Edward. To Invalid Corps, October 29, 1863.
Ward, Thomas. Died, March 19, 1863, of wounds received at Mechanicsville.
Wright, John. Honorably discharged, February, 25, 1863.

Company D.

Captains.

Richard Ellis, April 16, 1861. To major.
Thomas Canavan, November 11, 1863.

First Lieutenants.

John M. Curley, April 16, 1861. Honorably discharged on account of disability, November 25, 1862.
Thomas Canavan, May 9, 1863. To captain.
Robert R. Smith, February 17, 1864.

Second Lieutenants.

George Young, April 16, 1861. Honorably discharged, December 3, 1862.
Robert R. Smith. To first lieutenant.

Orderly Sergeants.

Samuel L. McKinney. Discharged, 1862.
Thomas Canavan. To first lieutenant. Wounded at Antietam.
John S. Firth. Appointed May 8, 1863.

Sergeants.

James Toomey. Color sergeant. Wounded at Mechanicsville and Gettysburg. To Invalid Corps.
Robert R. Smith. To second lieutenant. Wounded at Antietam.
John Grady. Appointed August 1, 1862.
William H. Dick. Honorably discharged, June 14, 1863.
David A. Nuttall. Died, August 23, 1862.
*Edward Sherry.
Philip S. Young. Appointed April 1, 1863.
Samuel Hopkins. Appointed February 1, 1864.
John Jones. Appointed February 1, 1864.

Corporals.

Smith Barker. Wounded at Antietam, September 17, 1862.
George W. Kendel. Wounded at Bull Run, August 29, 1862.
John S. McBride. Wounded at Gaines' Mill, June 27, 1862.
John Sagee. Appointed June 1, 1863.
Jacob Kreiss. Killed at Mechanicsville, June 26, 1862.

Musician.

Conner, William. Dishonorably discharged, 1862.

Privates.

Aitken, George W. Wounded at Mechanicsville. Honorably discharged, November, 1862.
Alexander, Samuel.
Atkinson, Robert. Reënlisted.
Baker, Albert C. Discharged to enter battery C, Fifth United States Artillery.

Barford, Jos. A. Honorably discharged. November, 1862.
Bassett, Samuel. Discharged to enter battery C, Fifth United States Artillery.
Blight, Jacob L. Wounded at Mechanicsville. Honorably discharged, August 27, 1862.
Bogia, Frederick F.
Bouvier, William.
Brines, Thomas J. Wounded at Antietam. Honorably discharged, December, 1862.
Brines, William. Honorably discharged, January, 1863.
Burgoon, Andrew. Reënlisted.
Clark, Gaven B. Honorably discharged, December 30, 1862.
Cope, Morris.
Covert, Isaac. To Invalid Corps, 1863.
Davis, Louis. Wounded at Fredericksburg. Reënlisted.
Dooling, Jeremiah.
Dungan, Levi. Honorably discharged, August 20, 1862.
Fisher, Joseph L. Killed at Mechanicsville, June 26, 1862.
Gardner, Asa C. Honorably discharged, May 15, 1862.
Glass, James. Discharged to enter battery C, Fifth United States Artillery.
Graham, Henry. To Invalid Corps.
Guy, Henry. Wounded at Gettysburg, July 2, 1863.
Hackett, Thomas. Killed at Mechanicsville, June 26, 1862.
Haffey, Charles. Drowned, July 23d, 1861.
Hamilton, William. Reënlisted.
*Harberger, John.
Harbison, James. Died, August 1, 1862.
*Hilt, Aaron.
Higgins, Francis. Wounded at South Mountain. Honorably discharged, December, 1862.
*Houston, Marcus.
Huly, William. Killed at Mechanicsville, June 26, 1862.
Kelley, John. Reënlisted.
Laws, Anthony A. Wounded at Mechanicsville. Honorably discharged, October 24, 1862.
Lauer, James.
Luckman, Edward.
*McEuen, Samuel.
McLane, William. Wounded at Glendale, June 30, 1862.
McNamee, Joseph. Reënlisted.
*Maines, James.
Miller, Charles F. Wounded at Gettysburg, July 3, 1863.
Mintzer, Andrew. Discharged to enter the Navy.
Morgan, James D. Discharged to enter battery C, Fifth United States Artillery.
Norris, Richard. Discharged to enter battery C, Fifth United States Artillery.
O'Kane, James. Wounded at Mechanicsville.
Palmer, John.

Parr, William N.
Patterson, Amos. Honorably discharged, November 21, 1862.
Peplow, Edward. Wounded at Glendale. Discharged January 8, 1863.
Reilly, John J. Killed at Mechanicsville, June 26, 1862.
Robinson, Benjamin.
Schoeber, Charles W. Wounded at Glendale. Discharged, December, 11 1862.
Shubert, John.
Smith, J. A. C. J. Detailed at Division Commissary.
Smith, Robert J. Died, September 13, 1862.
Steele, Joseph. Reënlisted.
Thompson, William.
*Tozier, James.
Vorhees, Albert B.
Walters, Henry.
Weller, William. Transferred to serve out time.
Wence, William.
Whiteman, George. Killed at Gaines' Mills, June 27, 1862.
Whiteside, Major. Killed at Glendale, June 30, 1862.
*Williams, James.

Company E.

Captain.

J. Orr Finnie, April 16, 1861. Wounded and prisoner at Gaines' Mill. Appointed Provost Marshal of Philadelphia, October 6, 1862.

First Lieutenants.

J. Baxter Fletcher, April 16, 1861. Killed at Glendale, June 30, 1862.
John Taylor, May 9, 1863. Appointed Aid-de-camp. Taken prisoner at Wilderness, May 5, 1864.

Second Lieutenants.

Alexander Black, April 16, 1861. Honorably discharged, October 25, 1862.
Andrew McLean, May 9, 1863.

Orderly Sergeants.

John Taylor. To first lieutenant.
Andrew McLean. To second lieutenant.
George H. Morrow. Appointed May 9, 1863.

Sergeants.

James McCormick. Appointed August, 1862.
John Reid. Appointed January, 1863.
William Mawhinney. Appointed May 9, 1863.

John Ringland. Appointed September 1, 1863.
James Stewart. Wounded and prisoner at Gaines' Mills. Honorably discharged.
Robert Ferguson. Wounded at South Mountain. Honorably discharged.
Michael McCauley. Reënlisted.
Thomas H. Humphries. Killed at Glendale, June 30, 1862.
William Prentice. Died of wounds received at Glendale, June 30, 1862.
Robert Linsenmeyer. Color corporal. Killed at Gettysburg, July 3, 1863.
*James Wilson.

Corporals.

James Nicholson.
Balthasar Steese.
John C. Young. Wounded at Antietam, September 17, 1862. Honorably discharged.
Robert Hill. Honorably discharged, December 11, 1863.
James Patton. Wounded at Antietam, September 17, 1862. Honorably discharged.
William B. Jones. Killed at Glendale, June 30, 1862.
Thomas Smith. Killed at Glendale, June 30, 1862.
Andrew Beckett. Color corporal. Died of wounds received at Gaines' Mill.
Edward Booth. Killed at South Mountain, September 14, 1862.
William McKechnie. Killed at Antietam, September 17th, 1862,
George Stewart. Died of wounds received at Gettysburg, July 26, 1863.

Musician.

John McLaughlin. Honorably discharged, February 25, 1863.

Privates.

Aitken, Julius C. Wounded at Mechanicsville. Honorably discharged.
Brown, Henry. Wounded at South Mountain. Honorably discharged
Birnie, George. Honorably discharged. December 17, 1862.
Burns, William. Killed at Glendale, June 30, 1862.
Collier, Thomas. Killed at Glendale, June 30, 1862.
Chandler, George. Reënlisted.
Chandler, William. Wounded at Fredericksburg, December 13, 1862.
*Cunningham, James.
Catanach, John A. Discharged to accept a commission.
Detwiler, Leonard. Wounded at Fredericksburg, December 13, 1862. Reënlisted.
Dunlap, Samuel. Wounded at Gettysburg, July 2, 1863. Reënlisted.
Elder, Thomas. Reënlisted.

Fry, Henry. Reënlisted.
Ferkler, Frank H. Honorably discharged for disability.
Grim, Christopher. Wounded and prisoner at Glendale and Fredericksburg. Honorably discharged.
Grier, James.
Graham, James. Died of wounds received at Mechanicsville.
Henry, William. Killed at Spottsylvania Court House, May 12, 1864.
Hamilton, Leslie W. Honorably discharged, December 22, 1862.
Harvey, Cassius P. Wounded and prisoner at Gaines' Mills. Honorably discharged.
Howard, John. Honorably discharged for disability, November 28, 1862.
King, Peter. Reënlisted.
Leight, Andrew M. Reënlisted.
Leight, James H. Reënlisted.
Lindsay, Joseph H.
Lappin, John. Honorably discharged for disability.
Laird, Samuel. Honorably discharged for disability.
McAdams, William.
McAllister, Archibald.
McCall, Archibald.
McCall, Alexander. Honorably discharged for disability, August 30, 1862.
McDonald, William. Wounded and prisoner at Gaines' Mills. Honorably discharged.
McFarland, William. Wounded and prisoner at Mechanicsville.
McGarvey, Samuel. Drowned in James river, August 16, 1862.
McHenry, Joseph.
McKeller, Gilbert. Killed at South Mountain, September 14, 1862.
McKinney, James. Wounded at Glendale, June 30, 1862.
McMichael, William.
McMillan, George. Wounded at Bull Run. Honorably discharged, May 24, 1862.
*Mackey, Thomas.
Macklin, William. Killed at Glendale, June 30, 1862
Markley, William. Reënlisted.
Morrison, James. Reënlisted.
Morrison, William.
Nelson, William.
Patterson, Robert. Wounded at Bull Run. Taken prisoner at Bristoe Station. Dead.
Potts, James. Killed at Glendale, June 30, 1862.
Query, John R. Died of wounds received at Gettysburg, July 2, 1863.
Roadermel, Christian A. Reënlisted.
Shannon, Samuel. Killed at Glendale, June 30, 1862.
Simpson, Joseph. Killed at Mechanicsvlle, June 26, 1862.
Smith, Charles H. Honorably discharged, February 24, 1863.
Stewart, Samuel. Wounded at ——. Honorably discharged, May 24, 1863.
*Tweedle, Edward.

*Tweedle, John.
*Tweedle, William.
Wallace, George M. Discharged for minority.
Ward, Samuel.
Whelan, John.
White, Calhoun. Killed at Mechanicsville, June 26, 1862.
Wilson, John. Wounded at Gettysburg, July 3, 1863.
Wilson, James W.

Company F.

Captains.

T. F. Bringhurst, April 20, 1861. Honorably discharged, August 27, 1861.
J. E. Barnacle, May 14, 1862, Resigned.
John M. Clark, August 1, 1862.

First Lieutenants.

Geo. W. Kite, April 20, 1861. Honorably discharged August 27, 1861.
John M. Clark. To captain.
Robert J. Clark. November 23, 1862. Wounded at Wilderness. Died June 9, 1864.

Second Lieutenants.

Wm. Edwards, April 20, 1861. Honorably discharged, August 27, 1861.
Isaac Mourer, May 14, 1862. Dismissed.
Robert J. Clark. To first lieutenant.
William Ambrose, May 1, 1863.

Orderly Sergeants.

Wm. Ambrose. To second lieutenant.
James T. Moore.

Sergeants.

William H. Wilgis. Died in hospital, November 16, 1862.
Harrison Cressman.
James B. Reed. Wounded at Wilderness, May 5, 1864.
Thomas S. Coleman.
Charles E. Laub.

Corporals.

John Smith. Wounded at Wilderness, May 10, 1864.
Philip Kraft.
David Cassidy. Wounded at Wilderness, May 12, 1864.
Christopher Souders.

Samuel A. Louder. Taken prisoner at Bristoe Station, October 14, 1863.
William B. Snyder.
Nicholas Hubert.

Drummer.

John Mace.

Privates.

Black, Samuel. Drowned in Rappahannock river, September 3, 1863.
Burns, John.
Bowman, Peter. Wounded at Gettysburg, July 2, 1863.
Bowman, Michael.
Bressler, Mahlon H.
Brown, William. Wounded at Gettysburg, July 2, 1863.
Beatty, Oscar. Discharged for disability, June 10, 1862.
Cornelius, David.
Carter, William B.
Chartres, William.
Cherry, Alfred. Killed at Wilderness, May 12, 1864.
Cornelius, Isaac.
Curfman, Joseph C. Wounded at Wilderness, May 10, 1864.
Cassidy, George W.
Decker, William S.
Delaney, Daniel.
Davis, John P.
Figart, Andrew M.
Gehrett, Adam. Wounded at Wilderness, May 10, 1864. Died May 16, 1864.
Glunt, William C.
Green, Benjamin F.
Green, Martin. Transferred to serve out time.
Hoover, John. Wounded at Bristoe, January 24, 1864. Discharged, June 17, 1864.
Houck, Marshall. Wounded at Wilderness, May 10, 1864.
Halsel, George J. Taken prisoner, May 10, 1864.
Hollingshead, John.
Hoffer, Alexander. Wounded at Gettysburg, July 2, 1863. Died, July 22, 1863.
Holl, Adolphus. Discharged for disability, September 2, 1862.
Hopkins, Wm. M.
Lindsay, William. Killed at Bristoe, March 27, 1864.
Labold, John. Taken prisoner at Mine Run, November — 1863.
Maurer, Abraham.
Moyer, George. Wounded at Gettysburg, July 2, 1863. Died, July 26, 1863.
Moore, William.
Murty, James T.

Meadeville, Joshua.
Phillips, Patrick.
Quarry, Alfred. Transferred to serve out time.
Quarry, Levi.
Quarry, Michael. Transferred to serve out time.
Reid, William J.
Ring, Charles P. Discharged for disability, February 10, 1863.
Rutherford, James.
Riggle, Martin A. Wounded at Gettysburg, July 3, 1863. Died, August 19, 1863.
Riggleman, Jonathan.
Shank, Nicholas.
Stewart, Samuel. Killed at Gettysburg, July 3, 1863.
Smith, Abraham L. Killed at Wilderness, May 10, 1864.
Sneath, Robert.
Straitliff, John. Transferred to serve out time.
Sharrow, William.
Sherman, Robinson T. Wounded at Gettysburg, July 3, 1863. Wounded at Wilderness, May 12, 1864. Died, June 3, 1864.
Shaffer, Jonathan. Transferred to serve out time.
Steele, Louden.
Thompson, Austin. Wounded at Wilderness, May 12, 1864.
Treawe, Elihu. Transferred to serve out time.
Vanzant, Wm. R.
Wall, William S. Wounded at Wilderness, May 12, 1864.
Webb, John B. Wounded at Gettysburg.
Webb, Henry. Drowned in Rappahannock river, May 27, 1862.
Wright, John F.
Wright, Levi. Discharged for disability, September 16, 1862.

COMPANY G.

Captains.

E. M. Woodward, April 20, 1861. Honorably discharged, August 27, 1862.
Wm. D. Reitzel, July, 1862. Resigned, December 7, 1863. To Captain one hundred days men.

First Lieutenants.

Henry Sheetz, April 20, 1861. To aide-de-camp to General McCall.
John K. Brown, July 20, 1861. Honorably discharged, August 27, 1862.
John L. Rhoads, March 20, 1862. To adjutant, September 23, 1863.

Second Lieutenants.

John K. Brown, April 20, 1861. To first lieutenant.

Charles F. Hoyt, July 16, 1861. To captain and commissary subsistence, volunteers.
Max Wimpfheimer, July 2, 1862. Killed at Antietam, September 17, 1862.
Elisha P. Woodward, September 17, 1862. To captain company C, 191st regiment, Pennsylvania veteran volunteers.

Orderly Sergeants.

Abram H. Witmer. Died April, 1863.
Elisha P. Woodward. To second lieutenant, September 17, 1862.
Martin Devine. Killed at Spottsylvania Court House.

Sergeants.

Hiram C. Hostetter. To sergeant major. Died, July 24, 1863.
George L. Myers.
George Brittain. To hospital steward.
Frederick K. Ort.
John A. Hull. Wounded at Antietam. Killed at Spottsylvania Court House.
Rudolph M. Graeff. Killed at Spottsylvania Court House.
William Brighton. Taken prisoner Ream's Station.

Corporals.

*Charles W. Stout.
Wm. H. K. Bush. Wounded at Antietam. Wounded and prisoner at Spottsylvania Court House.
Charles Gartner.
John A. Ziegler. Died August, 1862.
John Lytle. Wounded at Fredericksburg. Prisoner at Ream's Station.
Jeremiah Fritz. Died of wounds received at Antietam.
Thomas M. Fisher. To first lieutenant 191st regiment Pennsylvania Veteran Volunteers.
Franklin E. Jones.

Musicians.

Marshall Green.
William J. Kendig.

Privates.

Allgier, Samuel. Honorably discharged, September 22, 1862.
Allbright, John. Honorably discharged, May 21, 1862.
*Bauer, Jacob.
Bitterman, Francis. Wounded at Fredericksburg.
Blankhorn, Andrew. Wounded at Fredericksburg.
Block, Hugo. Transferred to battery C, 5th United States artillery.
Carter, Jacob. Wounded at Gettysburg.
*Cramer, Charles.

Daveler, George F.
Davis, Amos.
Ely, Thomas S. Died on the march.
Erhne, Adam. Wounded at Gettysburg. Killed at Spottsylvania Court House.
Emswiler, Michael. Prisoner at Ream's Station
Eckhart, Charles. Prisoner at Ream's Station.
*Green, Alexander.
Grab, Joseph. Prisoner at Ream's Station.
Gerkhart, John H.
Harnish, Jacob. Prisoner at Ream's Station.
Horst, Martin. Died October 21, 1862.
Hartman, Benjamin. Prisoner at Ream's Station.
Hahnlan, John.
Hart, John. Wounded at Gettysburg.
Harter, Joseph. Killed at Fredericksburg, December 13, 1862.
Kennedy, Andrew P. Killed at Fredericksburg, December 13, 1862.
Kepler, Isaac. Honorably discharged for disability, January, 1863.
Kais, Sebastian. Honorably discharged for disability, January 26, 1863.
Ludwig, George J. Honorably discharged for disability, April 20, 1863.
Lex, Charles. Honorably discharged for disability, January 28, 1863.
*Light, Absolom.
Leed, George W.
Lithgow, George W.
Lippold, Charles. To Veteran Reserve Corps, April 4, 1864.
Myer, Christian. To battery C, Fifth United States artillery, October 20, 1862.
Mull, Franklin. To Veteran Reserve Corps, February 13, 1864.
Means, Henry W. Died, November 28, 1862.
Neild, Thomas H. To United States Navy, May 1, 1864.
*Nichols, Samuel.
Paine, Samuel J. Honorably discharged for disability, May 8, 1863.
Price, Lyman S. Wounded at Antietam.
Pierce, Davis O.
Reagan, Charles. Wounded at Antietam. Honorably discharged, February 17, 1863.
*Rick, Charles.
Stackhouse, Park J. Wounded at Gettysburg. Honorably discharged.
Schmeidel, Augustus.
Sohm, John. Honorably discharged for disability, July, 1862.
Schoen, John.
Steinruck, John.
Shivers, James. To Veteran Reserve Corps.
Sucker, Augustus. Killed at South Mountain.
Schalck, John P. Wounded at Fredericksburg. Prisoner, May 5, 1864.
Shilling, Henry.

Stevenson, William. Honorably discharged for disability.
Schlotte, Wm. G. Honorably discharged for disability, January 13, 1863.
Schnaeder, Michael.
Shoemaker, John. Wounded at Fredericksburg.
Young, George W. Died, August 27, 1862.
White, John. To Veteran Reserve Corps.
*Weldon, James.
*Waltze, George.

COMPANY H.

Captain.

Timothy Mealey, April 17, 1861. Wounded at Antietam and Fredericksburg.

First Lieutenants.

Peter Somers, April 17, 1861. Resigned February 12, 1862.
Hugh P. Kennedy, February 19, 1862. Wounded at Gaines' Mills. Resigned, December 25, 1862.
Richard Clendining, December 25, 1862. Wounded at South Mountain.
Joseph Benison, September 11, 1863

Second Lieutenants.

Richard Clendining, October 17, 1861. To first lieutenant.
William McGlenn, December 25, 1862. To first lieutenant.
Joseph Benison, March 17, 1863. To first lieutenant.
Samuel W. Wallace, September 11, 1863.

First Sergeants.

Samuel Wallace. Made first sergeant, May 9, 1863.
James Cook. Made first sergeant, May 1, 1864. Reënlisted. To lieutenant 191st regiment P. V.

Sergeants.

Francis Kane. Discharged for disability, February 3, 1862.
William J. Fulton. Wounded at Antietam. To lieutenant Invalid Corps.
John Donnelly. Reënlisted. Wounded at Ream's Station.
John Barnes. Made sergeant from private, May, 1864.
Robert Cunningham. Made sergeant from private, May, 1864.
Thomas M. Savage. Made sergeant, June 1, 1863. Killed at Gettysburg, July 2, 1863.

Corporals.

Thomas H. Gouldey. Appointed corporal, February, 1863.
Hugh J. Strain. Appointed corporal, February, 1863.

Elwood Haas. Appointed corporal February, 1863.
John Collins. Wounded at Charles City Cross-roads. Discharged, January 10, 1863.

Musician.

George W. Leeti. Reënlisted. Wounded at Ream's Station.

Privates.

Azpell, Clinton.
Allen, James. Discharged for disability, April, 1863.
Blackwell, George. Discharged December 24, 1863.
Baskerville, James.
Burns, Thomas G. Killed at New Hope Church, Va., November 28, 1863.
Burns, Peter.
Coligan, Francis. Wounded at Bull Run. Discharged, November 1, 1862.
Connor, John. Transferred to serve out unexpired time.
Clendining, Samuel. Reënlisted.
Crilly, Thomas. Wounded at Charles City Cross-roads. To sergeant.
Dempsey, John. Discharged for disability, March 3, 1864.
Dempsey, Patrick.
Dempsey, Charles.
Dickinson, Benjamin. Transferred to Invalid Corps.
Dubois, Edward. To sergeant.
Dunn, Patrick. Killed at Gaines' Mills, June 27, 1862.
Farren, James J. Died, November 10, 1862.
Flaherty, William.
Frazier, John.
Finegan, Bernard. Wounded at Gaines' Mills. Discharged, December 23, 1862.
Fulton, Abraham. Wounded at Gaines' Mills, June 27, 1862.
Germain, Edward. Discharged for disability, July, 1861.
Gillespie, James. L. Discharged, July, 1862, to accept a commission.
Hackney, Ezekiel.
Harshaw, Samuel.
Haffey, Charles. Reënlisted.
Kincade, James. Wounded at Gaines' Mills. Discharged, April, 1863.
*Kuttler, Charles.
Loane, Abraham. Transferred to serve out time.
Long, John.
McGarvey, Henry.
Moody, Jonathan.
Myers, George L.
Myers, Isaac. Wounded at Antietam. Discharged, November, 1862.

Murdock, Alexander. Wounded at Gaines' Mills. Discharged, January 16, 1863.
McCann, John. Discharged for disability, April 21, 1864.
Murphy, Charles. Transferred to serve out unexpired term.
Montage, John. Transferred to serve out unexpired term.
Messmore, George. Transferred to serve out unexpired term.
McCormick, Edward. Discharged for disability, June, 1862.
McGonigle, Cornelius. Discharged for disability, February 3, 1862.
Mount, Michael.
Mackin, Henry L. Died, August 20, 1863.
Patton, Dennis.
Phillips, John. To corporal.
Porter, Thomas. Killed at Fairfax Station, Va., June 19, 1863.
Ryan, Andrew. Killed at Gettysburg, Pa., July 3, 1863.
Ritchie, Thomas. Died, March 6, 1863.
Ritchie, Jonathan.
Roe, James P.
Robb, William.
Siddall, George. Transferred to serve out unexpired time.
Shaw, William.
Smith, William.
Seddinger, John.
Thompson, Robert.
Waibel, George.
Wilson, Oliver. Transferred to serve out unexpired time.
Weaver, Charles. Discharged for disability, January 23, 1863.
Weaver, George E.
Walker, William.
Wilkins, William P.
Woodward, E. M. Promoted to sergeant-major, May 1, 1862.

Company I.

Captain.

William Knox, April 17, 1861. Honorably discharged, August 27, 1861. To sutler of the regiment.

First Lieutenant.

Thomas Weir, April 17, 1861. Honorably discharged, August 27, 1861.

Second Lieutenant.

John H. Jack, April 17, 1861. Honorably discharged, August 27, 1861. To first lieutenant company B.

Company K.

Captain.

P. I. Smith, April 15, 1861. Wounded and prisoner at Glendale. Wounded at Fredericksburg.

First Lieutenant.

Isaac J. Harvey, April 15, 1861. To captain Signal Corps.

Second Lieutenant.

James C. Justus, April 15, 1861. Acting quartermaster. Taken prisoner at Jericho Ford, May 24, 1864.

Orderly Sergeants.

David H. Pidgeon. To sergeant-major. Wounded at Glendale and Gettysburg.
Staughton George. Wounded at South Mountain. Honorably discharged. To second lieutenant Veteran Reserves.
Peter Gillis, Jr.

Sergeants.

Charles Macneil. Honorably discharged for disability.
George W. Nutz.
Thomas May. Reënlisted.
Joseph F. Sweeton. Color sergeant.
Charles C. Upjohn. Wounded at Spottsylvania Court House, May 12, 1864. Reënlisted.
Joshua T. Loyd.

Corporals.

Thomas Dugan.
Washington George.
James F. Morrison. Wounded and prisoner at Fredericksburg, December 13, 1862. Color corporal.
Henry J. Dewees. Honorably discharged for disability.
Richard C. Schriner. Honorably discharged for disability.
Henry C. Libe. Appointed May 1, 1864.
Jeremiah Barr.
Samuel G. Eglington. Appointed May 1, 1864.

Musicians.

George D. Massey. Drummer.
Rufus S. Read. Fifer. Reënlisted in battery M, Second United States Artillery.

Privates.

Andrews, John T.
Asch, Charles. Discharged for minority, June 27, 1861.

Barnes, Edward. Wounded at Mechanicsville, June 26, 1862.
Bartram, Joseph J.
Benzon, John L. To quartermaster-sergeant. To second lieutenant 191st regiment P. V.
Buck, John S. Discharged to enter battery M, United States Artillery.
Campbell, James. Teamster.
*Chamberlain, William.
Chew, Hiram F. Wounded at Antietam. Honorably discharged.
Coster, William H. Discharged to enter battery M, Second United States Artillery.
Cox, Joshua R. Wounded at Bull Run. Honorably discharged for disability.
Craft, Edward L.
Cross, Augustus T. Appointed sergeant-major, June 21, 1861.
Deitz, William K.
Donnelly, John. Reënlisted.
Edmonson, Thomas. Killed at Gaines' Mills, June 27, 1862.
Elliott, Frank M. Honorably discharged for disability. To first lieutenant 183d regiment P. V.
Errickson, Daniel. Reënlisted.
Everett, John. Reënlisted.
*Fell, Morton S.
Garrison, William B. Honorably discharged for disability.
Gibson, Robert S. Honorably discharged for disability, 1862.
Gougler, George. Wounded at Antietam. Honorably discharged.
Hanf, Charles. Wounded at Fredericksburg. Honorably discharged.
Hart, John H.
Hartman, Thomas. Taken prisoner at Glendale. Discharged to enter battery C, Fifth United States Artillery.
Hays, Michael. Discharged to enter battery C, Fifth United States Artillery.
McCollow, Joseph.
McNeill, Frank P. Killed at Glendale, June 30, 1862.
Manning, William J. Wounded at Antietam. Honorably discharged for disability. To captain 192d regiment P. V.
Mendenhall, Edward H. Discharged to enter battery M, Second United States Artillery.
Mingus, George W.
Morslander, Robert. Detailed to Signal Corps, August 29, 1861.
Murch, George B. Died, August —, 1862.
Newberry, John S.
Nolen, Daniel H. Honorably discharged for disability, September 30, 1861.
Poulson, Wilberforce. Killed at Bull Run, August 29, 1862.
*Powell, Robert T.
Quinn, James. Died at Smoketown Hospital, Md., October —, 1862.
Reel, Albert R. Wounded at South Mountain. Honorably discharged.
Rowe, George W. Honorably discharged.
Shaw, Thomas. Wounded and prisoner at Glendale. Honorably discharged.

Shaw, William. Died of wounds received at Gaines' Mills.
Simpson, William H. Killed at South Mountain. September 14, 1862.
Smile, John A. J. Honorably discharged for disability.
Snider, William. Reënlisted.
Snyder, Henry.
Stanley, Charles.
Supplee, John.
Swancott, George W. To Invalid Corps.
Thompson, Henry C. Honorably discharged for disability.
Towell, James.
Toy, Andrew J. Killed at Antietam, September 17, 1862.
Treadway, Harvey B.
Upjohn, Henry.
Vickers, George M. Honorably discharged for disability.

APPENDIX C.

MARCHES AND BIVOUACS.

1861.				MILES.
May	28-9.	From	Philadelphia to Camp Washington	66
July	24.	"	Camp Washington to Camp Curtin	107
"	25.	"	Camp Curtin to Baltimore	85
"	28.	"	Baltimore to Sandy Hook, Md.	80
Aug.	14.	"	Sandy Hook to Berlin, and back	10
"	17.	"	Sandy Hook to first bivouac	15
"	18.	"	First bivouac to Cotoctin creek	6
"	19.	"	Cotoctin creek to the Monocacy	8
"	21.	"	the Monocacy to Hyattstown	6
"	22.	"	Hyattstown to new camp	1
"	29.	"	camp to near Darnestown	8
Sept.	19.	"	Darnestown to Muddy Branch	8
"	25.	"	Muddy Branch to Tenallytown, D. C	15
Oct.	9.	"	Tenallytown to Camp Pierpont, Va	8
"	19.	"	Camp Pierpont to Drainesville	15
"	21.	"	Drainesville to Camp Pierpont	15
Nov.	20.	"	Camp Pierpont to Munson's Hill, and back.	16
Dec.	8.	"	Foraging expedition to Thomas', and back...	16
"	20.	"	The battle of Drainesville march	14
1862.				
March	3.	"	Camp Pierpont to Chain Bridge, and back...	8
"	5.	"	" " " " ...	8
"	10.	"	Camp Pierpont to first bivouac	15
"	11.	"	first bivouac to Camp Hawkhurst	2
			Carried forward	533

1862.			MILES.
		Brought forward	532
Mar. 14.	From	Camp Hawkhurst to near Difficult creek	6
" 15.	"	Difficult creek to three miles east of it	15
" 16.	"	bivouac to near Alexandria	13
April 9.	"	Alexandria to Rebel cabins near Bull Run	24
" 10.	"	the cabins to Manassas Junction	4
" 17.	"	Manassas Junction to near Brentsville	7
" 18.	"	Brentsville to Catlett's Station	6
" 26.	"	Catlett's Station to Elk Run	6
" 27.	"	Elk Run to White Ridge	8
" 28.	"	White Ridge to near Falmouth	17
" 29.	"	near Falmouth to camp below it	3
May 26.	"	camp to back of Fredericksburg	3
" 31.	"	Fredericksburg to near Falmouth	2
June 8.	"	Falmouth to Cedar Lane	7
" 9.	"	Cedar Lane to Gray's Landing	1
" 9-10.	"	Gray's Landing to mouth of Rappahannock River	150
" 10.	"	Rappahannock river to Yorktown	35
" 10-11.	"	Yorktown to White House	60
" 11.	"	White House to first bivouac	2
" 12.	"	bivouac to Dispatch Station	10
" 13.	"	Dispatch Station to Tunstall Station	8
" 15.	"	Tunstall Station to Dispatch Station	8
" 18.	"	Dispatch Station to Dr. Gaines' house	8
" 19.	"	Gaines' house to Ellison's Mills	2
" 20.	"	Ellison's Mills to Nanaley's Mills	1
" 24.	"	Nanaley's to Mechanicsville, on picket	1
" 26.	"	picket to Nanaley's	1
" 26.	"	Nanaley's Mills to Mechanicsville battle-field	4
" 27.	"	Mechanicsville field to Gaines' Mills	6
" 28.	"	Gaines' Mills to Trent's Hill	3
" 28-9.	"	Trent's Hill to White Oak Bridge	8
" 29.	"	White Oak Bridge to Glendale	3
" 29.	"	Glendale to picket	1
" 30.	"	picket to Glendale battle-field	1
July 1.	"	Glendale field to Malvern Hill	6
" 1-2.	"	Malvern Hill to Harrison's Landing	10
Aug. 15.	"	Harrison's Landing to Fortress Monroe	70
" 20.	"	Fortress Monroe to Aquia creek	145
" 21.	"	Aquia creek to Falmouth	12
" 22.	"	Falmouth to first bivouac	7
Aug. 23.	"	bivouac to Crittenden's Mills	17
" 24.	"	Crittenden's Mills to the Gold Mines	8
" 25.	"	Gold mines to near Bealton Station	10
" 26.	"	Bealton Station to near Warrenton	20
" 27.	"	Warrenton to Broad Run	12
" 28.	"	Broad Run to Bull Run battle-field	28
		Carried forward	1311

			MILES.
		Brought forward	1311
Aug. 30–1.	From	Bull Run field to Centreville	7
" 31.	"	countermarching around Centreville, picket and back	8
Sept. 1.	"	Centreville to near Fairfax Court-house	8
" 2.	"	Fairfax Court-house to Arlington Heights	14
" 3.	"	Arlington Heights to Arlington House	3
" 4.	"	Arlington House to Upton's Hill	4
" 6.	"	Upton's Hill to near Washington	9
" 7.	"	near Washington to Leesborough	10
" 9.	"	Leesborough to near Brookville	10
" 10.	"	near Brookville to Patuxent river	5
" 11.	"	Patuxent river to Poplar Springs	10
" 12.	"	Poplar Springs to near New Market	14
" 13.	"	near New Market to the Monocacy	4
" 14.	"	Monocacy to South Mountain battle-field	14
" 15.	"	South Mountain to Keedysville	7
" 16.	"	Keedysville to Antietam	2
" 18.	"	Antietam to near Sharpsburg	2
Oct. 26.	"	Sharpsburg to Berlin	14
" 29.	"	Berlin to Lovettsville	8
Nov. 1.	"	Lovettsville to Hamilton	12
" 3.	"	Hamilton to near Philomont	9
" 4.	"	near Philomont to bivouac	4
" 5.	"	bivouac to near White Plains	16
" 5.	"	White Plains to picket line	1
" 6.	"	picket line to beyond Warrenton	13
" 11.	"	Warrenton to Fayettsville	10
" 17.	"	Fayettsville to beyond Grove Churches	16
" 18.	"	Grove Churches to near Stafford Court-house	14
" 22.	"	Stafford Court-house to Brooks' Station	6
Dec. 8.	"	Brooks' Station to near White Oak Church	8
" 11.	"	White Oak Church to near the Rappahannock	3
" 12.	"	bivouac to Fredericksburg battle-field	3
" 15.	"	battle-field to picket on the north bank	3
" 16.	"	picket to camp	3
" 18.	"	camp to bivouac	5
" 19.	"	bivouac to camp near White Oak Church	1
1863.			
Jan. 20.	"	White Oak Church to Banks' ford	14
" 23.	"	Banks' ford to White Oak Church	14
Feb. 6.	"	White Oak Church to Belle Plains	4
" 7.	"	Belle Plains to Alexandria	59
" 12.	"	Alexandria to Fairfax Court-house	20
" 21.	"	Fairfax Court-house to Bull Run picket	9
Mar. 9.	"	Bull Run picket to Fairfax Court-house	9
" 28.	"	Fairfax Court-house to Fairfax Station	4
June 25.	"	Fairfax Station to bivouac beyond Vienna	10
		Carried forward	1727

				MILES.
			Brought forward	1727
June	26.	From	bivouac to Goose creek	18
"	27.	"	Goose creek to mouth of Monocacy, Md	15
"	28.	"	Monocacy to near Frederick City	15
"	29.	"	Frederick City to bivouac in woods	10
"	30.	"	the woods to beyond Uniontown	20
July	1.	"	beyond Uniontown to Pennsylvania line	10
"	1.	"	State line to bivouac	10
"	2.	"	bivouac to Gettysburg battle-field	10
"	5.	"	battle-field to first bivouac	6
"	6.	"	bivouac to near Emmittsburg	3
"	7.	"	Emmittsburg to near Frederick City	21
"	8.	"	near Frederick City to near Middletown	14
"	9.	"	near Middletown to near Keedysville	10
"	10.	"	near Keedysville to Delamont Mills	10
"	11.	"	Delamont Mills to Hagerstown pike on picket.	4
"	12.	"	picket to bivouac	1
"	14.	"	bivouac to Falling Waters	5
"	15.	"	Falling Waters across South Mountain	10
"	16.	"	eastern base of South Mountain to near Berlin.	23
"	17.	"	near Berlin to Lovettsville, Va	8
"	18.	"	Lovettsville to Wheatland	7
"	19.	"	Wheatland to Purcellville	7
"	20.	"	Purcellville to near Upperville	14
"	22.	"	Upperville to Rectortown	7
"	23.	"	Rectortown to Manassas Gap	25
"	24.	"	Manassas Gap to bivouac on the mountains.	5
"	25.	"	Mountain bivouac to first bivouac	15
"	26.	"	bivouac to near Warrenton	19
"	27.	"	near Warrenton to near Fayetteville	4
"	28.	"	Fayetteville to new camp, for water	1
Aug.	1.	"	camp towards Warrenton	2
"	3.	"	Warrenton towards Fayetteville	13
"	4.	"	Fayetteville to bivouac	1
"	8.	"	camp to Rappahannock Station	9
Sept.	16.	"	Rappahannock Station to near Culpepper Court-house	13
"	17.	"	Near Culpepper Court-house to camp	6
Oct.	10.	"	camp to Raccoon Ford	7
"	11.	"	Raccoon Ford to old camp	7
"	11.	"	camp to Rappahannock Station	19
"	12.	"	Rappahannock Station to Brandy Station	8
"	12-13.	"	Brandy Station to Rappahannock Station	8
"	13.	"	Rappahannock Station to Catlett's Station	10
"	14-15.	"	Catlett's Station to near Bull Run	15
"	15.	"	Bull Run to near Fairfax Court-House	11
"	17.	"	Fairfax Court-House to Centreville	6
"	18.	"	Centreville to Fairfax Court-House	6
"	19.	"	Fairfax Court-House to Bull Run battle-field.	13
			Carried forward	2208

Date		Route	Miles
		Brought forward	2208
Oct.	20.	From Bull Run to near New Baltimore	10
"	26.	" New Baltimore to New Auburn	7
"	30.	" New Auburn to near Warrenton	5
Nov.	7.	" Warrenton to Rappahannock Station	8
"	7.	" Rappahannock Station to Fordman's Ford	6
"	8.	" Fordman's Ford to Rebel cabins	2
"	10.	" the cabins to Mountain Run	4
"	24.	" Mountain Run towards the Rapidan, and back	5
"	26.	" Mountain run to near Chancellorsville	15
"	27.	" near Chancellorsville to New Hope Church	6
"	28.	" New Hope Church to Robinson's Tavern	8
"	29.	" Robinson's Tavern to Mine Run	3
Dec.	2, 3.	" Mine Run to Brandy Station	14
"	4, 5.	" Brandy Station to Bristoe Station	20
1864.			
April	29.	" Bristoe Station to near Warrenton Junction	11
"	30.	" Warrenton Junction to Culpepper Court-House	19
May	4.	" near Culpepper Court-House to Lacy's farm	22
"	5.–7.	Through the Wilderness	30
"	8.	From Wilderness to Spottsylvania Court-House	15
"	9.–13.	Around Spottsylvania Court-House	10
"	14.	To the River Po	15
"	15.–20.	Countermarching and taking up positions	20
"	21.	To Guinney's Station	18
"	22.–24.	Marching on Telegraph road	35
"	25–28.	Crossing the Pamunkey	30
"	29.	Around Bethesda Church	8
June	1.	Bethesda Church to White House	28
"	3.	White House to Washington	252
"	5.	Washington to Baltimore	45
"	5–6.	Baltimore to Harrisburg	85
"	7.	Harrisburg to Philadelphia	107
		Total distance marched by the Regiment	3071

Memoirs of the Queens of France. Written in France, carefully compiled from researches made there, commended by the press generally, and published from the Tenth London Edition. It is a truly valuable work for the reader and student of history. By Mrs. Forbes Bush. 2 vols. in one. Cloth. Price $1 75.

Memoirs of the Life of Anne Boleyn, Queen of Henry VIII. In the records of biography there is no character that more forcibly exemplifies the vanity of human ambition, or more thoroughly enlists the attention of the reader than this—the Seventh American, and from the Third London Edition. By Miss Benger. With portrait on steel. Cloth. $1 75.

Heroic Women of History. Containing the most extraordinary examples of female courage of ancient and modern times, and set before the wives, sisters, and daughters of the country, in the hope that it may make them even more renowned for resolution, fortitude, and self-sacrifice than the Spartan females of old. By Henry C. Watson. With Illustrations. Cloth. $1 75.

Public and Private History of Louis Napoleon, Emperor of the French. An impartial view of the public and private career of this extraordinary man, giving full information in regard to his most distinguished ministers, generals, relatives and favorites. By Samuel M. Schmucker, LL. D. With portraits on Steel. Cloth. $1 75.

Life and Reign of Nicholas I., Emperor of Russia. The only complete history of this great personage that has appeared in the English language, and furnishes interesting facts in connection with Russian society and government of great practical value to the attentive reader. By Samuel M. Schmucker, LL. D. With Illustrations. Cloth. $1 75.

Life and Times of George Washington. A concise and condensed narrative of Washington's career, especially adapted to the popular reader, and presented as the best matter upon this immortal theme—one especially worthy the attention and admiration of every American. By Samuel M. Schmucker, LL. D. With Portrait on steel. Cloth. $1 75.

LIFE AND TIMES OF ALEXANDER HAMILTON. Incidents of a career that will never lose its singular power to attract and instruct, while giving impressive lessons of the brightest elements of character, surrounded and assailed by the basest. By SAMUEL M. SCHMUCKER, LL. D. With Portrait on steel. Cloth. $1 75.

LIFE AND TIMES OF THOMAS JEFFERSON. In which the author has presented both the merits and defects of this great representative hero in their true light, and has studiously avoided indiscriminate praise or wholesale censure. By SAMUEL M. SCHMUCKER, LL. D. With Portrait. Cloth. $1 75.

LIFE OF BENJAMIN FRANKLIN. Furnishing a superior and comprehensive record of this celebrated Statesman and Philosopher—rich beyond parallel in lessons of wisdom for every age, calling and condition in life, public and private. By O. L. HOLLEY. With Portrait on steel and Illustrations on wood. Cloth. $1 75.

PUBLIC AND PRIVATE LIFE OF DANIEL WEBSTER. The most copious and attractive collection of personal memorials concerning the great Statesman that has hitherto been published, and by one whose intimate and confidential relations with him afford a guarantee for their authenticity. By Gen. S. P. LYMAN. With Illustrations. Cloth. $1 75.

LIFE AND TIMES OF HENRY CLAY. An impartial biography, presenting, by bold and simple strokes of the historic pencil, a portraiture of the illustrious theme which no one should fail to read, and no library be without. By SAMUEL M. SCHMUCKER, LL. D. With Portrait on steel. Cloth. $1 75.

LIFE AND PUBLIC SERVICES OF STEPHEN A. DOUGLAS. A true and faithful exposition of the leading incidents of his brilliant career arranged so as to instruct the reader and produce the careful study which the life of so great a man deserves. By H. M. FLINT. With Portrait on steel. Cloth. $1 75.

LIFE AND PUBLIC SERVICES OF ABRAHAM LINCOLN. (In both the English and German languages.) As a record of this great man it is a most desirable work, admirably arranged for reference, with an index over each page, from which the reader can familiarize himself with the contents by glancing through it. By FRANK CROSBY, of the Philadelphia Bar. With Portrait on steel. Cloth. $1 75.

LIFE OF DANIEL BOONE, THE GREAT WESTERN HUNTER AND PIONEER. Comprising graphic and authentic accounts of his daring, thrilling adventures, wonderful skill, coolness and sagacity under the most hazardous circumstances, with an autobiography dictated by himself. By CECIL B. HARTLEY. With Illustrations. Cloth. $1 75.

LIFE OF COLONEL DAVID CROCKET, THE ORIGINAL HUMORIST AND IRREPRESSIBLE BACKWOODSMAN. Showing his strong will and indomitable spirit, his bear hunting, his military services, his career in Congress, and his triumphal tour through the States—written by himself; to which is added the account of his glorious death at the Alamo. With Illustrations. Cloth. $1 75.

LIFE OF KIT CARSON, THE GREAT WESTERN HUNTER AND GUIDE. An exciting volume of wild and romantic exploits, thrilling adventures, hair-breadth escapes, daring coolness, moral and physical courage, and invaluable services—such as rarely transpire in the history of the world. By CHARLES BURDETT. With Illustrations. Cloth. $1 75.

LIFE OF CAPTAIN JOHN SMITH, THE FOUNDER OF VIRGINIA. The adventures contained herein serve to denote the more noble and daring events of a period distinguished by its spirit, its courage, and its passion, and challenges the attention of the American people. By W. GILMORE SIMMS. With Illustrations. Price $1 75.

LIFE OF GENERAL FRANCIS MARION, THE CELEBRATED PARTISAN HERO OF THE REVOLUTION. This was one of the most distinguished men who figured on the grand theatre of war during the times that "tried men's souls," and his brilliant career has scarcely a parallel in history. By CECIL B. HARTLEY. With Illustrations. Cloth. $1 75.

www.ingramcontent.com/pod-product-compliance
Lightning Source LLC
LaVergne TN
LVHW010142110826
845151LV00002B/407

9781425538989